Earn Income with Your Index Investments

A Complete Guide to Portfolio Overwriting for
Passive and FIRE Investing

by

Matthew J. Chamberlain

How to Generate Cash and Retire Sooner by
Selling Covered Calls

Front Matter

Earn Income with Your Index Investments

*A Complete Guide to Portfolio Overwriting for Passive
and FIRE Investors*

Paperback ISBN 978-0-578-33963-4
Hardcover ISBN 979-8-9878185-0-3

LCCN 2022901997

1st Edition

Call to FIRE, LLC

Disclaimer

The information contained in this book (henceforth referred to as "text") is in no way financial or investment advice of any kind.

All information presented in this text is meant for entertainment and educational purposes only.

There is no endorsement or solicitation of any investment strategy or any specific investment contained within this text.

No guarantee of returns is stated or implied by this text.

The author of this text does not give financial or investment advice of any kind.

The author of this text is not a financial advisor, registered investment advisor, or broker-dealer. The author of this text holds no financial certifications or licenses, or any formal financial training of any kind whatsoever.

Options are not suitable for everyone, and as such, should be discussed with a licensed professional prior to taking any action.

Any action taken by readers of this text is taken of their own volition, is solely their responsibility, and no fiduciary relationship is established between Call to FIRE, LLC or the author of this text and its readers.

Although the aim of this text is to provide accurate information, no claims of veracity, accuracy, validity or being "up-to-date" are made or guaranteed. Call to FIRE LLC and the author of this text are not liable for any errors or omissions contained herein, and therefore the information contained herein should not be relied on for any financial decisions, or in any other way whatsoever. This text provides no warranties or guarantees

Before you can trade options, you must read "Characteristics & Risks of Standardized Options," also known as the options disclosure document (ODD), which is located at: http://www.optionsclearing.com/ about/publications/ publication-listing.jsp

This book contains cartoons of wizards and
should not be taken seriously.

8

Dedication

This book is dedicated to my parents. I only realized with age just how lucky I was to have two wonderful people doing their best to raise me. I hope to be the best of both of you.

And to my beautiful, intelligent, and considerate fiancée Dr. Mary Cole, who has always supported me in everything I do, and draws pretty great wizard cartoons.

Epigraph

"Money is a problem to be solved."

—Franklin Parker, CFA

Contents

CHAPTER 1

An Example, to Start

Nother day on the path to FIRE [1] . It's nice, but it's a grind. You wake up, make your own coffee, pack a lunch, go to work (hopefully by bike), and operate alongside everyone else at a job you may have mentally categorized as temporary.

Like many of your colleagues, you are investing in a group of index funds. Unlike many of your colleagues, you plan to hit the escape hatch[2] whenever the value of your investments reaches 25 times your annual spending. It's not necessarily a bad thing, and in fact, eventually it's going to turn out to be the best thing... but could you make the stretch of days until you retire early better?

---

[1] Financial Independence/Retire Early
[2] Stop working, at least at your regular job.

1

Figure 1.1: *Artist's representation of me in the morning as a wizard, trying to un-groggy myself with a cup of coffee.*

1.1 The Proposed Improvement

Figure 1.2: *My gallant steed— a used Giant Escape 3 bike I got off Craigslist.*

Better could mean a lot of things, but let's say better means "generating income with your index fund shares on the path to FIRE, without ever having to sell them for less than the price you purchased them." [3] What you do with the income itself is up to you. Since we all know by now that money itself doesn't make you happy, you might want to use the income to speed up the path to FIRE by purchasing more shares of VTI (Vanguard's Total US stock market index fund) or your chosen index fund, or wisely spend some on experiences to make the years of saving seem much less austere, potentially a bit luxurious. You might even use some of the income to fund a side hustle that really speeds up the clock on hitting your FIRE number.

In all seriousness, generating income off your FIRE fund without selling shares could allow you to weather an unexpected expense, endure a sudden job loss, help a friend in need or donate to charity.

Really pause and ponder: creating income without selling shares can reduce the sense of scarcity that exists pre-financial independence, and make you feel more empowered. Even better, the type of trading this book describes works best in flat or slowly rising markets, so you can still generate cash even if the market is floundering. For these

---

[3]If you have to sell them at all.

Figure 1.3: *Knowledge of covered calls as an emergency tool.*

reasons, I think everyone should at least know how to sell covered calls in the case of an emergency, even if they don't do it regularly.

1.2 My Investments Can Make Me Income?

So, am I telling you that there is a way to make the journey better without destroying the precious FIRE nest egg?

Yep.

Yes.

You bet.

Absolutely.

As mentioned, you can sell covered calls against your VTI shares, aka "portfolio overwriting".

It's one of the simplest forms of options trading (that is, simple in theory, complex in practice), and it can get you an extra "dividend" every month from your held VTI shares.

And no, not all options are very risky— only specific types of options trades. In the case of covered calls, the risk/reward is limited and explicitly known from the outset, and you never stand to lose more on the downside than the value of the shares you hold (which, as an index investor, is the risk you are taking anyway).

Depending on how you choose to execute the trade, an extra 0.5%[4] of the stock price is a normal monthly premium for a total market ETF like VTI, or large index ETF like SPY. To be clear, portfolio overwriting isn't a magic strategy that gets you an extra 12% per year[5] . It can, however, give you intermittent, incremental returns in the form of extra cash, *without requiring you to sell your shares for anything less than you bought them for.*[6]

1.3 For Example:

At the time I wrote this, VTI was $168.32 a share, and I could have sold someone the right to buy 100 shares from me, at the price of $170[7] per share, for a premium of $1.66 a share. That would have been $166 in my account, and I would only have had to sell my shares if they had risen to more than $170 when the option contract expired[8]. Of note, $170 is more than what I purchased them for ($168.34), so I'd be selling my shares for an additional $176 [9] gain on top of the $166 I got when I sold the contract.

For the frugal FIRE investor, $166 extra can make for quite a

---

[4]Usually it's between 0.25–1.2% depending on the index and market conditions

[5]It could, depending on the strikes you choose, how the market moves, and how lucky you are on any given day, but that's very rare. And it's not the goal.

[6]In fact, you pick the price you are obligated to sell shares at when you sell a covered call— it can be as high above the current index price as you want.

[7]You chose this price as the option seller.

[8]You also choose the date as the option seller— one month in the future in this example.

[9]$1.76 per share x 100 shares

luxurious month, or buy yet another share of VTI.

Just picture yourself waking up, making some income off your shares for the month, and then biking to work and checking off another day towards FIRE, all the while knowing you have the "magical" options trading skills of a FIRE wizard.

CHAPTER 2

Why You Should Care

Earning how to trade stock options? Selling covered calls to make money by portfolio overwriting? Why would I want to do that? It sounds exhausting.

2.1 Selling Covered Calls Makes You Money

I guess I'll open with the biggest selling point:

Covered calls make you money.

More interestingly, selling covered calls makes you money in a flat market (!). If you own shares of anything and aren't excited about this prospect, I'm not sure you're technically alive.

7

In fact, the covered call seller does best in situations with no appreciation or a small amount of appreciation over time. The covered call seller also outperforms the buy-and-hold investor if the price of the shares the call was sold against declines. The simple reason is that the covered call seller has made a premium that the buy-and-hold investor hasn't, and if the price of the underlying stays below the strike price of the call contract, the covered call seller has not incurred upside risk[1] and will not have to sell their shares.[2]

2.2 Selling Calls Provides Immediate Liquidity

The money that selling a covered call gets you is also deposited directly into your account, immediately. This liquid cash is fundamentally different from share price appreciation; until you sell your shares, profits are never locked in, and their value could decline to zero. Contrast that with actual liquid funds you can use to buy and sell securities, or transfer to your checking account.[3]

---

[1]The buy and hold investor would outperform the call seller once the price of the underlying security rises past the strike plus the amount of premium the call seller received. Don't worry- we get into this in depth later.

[2]If the price of shares is above the strike price of the call the day the contract expires, it will automatically be exercised, meaning your shares will be sold to whatever anonymous counterparty owns the call you sold. Buyers of call contracts who do not wish to buy shares are not presented with the option to exercise on expiration Friday— instead they would have to sell-to-close their contract if they did not want to have it automatically execute and buy shares at the strike price.

[3]To be clear, selling an option creates a short position in your account equal to the premium you receive, so it's not entirely magical money from nowhere, but it does increase your cash balance immediately. The call you sell is considered short because you have created an obligation in your account you you must fulfill in the future if the contract is exercised, namely providing shares at a certain price. For the covered call seller, this is not a risky proposition, as you are "covered" and own the shares that you may have to provide. For someone selling a "naked" call (where they don't own shares), it is a risky proposition indeed, as they must in the future buy shares on the open market to fulfill the naked call contract if the

For this reason, the cash you receive when selling a covered call can be considered a form of income, and some investors sell calls monthly and treat it that way. There are even ETFs that sell covered calls to generate monthly "dividends" for you . This book aims to teach you how to do the same thing yourself and avoid the fund management fees![4]

2.3   Options Are an Essential Addition to Any Investor's Toolkit

I consider a basic knowledge of single-leg[5] options an invaluable tool for anyone's investing, even passive index investors. If you understand how a call works, and then you figure out how puts[6] work, every other option trading strategy available to retail investors is just a combination of the two! Even better, a call is just the opposite of a put, so learning one gives you a fundamental intuition for the other.

Not knowing how options work seems almost irresponsible to me if you are an active investor (or an investor, period). Trading stocks without trading options is like playing a sport and not knowing how to lift weights. You might have all the talent and practice in the world,

---

underlying share price rises above the strike, no matter how high it rises. I do not practice, advocate, or describe this type of trading, which presents a theoretically unlimited risk.

[4] "Expense ratio" is a four-letter word.

[5] The options available to a retail investor are the call and the put, and you can trade one or many options at once, up to four per position. Buying or selling just a call or a put is considered a "single-leg" strategy. Trading many options at once to create a complex position is called a "multi-leg" strategy.

[6] A put is the right to sell someone a stock at a specified price. You can buy a put and own the right to "put" stock to someone, or sell a put and sell the right to have stock "put" to you. Conversely, a call is the right to "call" stock from someone. When you sell calls (the topic of this tome) you are selling someone the right to "call" a stock from you. A call buyer, by extension, owns the right to "call" stock from someone else.

but you could probably be better if you added some explosiveness,
strength or endurance to your game.

Figure 2.1: *Ross Enamait— boxing trainer, publisher of some of the
best fitness material ever made, and a generally stand-up dude. He has
a real passion for fitness and making it accessible to anyone. I would
recommend any of his books or DVDs. They are all high-content and
worth every penny, and made such an impression on me when I was
much younger that they eventually helped inspire this book.*

2.4   Options Offer More Control

I cover this again in later chapters about emotional investing, but I
have to touch on it here. Trading options, to me, is a lot more enjoyable
than just buying stocks and hoping they go up. Because of the myriad
of ways you can set up an options trade, you have a lot more control
over what happens with your trading, and can buy and sell options
that make money when a stock goes up, down[7], or sideways.

To me, this feels much better than just buying a stock and hoping

---

[7]As mentioned, covered calls actually make money when the price of an underlying security decreases, and it's frankly quite nice seeing some green on a red
day.

it appreciates in price, hoping you bought it at the right time, and then wondering when you should sell. Options let you make moves and dance around your positions instead of passively observing.[8] Investing in the market can be like swimming in rough seas. When things look choppy, knowing how to surf changes the game. You can see what's coming, catch your breath, time it and paddle in, and try to go with the waves rather than be thrown by the currents. Options can be the board that helps you ride the wave.[9]

2.5 "Options are too risky" is Flat Wrong

"Options are risky" is a wildly misinformed statement. I *cringe* when I hear it. Some types of options are very risky— covered calls... not so much.[10]

Fact: Selling covered calls has less *downside* risk than owning a

---

[8]Selling covered calls can be as time consuming as you want it to be. Selling a call at the beginning of the month takes less than a minute on most brokerage apps, and you can simply let it run to expiry knowing your initial profit and loss risk. You can also spend lots of time attempting to squeeze out extra profits by buying back your calls and selling new ones if you so desire, the how-to of which (called position management) comprises a major portion of this book. Chapter 42 is a parable of 3 investors, featuring more detail on the different types of investors and style of portfolio overwriting and corresponding time commitment that is best for them.

[9]Cowabunga. I was really torn about including a surfing metaphor, yet here we are. It's actually quite an apt analogy, because standing in the surf and trying to predict the characteristics of the next ten waves that will hit you is on par with the level of difficulty of predicting (random) price movements in the market.

[10]Traditionally, covered calls were the first type of options any retail account would be approved for, and investors would only be able to trade more complicated and risky options once they had traded covered calls for some duration. At the time of writing this, however, many new app-based brokerages have an online options application form that allows people to state that they have any level of experience without any burden of verification, and immediately begin trading very risky options with little or no actual prior experience.

stock or index. This is simply because the premium you are paid when you sell a call offsets a loss of share price of the same amount. Compared to buy and hold, you will have always "made" the premium in returns.

Additional Fact: There is more *upside risk*, which is a form of lost profits (i.e., missing out on gains you could have had), and I cover this thoroughly. In fact, I believe my biggest responsibility is showing you the risk, because I myself have read and own A LOT[11] of books about options trading and too many of them present an overly rosy view of the endeavor, which leads to over-optimism and eventual letdowns.[12]

Other options strategies are risky, but most, including portfolio overwriting as described in this text, have an explicit and known risk at the outset. If you buy a put, you make money if the stock goes down, but never lose more than the price of the put you purchased. Compare that to shorting[13], where if the stock you shorted goes to the

---

[11] At this point, I have compiled what could be considered a small library on the topic of options trading.

[12] Because I'm not trying to sell any subscriptions to investing services, I am in the unique position where I can genuinely present the risks and downsides, and not have to market myself as a guru with any extra secret knowledge you'll need to pay for. Everything I know is in this book, which is intended to be a standalone guide to selling covered calls.

[13] When you own a security (stock or option) it is referred to as being "long". A position in your account that you do not own is referred to as "short". This is a very confusing concept initially.

In the case where you "short" stock, you borrow shares from a brokerage at the current price to create your "short" position. If shares decline in price, you can buy them at a lower price to fulfill your "short" position, and you make the difference between the price you borrowed them for and the (now lower) price you paid to fulfill your short position. If the price of the stock goes to a million dollars a share, you still have to buy those shares on the open market to fulfill your short position at some point, which is why "shorting" has theoretically unlimited risk. I say theoretically because share price doesn't usually go to infinity.

When you sell a covered call, the option is short in your account, but your short call is "covered" because you own the shares and can deliver them at any time. Unless you are approved for margin and higher levels of option trading, your broker will not allow you to make an unlimited risk trade. Sidenote: I do not trade on margin or make unlimited risk trades, ever; I like being able to sleep at night.

moon, you might have to take out a second mortgage on your home in order to pay your broker when you get margin called.

2.6 Your Money Makes Money in Real Time

Understanding delayed gratification is one of the major struggles we face as an intelligent animal. Pop psychology has the famous "marshmallow test", and we know from FIRE that frugality now leads to outsized rewards later. Although this is easy to understand abstractly, it's hard to really internalize the benefits that years of self-control will have far, far in the future. But when you sell a call, money is deposited into your account right away, and it can be a game-changing motivator for people who aren't as easily swayed by the promise of a better tomorrow in exchange for restraint today. So portfolio overwriting can be an excellent motivator for the crowd that finds index investing to be a daunting, boring task.[14]

2.7 Finally, Learning = Good

Learning keeps your mind limber, and if you're interested in a topic and it's your choice to learn it, learning isn't hard at all. As a FIRE investor, I'm assuming you have the same motivation and desire to think outside the box as the rest of the community, which is more than enough of the moxie required to grock[15] covered calls. Also, the

---

[14]This may be the best reason to learn portfolio overwriting. Seeing the long-term rewards of investing is very difficult for most people. If creating some income now via selling calls is enough motivation for someone to build a portfolio that they otherwise would never even start, the benefits extend far beyond the call premiums.

[15]Meaning to understand intuitively, grock (alternate spelling: grok) is one of my favorite words, coined by author Martin Heinlein in the 1961 novel Stranger in

only math you need to know in order to understand and sell covered calls at the retail level is arithmetic.

a Strange Land. Primarily it has found use as part of the hippie lexicon.

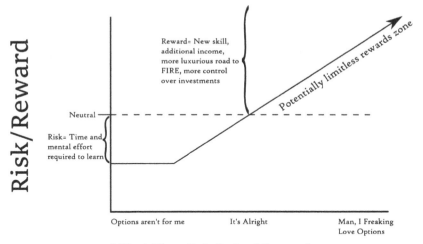

Risk/Reward

Reward= New skill, additional income, more luxurious road to FIRE, more control over investments

Potentially limitless rewards zone

Neutral

Risk= Time and mental effort required to learn

Options aren't for me   It's Alright   Man, I Freaking Love Options

What You Get Out of Learning
Portfolio Overwriting with Covered Calls

Figure 2.2: *A risk/reward chart of learning how to trade options.*

Above is a graphical representation of the risk vs the reward of reading this book and learning portfolio overwriting. Spoiler alert: it's roughly the same as a long call risk-reward graph. [16]

Hopefully I made a good argument for continuing to read this book, so let's lay out a roadmap in the next chapter so you know what's in store.

---

[16]A long call (or "being long a call") is when you own the call. This book primarily focuses on when you sell a covered call, which would be referred to as being "short" a call.

Profit and loss (aka P&L) graphs like this are a great tool for understanding how much money you stand to lose or make when you enter an options trade based on the price at expiration, and will be used and will appear one more time in chapter 23 to help visualize "upside breakeven." Although we don't use them much for portfolio overwriting, they are invaluable for understanding more complex strategies, as they can visually represent the combination of two or more different profit and loss trades, combined into one.

CHAPTER 3

Outline

---

had a semblance of intelligent design when I laid it all out; here's the underlying logic—

First, the thought map I made before I started writing. It went through about a million changes:

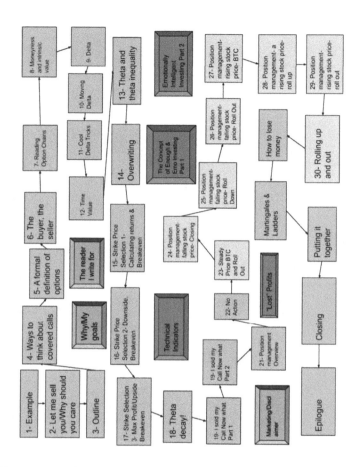

Figure 3.1: *A very early mind-map of what I wanted to explain.*

3.1   Pace and Pueo

You might notice at first that there are a large number of chapters, but you'll notice just as quickly once you start reading that most of them are brief and digestible. My vision was something you can read, at your convenience, at your pace, and come back to as a reference whenever you need to.

Figure 3.2: *This is a cool picture I took of a Pueo on my pre-wedding honeymoon. I hope that does the trick for you. It has nothing to do with covered calls.*

If you work your way through it all, you should have all the skills and preparation necessary to do some portfolio overwriting.

You'll also notice most technical chapters feature only one or two examples, but they are covered in depth. I want to conversationally explain everything at a pace conducive to learning with some fun pictures here and there.

There will be lots of technical pictures as well. There already exists a glut of educational material featuring intimidating blocks of text that I feel are a hurdle to most people. Those sources are great places to get other perspectives and more examples after learning solid foundations here.

3.2   The Path

The chapters take you through the basics of what an option is, and
how to understand options, specifically how to trade covered calls and
manage positions. Learning the basics of what a covered call is and
how to sell one is simple— a quick internet search will give you the
basic idea.

The complicated part all happens after you initially sell a covered
call.

One could learn the basics and how to sell a call very rapidly, and
most brokerages offer video tutorials online.[1] Unfortunately, like most
things, it's not as simple as it seems.

The call you sell, like a stock, changes in price over time in tandem
with the underlying stock, and you have the ability to trade it up
until expiration, buying back the initial call you sold, or rolling[2] it
into another call. This is called "position management", and the topic
comprises much of the latter half of the book.

As a portfolio overwriter, you can be as active or passive in this
endeavor as you desire.[3] Some portfolio overwriters frequently trade
calls with the aim of locking in gains and generating more premium
at every possible opportunity. Others just take a few minutes and
sell calls every month or two, taking a more passive and less time-
consuming approach. Wherever you fall on this spectrum, the lion's
share of skill and knowledge lies in position management, and you need
to know how to competently perform it— mainly because it is easy to

---

[1]I recommend learning the how-to nuts and bolts of what to click or tap when
selling a call via your brokerage's website or educational materials, as they are all
very simple but have slightly different interfaces.

[2]"Rolling" is buying-to-close your current call and simultaneously selling to
open another, effectively "rolling" your contract into a different trade. This is
covered in-depth in future chapters, as it comprises a large majority of portfolio
overwriting.

[3]A later chapter on emotionally intelligent investing covers this in-depth.

lose money here if you don't understand what you are doing.

3.3   An Index Bias

I'm writing mostly from the perspective of how to portfolio overwrite a total stock index (if you don't know what this means, don't worry!) because I'm gearing this all towards my FI crew, but this book would also be useful to anyone who trades individual securities and wants to know how to sell covered calls.

Portfolio overwriting is a very specific goals-based strategy when it comes to selling covered calls, aiming to sell calls against shares you would like to hold long-term and would prefer not to sell. But there are other ways to invest with covered calls, and this book is a comprehensive introduction to selling covered calls in general.

After reading this book, you will not only understand portfolio overwriting against indexes, but also have a strong basis in call options (and options in general) that will allow you to explore other avenues with confidence and ease, if you so desire.[4]

3.4   Bonus Material

There are also some ancillary chapters: some that directly explain technicalities and some that give a more holistic sense of what I'm up to and why, as well as some (hopefully) insightful thoughts on how I view trading in general. They are, imho, the most valuable ones... but

---

[4]I have in the past, but it is extremely time consuming, stressful, and difficult. The fact that I consider myself a "reformed" active investor and almost entirely adhere to index investing with some portfolio overwriting as described in this book should be telling to the reader about what I've found works, what doesn't, and most importantly what's worth my time.

that's just like, my opinion, man.[5]

Figure 3.3: My "Desktop Dude"

---

[5]The Big Lebowski is one of my favorite films. I'm even a certified Dudeist Minister if anyone reading this needs their pets married (I don't ordain human covenants— too many ins and outs, and what-have-yous). If you'd like some awesome Lebowski art check out Chuck Hamilton's portfolio on the website for A. T. Hun art gallery in Savannah Georgia http://www.athun.com/

CHAPTER 4

Thinking About Covered Calls

love metaphors. Pictures, too. I'm going to use them to help conceptualize covered calls.[1]

---

[1]None of these metaphors are truly accurate. The idea of "extra dividends" or a "holding fee" are nice ways to look at covered calls, but they are not precise. The real estate prospecting example comes closest, but I am mentioning this primo in the chapter so you don't have an overly-rosy view of covered calls being "free money". You are selling an asymmetric option- a claim on the potential returns of an underlying asset above a certain price. That possibility, the possible futures that include profit, are what transacts. Although abstract, it has real value, which is why you are paid for it.

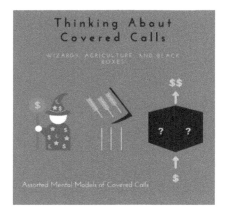

4.1   Artificial Dividends

The first thing I thought when I learned about covered calls: they're like a dividend that you create. Dividends are pretty slick, because they turn your shares (basically a theoretical claim on corporate profit) into an instrument that generates real income. You may have heard of "dividend investors" or "dividend FIRE", where one keeps accumulating shares of dividend-paying stocks until they pay out enough to replace the income from one's day job.

But what if you could make your own dividends? And what if the dividends you were conjuring out of thin air yielded much more than traditional dividend stocks? Covered calls can do that!

When you sell a call you are, in one sense, collecting money for the "task[2]" of holding shares. To me, this concept was stellar. Sounds too good to be true? At the time of writing this, if you own 100 shares of PFE (Pfizer) for \$37.36 a share, someone will deposit \$90 in your account, right now, for the right to buy the shares from you for \$38.00

---

[2]Aka "risk"

a share (yes, a price that is **more than you paid for it**) in one month.

Figure 4.1: *The first time I learned that, I felt like I had been imbued with the power of a financial wizard, privy to the secret arcane arts that normal mortals fear and revere.*

Ruminate on that for a moment.

The possibilities seem endless, don't they? Just think: every time you sell a call against shares you hold, your shares pay for themselves just a bit, lowering their own cost basis. It's like using your car to drive Uber and then using the Uber paycheck to make your car payment. In fact, some people try to sell calls perpetually, hoping to eventually own shares that, over time, will have paid for themselves.

Owning assets that produce income is another big shift in thinking compared to just saving, and is repeatedly harped on in personal finance advice... But for me, I have no interest in managing a franchise[3] or rental property.[4] Also, not everyone has the six figures required for most traditional income-producing assets, and selling calls can get you started making money with your money for a much lower entry fee.[5]

---

[3] In my experience, numbers are typically easier to deal with than people.

[4] I did it once and it was a disaster

[5] Specifically, the price of 100 shares of any stock with options. Although indexes like VTI and SPY can be quite expensive, there are optionable stocks across the spectrum of share prices. SPYG and SCHD are good, lower cost, optionable funds that track the "growth" and "dividend" subsets of SPY, and may make for a suitable, less capital-intensive alternative. There are also some optionable stocks under $5, that would make for great practice before selling options against indexes, but at that point paper trading may be preferable than "stock-picking" for the

Or, you could sell calls on a stock that already pays dividends and think of it as making...EVEN MORE DIVIDENDS![6]

But we have to be more precise in our thinking; I may have misled you already. You aren't really getting paid for the task of holding the shares and the associated risk of share price falling; rather, you're selling someone the **option** to buy the shares from you. The option itself is a contract for the future sale of the shares.

4.2   Real Estate Prospecting

Let's make up an imaginary real estate scenario to explain it better. Say you own a swank abode. I personally would get a home from Utopian Villas and plunk it down in Ouray, CO if I had my pick of locale and domicile.

Figure 4.2:   *The Utopian Villas Denali...look at that tiny living dream!!!*

So, in this example, your place has big windows, a roomy kitchen, a fancy bathroom, and stainless steel as far as the eye can see...but

---

average Mustachian.

[6]This is just the tip of the iceberg.

Figure 4.3: *It even has a rooftop deck....whaaaaat?*

suddenly a knock at the door. A smooth talking real estate developer is waiting on the other side, telling you that they think they might want to buy your house in a year. But they aren't sure, and therefore aren't willing to buy it right now.

To be precise, the real estate developer doesn't want to buy your crib, but rather wants to buy the right to buy your crib. Specifically they tell you they want to buy it in a year, for more than it is worth now. Now, they are still going to be paying you less than what they think it will be worth next year, because they are speculating[7] and need to turn a profit.

So let's put some numbers to the example.

---

[7]This is the whole reason that options exist— uncertainty about future prices. Options distill the market's expectations about future prices into a real number today. This area where rubber meets the road with probability is super cool and of great intellectual interest to me.

Because options are linking the uncertain future to the certain present, they are relatively straightforward and simple instruments with a variety of functional applications.

Options can provide outsized leveraged returns, or provide protection by using options as a kind of insurance. This book details how they allow shareholders like us to sell someone else the right to buy our shares, because selling that right generates income!

Figure 4.4: *Imagine all the bottle rockets you could shoot off that thing.*

Figure 4.5: *Lots of sun inside, too.*

Hypothetically:

- You bought your place for $220k.

- Your place is now worth $280k.

- A real estate human wants to buy it for $320k next year, if and only if[8] they feel like it.

---

[8]To equate this example to stock options more, we will assume that if your house is worth more than $320K that the speculator WILL feel like buying it.

First of all, the savvy homeowner will appreciate that giving some-one an exclusive right to purchase your home should be worth some-thing; after all, you are reducing the developer's risk and providing them the possibility of making an outsized return, while at the same time constraining yourself a bit. By selling the right to buy your house at a fixed price in the future, *you transfer your potential to make profits* to the speculator.

But what is that exclusive right worth? $1,000? $5,000? $10,000? A lot goes into that arithmetic!

Firstly, how much do you like where you live? Are you treating your house like an investment, or does it have more than just financial value to you? Would you rather wait and see if the value goes up next year and sell it yourself, maybe for even more than the $320k real estate speculator is offering? Do you know of any secret problems with the house (ghosts) or surrounding area (active fault lines) that might make you want to sell and move soon? Do you think that if you are forced to move that you'll be able to get another house that is just as valuable to you next year for $320,000? How much is it going to cost you to move? Is a tech giant going to build a satellite campus down the street and make the local economy explode with prosperity?

So you think about it, do some bickering, and decide on $12,000. You feel like an extra $1,000 a month would be nice, and since you bought the place for $220k and will be selling for $320k, you will have made a smooth $100k plus a $12,000 contract premium, which could cover moving costs and/or part of at least a down payment on a new house.

So you mock up this weird fantasy contract, shake hands, and you get a check for $12,000. Now what?

If your local real estate market doesn't change one bit over the next year, you'll end up having made $12,000 and won't have to sell your house, because the developer is never going to exercise the option and pay $320K for a $280K house.

If, however, it turns out that some tech giant actually does build a new campus near you and your locale morphs into San Francisco 2.0, your place might end up being worth $500K. In which case, you'll get a $100K return from your purchase price of $220k if you sold it to the developer for $320K, but will miss out on making the extra $280K from selling it yourself, post-housing boom.[9]

Given that misfortune, you might be kicking yourself, or you might be ok with the fact that you can't predict the future and made $100K plus the $12K contract price (take note, you'll see this theme a lot).

Figure 4.6: *A $2 Million San Francisco Home*

Or, if the value of your home dropped to $268K, you'd break even since you made $12k in a year— in which case you'd feel pretty smart.

In the above scenario, your house would be equivalent to a stock, the future contract to sell would be a covered call stock option you sold, $320K would be the strike[10] price, and the $12K would be the option premium you receive as the call seller.

So why doesn't everyone do this, all the time? Just like when the price of the house skyrocketed in our example, selling a call "caps" your profits on the underlying stock (or other investment, such as an

---

[9]This is known as "upside risk", which we will come back to again and again throughout the book. It is the most overt and ever-present risk that you should have a full understanding of when selling covered calls.

[10]Covered in more detail later, the "strike price" is the price that the owner of the call option has the right to buy shares at, up until the date the contract expires, regardless of what the share price actually is.

ETF or index fund). This is called upside risk, and it **can** reduce your gains over time compared to buy-and-hold investing.

More concerning, if you are not disciplined with portfolio overwriting (only ever selling calls above your cost basis, and only against a small portion of your portfolio, and never rolling the position for a loss) you can actually *lose* money selling calls. This can be hard for some people to handle. If you aren't able to sell a call only above your cost basis, let the shares go when necessary, and resist the temptation to chase profits, you will likely find yourself losing money.[11] This book repeatedly emphasizes how money is lost to things other than upside risk, and repeatedly emphasizes how you can avoid it.[12]

Initially, I was happy letting shares get called away.

Figure 4.7: *Goodbye, shares. If you love something, let it go.*

I began to think of covered calls like a cash machine, short term investment where I could use my money to buy new shares, sell new

---

[11]More to the point, as we will see and discuss in depth later, selling covered calls is more suited to income generation than growth.

[12]The good news is this usually boils down to nothing more than being patient, and either waiting for the right time to sell a call, or selling a longer-dated call.

calls, and make a % every month[13] that would compound my account value to the millions in a matter of years. Seemed like a great deal to me!

But I was wrong. It's not that easy.[14] Instead of a black box that gives you money, it turned out to be more of a slot machine where you have some modicum of control.[15]

4.3   Harvesting

In another way, selling calls after a stock has gone up can "lock in" some profits without requiring you to sell any shares. It's a bit like picking mint leaves from your herb garden without uprooting the whole plant. Anyone who has invested knows the eternal dilemma is when to buy and sell, and selling calls partially circumvents the decision. It

---

[13]Is this a bad view? Not necessarily. Treating covered calls and the underlying shares purely as a monthly income vehicle is an interesting view to take and a more difficult strategy to implement. The monthly returns are not as consistent for individual stocks due to underlying volatility and trade-off of upside potential for premiums. Worse, the risk of share price decline usually outweighs the premiums made over time; one stock tanking can wipe out months of accumulated premiums.

This book essentially describes a variation of that strategy that hinges on some important differences. We use a smaller portion of our shares, with an index we would be invested in indefinitely anyway (we accept the downside risk) as the underlying, with the aim of making very modest returns, only selling contracts with a higher strike price than our cost basis, usually above the current market price, that hopefully won't result in us selling our shares.

I may cover my experiences with more aggressive options elsewhere in the future, and the spoiler alert here is that it would be a mostly cautionary tale. But this is portfolio overwriting for Mustachians, not active investing for degenerate (just kidding) traders.

[14]Don't believe anyone who tells you that it is.

[15]A large portion of my time spent selling covered calls was against individual securities— mostly biotech. I learned along the way that the higher premiums were often not outweighed by the added risk. After discovering FIRE, I learned that I far preferred occasionally portfolio overwriting some of the shares I plan to hold forever for some extra scratch. Most appealing was the knowledge that pullbacks were a temporary and natural part of the long-term outlook I had embraced, so it was infinitely less stressful than trying to beat the market.

allows you to make some money and keep your shares if the price of the underlying investment falls.

Figure 4.8: *My very modest herb garden— the one on the right is catnip.*

All sound too good to be true? For some reason, a lot of people who have traded stocks their entire investing career have no idea how options work. This is a mystery to me, but I'm guessing it comes from a few places: misinformed prejudice that all options are risky, a fear of the difficulty learning to trade options, or a lack of exposure.

As far as riskiness goes, there are lots of options strategies that have limited, explicitly know risk. In terms of difficulty, the math involved to trade options in the retail setting is limited to simple arithmetic.[16] And as far as exposure goes, this book is here to help with that!

---

[16]If you want to understand the Black-Scholes formula or binary pricing models (some of the dominant theoretical mathematical models used to price options by investment firms) in depth, you will need some higher level math...but that isn't absolutely necessary for selling covered calls at the retail level.

CHAPTER **5**

When Does It Make Sense to Sell Calls

---

ow that you have an idea of how a covered call works, you might be pondering exactly when it would be useful to sell one against your shares.

5.1 You're Going to Spend the Money Anyway?

A not-entirely-accurate but often provided answer is "when you would be spending the money anyway." Say you needed to purchase an automobile for $40,000 (arguably too expensive, but it is roughly the same price as 100 shares of SPY at the time I'm writing this). Also imagine you did not have the option to lease— this is a car that your good friend bought and only drove once, but they need money now and can't finance like a bank would. The classic pro-covered-call argument goes "rather than cash out right away, sell a covered call. You get the premium, and if shares get called away, use them to pay for the car. You still bought your car but now you have the extra premium as well."

This seems sound at first glance— but let's consider possible futures for a moment to poke a hole in the logic.

In a future where the S&P stays the same or rises above your strike, this makes sense.

But in a different future, there is a huge dip in the S&P. You still have to pay for the truck. Your friend needs the money, and you owe it to him, but the index tanked due to some major market event and your shares are only worth $250 each— $25,000. Not good!

5.2   You're Going to Spend the Money Anyway, Over Time?

So the next clever argument is "what about when you do have the option to lease? Sell a call, make the first payment with premium, and assume the entire market doesn't crash so badly that you could afford to sell shares to make payment #2 if needed." This argument is a bit better, but still has to contend with the fact that selling your shares outright when they were worth about $400 each would have been a better move if the index dipped to $250 per share like above.

Before you discount it, keep in mind you made a premium you wouldn't have otherwise. And consider another future where the S&P stays the same all month, or dips and then bounces back. In these cases you made the premium and didn't lose any index value, and you can do it again (and again, hopefully).

The point here is that portfolio overwriting wins... in some timelines. It harkens back to the fact that selling calls outperforms in down or sideways markets, but it's not the most ideal strategy for all situations. Nothing is.[1] Especially if you have a small acount and have to sell a few shares at market-crash prices to make next month's payment, and no longer have the required 100 shares necessary to sell covered calls.

So how can we improve the endeavor overall?

5.3 You're Going to Spend the Money Anyway, Over Time, but You Aren't on a Strict Timetable?

Consider a third example, where you decided to give $40,000 to charity. But rather than a lump sum, you decide to provide the charity with money over time. The money is no longer mentally "yours", and there isn't as strict a timetable. In this case, it would be very nice to sell covered calls. If you only sold calls at cost basis or above, you'd know your charity of choice would get at least the $40,000 plus one month's premium, and you wouldn't be on the hook for something like a car payment. You could wait for the index to rebound to your cost basis before doing it again. In this case, time and flexibility are your friends.

But you may not be at the Pete Adeny[2] level of giving yet. So

---

[1] With covered calls you are still exposed to downside risk, but the rub is that you intrinsically accept that risk as an index investor. It makes the portfolio overwriting for FIRE mindset and risk/reward profile vastly different than selling covered calls on individual securities with much larger downside risk.

[2] Pete Adeny is Mr. Money Mustache's real name. He's given away $100,000 multiple times and described the process in blog posts, starting with one in October 2017. As far as I'm concerned that makes him a G-D national treasure and inspirational role model we need. We have enough people showing off the material things you can buy with money. I have a fantasy in my head of convincing MMM to set funds aside and try making contributions with premiums generated from covered calls, but more likely than not I'd probably receive a patented Mr. Money

what kind of situation would someone have to be in where they didn't need set income and had a sizable chunk of shares sitting around to leverage? Someone that maybe wanted to withdraw 4% a year of some investment, while patiently holding with the other 96% forever? Someone that might like the idea of potentially NOT having to sell shares from their FIRE funds?

You probably see where I'm going here.

The perfect setup exists for someone with a frugal lifestyle and minimal expenses that is going to be cashing out at some point, but has an excess reserve of shares they can sell calls against a portion of.

5.4 You Have the Extra Funds Available to Allocate a Portion of Your Portfolio to an Income-Producing Asset.

I need to make a very abstract, very important point here. What you are doing by selling calls is, in a way, taking a part of your portfolio and turning it into a different financial instrument. Rather than just shares that go up and down with the market, you have created a position that outperforms in sideways months, down months, or months with slight appreciation. This is the whole idea behind a hedge[3] fund or diversification to an asset class like bonds, or real estate. When people reach a certain level of wealth, expanding to assets that perform well when the overall market does not is arguably the logical move. The difference with portfolio overwriting for FIRE is that the modest premiums can make a huge difference to the frugal FIRE adherent, and it leverage the indexes you are already holding!

Mustache Facepunch for advocating any kind of active investing

[3]It "hedges" your bets (portfolio holdings).

> **As far as Mustachians are concerned, this book can be seen as describing a side hustle you can choose to invest some of your funds in.**

It should be apparent to the reader that these conditions are the same that one would use to determine when to make ANY alternative investment— namely, when you are in a financially sound place to do so. Not exactly the most insightful and original thought, but that is how you should be treating funds allocated to portfolio overwriting— as a type of investment!

If you buy a rental house, you might not make money every month— there are occupancy issues, repairs, natural disasters etc. It's the same thing with portfolio overwriting. In my opinion, it should exist as a supplement, a diversification, rather than your entire portfolio.

5.5 The Best Side Hustle to Ever Exist

Speaking of rentals, I view portfolio overwriting as by far the best side hustle that ever existed. The income may be less consistent than others[4], but in terms of time spent (very little) and paucity of headaches, it can't be beat.

- No sales

- No customer service

- No tenants asking if they can repaint your bathroom blue, which you agree too, only to find out that by "paint" they meant spray-paint with artistic graffiti (this happened to yours truly)

---

[4]When portfolio overwriting, you only sell calls with a strike price above your cost basis, and if the market tanks you may have to wait until the share price of your index recovers back to the point where a strike price above cost basis gets you a substantive premium.

It's also a fantastic way for people who may be newer to investing or have never had an entrepreneurial endeavor to see their money make money. As someone who has worked since the age of 15, the first time I sold a call and saw a premium get deposited into my account, it changed the way I saw the world. An older acquaintance[5] once told me "one day you'll wake up and realize your money can work harder than you" and it never truly clicked for me until I sold a call.

And if you do want to do a traditional side hustle, a backup portfolio overwriting fund can be a great "safe haven" cushion for that endeavor.[6] Unexpected expenses can destroy businesses, especially in the early phases.[7] I wouldn't advocate for replacing your business savings and checking with an index you plan to sell shares against, I'm just trying to illustrate that income from portfolio overwriting can be used for anything.

Premiums can also be invested into more index shares to turbo-

---

[5]This gentleman was a trader by profession, and was offering me advice before I knew how valuable it was. Unfortunately I didn't properly value the opportunity at the time, but I thankfully retained this lesson. To give you an idea of how old-school and experienced he was, he used point-and-figure charting, a very old and now obscure method of "technical analysis" where you try to predict the moves of stock by studying the past moves— the "shape" of the chart.

[6]A dissenting opinion that I hold: Traditional finance would balk at a haven of invested funds set aside for the express purpose of supporting a business venture. Not only would it be a gross example of unutilized capital (money that could be invested in the business to generate more profits), it would be an indication that the business itself was unprofitable. I personally think this type of efficiency maximization lacks any higher order reasoning, only thinking in the numerical accounting dimension. Although this seems a common sense diversification to an uncorrelated asset to me (selling widgets and investing some of the widget profits into an income producing investment in case a pandemic or something similar slows down your widget sales), the same people that would tell me I'm wrong would likely have taken classes in modern portfolio theory and diversification, remaining blind to the parallels.

[7]It happened to me with my brief, disastrous foray into owning rental properties, which is one of the main reasons I prefer portfolio overwriting to real estate. Had I been portfolio overwriting at the time, I could have floated my property's mortgage payments during times of vacancy and repair costs with call premiums rather than having to end up selling the property, at a loss, only to watch it appreciate about 700% (gentrification) from the price I unloaded it at. See above footnote.

charge compounding, or any other form of investments, whether it is a rental property, food truck, or something even riskier. And if those invested premiums support growth in a different area, your returns are going to be above and beyond whatever % monthly you made from the premium.

So why am I appealing to the Mustachians? Why would I plead my case to one of the most notoriously anti-active investing crowds to ever exist? Because we are perfect for it, and I'll explain why next.

CHAPTER 6

Mustachians and Overwriting

---

know mustachians are about as anti-active investing as you can get, but a more perfect crowd for portfolio overwriting doesn't exist! Not knowing how to portfolio overwrite as a FIRE adherent would be like Einstein deciding that he should stick to patents.

6.1 Mustachians Know What Money is Worth

Firstly, Mustachians are frugal. Keeping expenses to a minimum means you really understand what's important in life. It also means you have a built in, experimentally verified marginal return on utility. I only mention this because it is a really neat concept that can be understood with a simple picture.

Swiss Mathematician Nicholas Bernoulli posited that different people have different utility (use/value) for a given amount of money. This intuitively makes sense— if I am completely broke, $1,000 will mean a lot more to mean than it would a billionaire. Illustrated below, it shows wealth on one axis and utility on the other axis, with utility dropping off bigtime after a certain point in wealth.

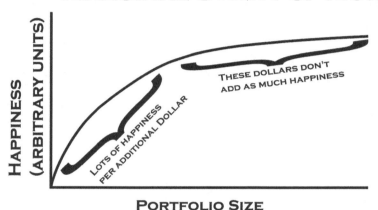

Figure 6.1: *A typical marginal utility of money graph.*

Adjusted for FIRE, your 25x is the biggest boost. After that it's all gravy, but it's not as important as that first 25x. As such, the Mustachian version might look something like this:

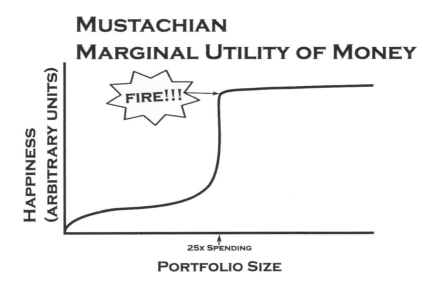

Figure 6.2: *The Mustachian Marginal Utility of Money Curve.*

6.2 Mustachians and Index Investors Have Unshakeable Investing Faith

Second, your conviction in the underlying security— namely the US market over time— is indestructible. Bogleheads, like the FIRE crowd, believe in buying and holding the overall US market with religious fanaticism, and with good reason.[1] This ability to buy and hold forever is a skill not routinely found among active investors.

---

[1]It's kind of crazy to think about how a lot of the world's inhabitants don't even have access to this luxury. The fact that Americans have direct access to participating in the gains of a (seemingly) ever-upward trending economy is like being able to put money down on an EZ-made millionaire machine that only requires patience, and not buying stuff you don't need, is astounding. The fact that a lot of people with the means to participate in it simply don't equally baffling.

Compare the Boglehead investor to active investors working with options trading and selling covered calls for income. A large portion of this crowd treats securities as interchangeable, buying stocks and selling a call on them based on momentum[2], without full faith in each underlying stock's long term prospects. This crowd will forever be plagued with uncertainty of their underlying thesis, and concerned with maximizing return on capital. They might lack the financial stability and patience[3] required to wait for a recovery from a dip in price to ensure they sell covered calls at a strike price above cost basis.

6.3   People Pursuing FIRE End Up with a Large Portfolio of Index Funds

Depending on funds, you can also leverage your financial stability into accepting smaller, more consistent returns that allow for sizable upside potential, mitigating your upside risk. Allow me to illustrate:

- When I wrote this, the S&P 500 was $420[4] a share

- The $505 LEAPS call sells for $2.30 a contract

- If you had 2,000 shares in excess of 25x, you could sell 20 calls at $2.30, netting yourself $4,600

- Depending on your spending, $4,600 is probably a normal Mustachian monthly budget

---

[2]Or news, or technical analysis, or social media like Fintwit, or Reddit

[3]This patience can also allow for an ultrahedger/LEAPS strategy. Covered in more detail in chapter 22, LEAPS is an acronym for a "Long-term Equity AnticiPation Security". Simply put, it is an option with an expiration date 1–2 years into the future.

[4]Nice.

- Selling the \$505 call allows for about 20% upside. So, even if you did allow those shares to be assigned, [5] you're making a \$170,000 profit. Probably something you'd be happy with.

Having this many excess shares (about \$840,000 worth) to sell calls against is a lofty goal[6] , but combined with the ability to wait a year and not think about it, it's a pretty good deal overall.

Simply said, having more funds and small expenses allows you to make trades that are very safe from an upside risk perspective, but still impactful on your (low) living expenses.

6.4 Anyone Seriously Pursuing No Longer Having to Work Is Nonconformist

Additionally, Mustachians as a whole are iconoclastic.[7] The fact that you even wanted to escape the rat race and sunder your meaning in life from your source of income means that you are already thinking outside the box that others may be trapped in. That's all the iconoclastic mentality and motivation that it takes to learn a complex topic like options... and you've already got it.

---

[5] You aren't locked into assignment— we cover this and other position management techniques in future chapters

[6] I am nowhere near that level of wealth at the time of writing this, but I'm working on it.

[7] I guess if you are an iconoclast by virtue of being a Mustachian, and you choose to sell calls (with active investing being anti-mustachian) then that makes you a... meta-iconoclast?

6.5   Even the Best Mustachians Worry About Withdrawal Rate

Even the most frugal indexers can still have worries about SWR (Safe Withdrawal Rate— most commonly agreed to be 4% per year). Return sequence risk is a very real thing, where withdrawals made during down years greatly decrease performance over time.[8] It is the fear of every Mustachian about to FIRE that the market will crash and stay crashed the moment that they retire early.

The good news is that covered calls do great in flat or slowly decreasing markets, and can keep you from selling your shares if your index dips after you sold a call.

6.6   Options Just Might be Fun for You

Finally, there's the off chance that you might fall into the unique category where this FIRE wizard (yours truly) exists. If you enjoy probability, risk, mathematical thinking, strategy, and the possibility of gains above the market then this is a great hobby to read and learn about. I'm not going to try and pull you into an active investing rabbit hole in the pages of this tome,[9] but suffice to say making some extra money every month via safe, conservative index portfolio overwriting using only your smarts and some trades feels pretty good.

---

[8]To learn the concept intuitively by playing with a free calculator and Monte Carlo simulation, check out `http://www.winchfinancial.com/financial-planning/risk-management-insurance/sequence-returns-calculator/`

[9]In fact, I wouldn't recommend it. As such, throughout the course of this book I'll mostly be deterring you via good-natured self-deprecation and cautionary tales.

CHAPTER 7

A Formal Definition of Options

Riting this makes me shudder. Prepare yourself for the most boring statement ever devised to academically describe one of the most interesting topics in existence:

> **An option is the right (but not the obligation) to buy (or sell) a stock for a predetermined price on (or before) a specified date.**

I hope to gawd you're still with me. I'm sure a percentage of eyes glazed over and lost attention because of that one sentence. I think most people lose interest the exact moment that definition gets thrown at them. There's no cool way to say it, and it's not compelling in that format. It's an industry standard hurdle you just have to jump over before you get to the good stuff.

Figure 7.1: *I tried— still not very cool.*

7.1 The Breakdown

Don't worry... it's simple...

An option is the right (but not the obligation) to buy (or sell) a stock for a predetermined price on (or before) a specified date.

- Option = Option[1]

- Right but not obligation = whoever owns the contract can buy (or sell) the underlying stock *if they want to*[2]

- For a predetermined price = this is the "strike price", and you choose it when you buy or sell options.

- On (or before) a specified date = at some point in the future, because our perception of time is linear and unidirectional. In American-style options, the right can be exercised anytime before the contract expires (the "expiration date"). This date is also chosen by the option buyer/seller.

Important note: options are sold in lots of 100, so you are always buying or selling an obligation tied to 100 shares. This is a given, and I will sometimes switch between talking about a per share gain/loss and a total gain/loss, so I'm warning you now it may be confusing. Unfortunately, it is the lay of the land in the options world. Fortunately, you can get accustomed to it here before venturing out to other sources that assume you have more of a knowledge base.

---

[1]Mono = One and Rail = Rail. This is a Simpsons reference.

[2]Contracts that expire "in the money" are automatically exercised on expiration day after market close, but can also be exercised prior to expiration day by the contract owner. As call sellers you do not own the call (you sold it), and therefore would not have the option of exercise.

7.2   How Does This Make Me Money?

Options aren't free for the buyer. If you sell one, you get paid immediately to enter that obligation. What you are paid is known as the "options premium". The converse is also true if you are the one buying the option— you have to pay for it right away.

With this book I intend to teach you how to be a covered call seller[3]— the one getting paid to hold something you already plan on holding indefinitely. You will also know exactly how much you are paid, and how much you can earn (or lose) when you make this trade.

The basic idea is to buy 100 shares of stock (or use 100 shares of an index if you are an FI-oriented Boglehead), sell someone else the right to buy the 100 shares at a higher price, and collect the premium.

But before we can sell options, we need to learn a lot. For starters, we have to understand who buys and sells the call.

---

[3]The call "seller" is also known as the call "writer" when it comes to options. The seller "writes" the contract when they sell the option.

CHAPTER 8

The Buyer and the Seller

---

ost people have trouble keeping the concept of call buyer and seller straight, so this chapter with lots of pictures should help.

For this example, you'll be the call seller.

8.1   The Setup

So you have a funny hat, and 100 shares of VTI (100 shares is one
"lot", and all call contracts are sold by the lot). The other person is
an investor looking to speculate, and wants to pay you for the right
to buy those shares at a certain price (this price is the strike price of
our sample contract).

8.2 Selling the Call

That investor person gives you some money, and they buy a "call" contract from you for the right to buy those shares. They are the call buyer.[1]

You sell the investor person the "call" contract to buy shares from you for a set price.[2] You get the cash (the call premium), and they now own the contract (the call option) you sold them. You are the call seller, since you sold them the call.

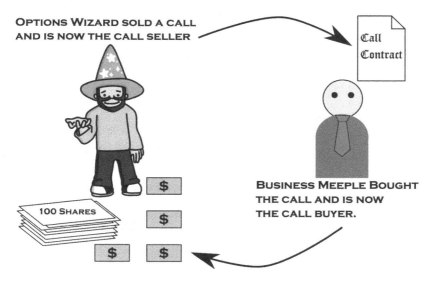

OPTIONS WIZARD SOLD A CALL AND IS NOW THE CALL SELLER

Call Contract

100 SHARES

$ $ $ $

BUSINESS MEEPLE BOUGHT THE CALL AND IS NOW THE CALL BUYER.

---

[1]Who is this call buyer? Some unknown person who thinks they can make money by buying the call, randomly assigned by your brokerage. When you sell and buy back calls, it may not even be from the same person; your brokerage handles the transaction and it is anonymous.

[2]Higher than what the shares are trading at today, if you are doing portfolio overwriting. This is an OTM (Out of The Money) call. We cover the details of what makes a call OTM later.

8.3   If the Price of the Stock Goes Up

If the price of the stock goes up the call buyer is happy. The person holding the call has a right to appreciation above the strike price. You still have the premium and appreciation up to the strike price, but you would miss out on any gain above that, as it would go to the call holder. Additionally, you may have to sell shares if they remain above the strike until expiration and you don't buy the contract back.

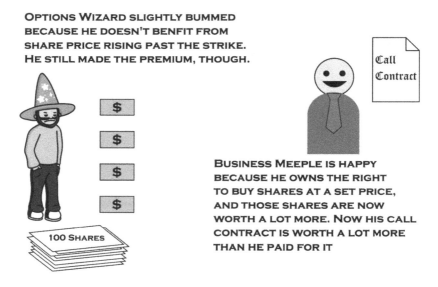

OPTIONS WIZARD SLIGHTLY BUMMED BECAUSE HE DOESN'T BENFIT FROM SHARE PRICE RISING PAST THE STRIKE. HE STILL MADE THE PREMIUM, THOUGH.

100 SHARES

BUSINESS MEEPLE IS HAPPY BECAUSE HE OWNS THE RIGHT TO BUY SHARES AT A SET PRICE, AND THOSE SHARES ARE NOW WORTH A LOT MORE. NOW HIS CALL CONTRACT IS WORTH A LOT MORE THAN HE PAID FOR IT

8.4 If the Price of the Stock Stays the Same, or Declines a Little

If the price of the stock stays the same or only goes up or down a bit, the call buyer is sad because his call isn't worth much (if anything) when the contract expires. You (the call seller) are happy because you made the call premium that you wouldn't have made otherwise. You'd also be happy if the stock only went up to your strike price or a little bit past it, because the call premium might be worth as much as the rise in price, so you didn't "miss out" on much of the price appreciation.

OPTIONS WIZARD HAPPY BECAUSE HIS SHARES DIDN'T CHANGE IN PRICE, BUT HE STILL MADE A PREMIUM HE WOULDN'T HAVE OTHERWISE ON SHARES HE WAS GOING TO HOLD ANYWAY

BUSINESS MEEPLE IS UNHAPPY BECAUSE SHARE PRICE DIDN'T GO UP ENOUGH, AND HIS CALL CONTRACT IS WORTH LESS THAN HE BOUGHT IT FOR. IF SHARES DON'T RISE PAST THE STRIKE BY EXPIRATION, IT WILL EXPIRE WORTHLESS

8.5   If the Stock Tanks

If the price of the stock dropped a lot, you'd both be sad. The call buyer's call expires worthless, and you lost money on your shares, but *not as much as you would have lost if you hadn't sold the call*— the premium you received mitigates the loss on shares.

**OPTIONS WIZARD IS BUMMED BECAUSE
SHARE PRICE DROPPED, BUT NOT TOO
BUMMED BECAUSE HE WAS A BUY AND HOLD
BOGLEHEAD INVESTOR AND MADE A
PREMIUM HE WOULDN'T HAVE MADE OTHERWISE**

100 SHARES

**BUSINESS MEEPLE IS UNHAPPY
BECAUSE SHARE PRICE DROPPED
AND HIS CALL CONTRACT IS NOW
NEAR WORTHLESS**

8.6   Buying Back the Call You Sold

And if the call contract isn't worth much anymore (because the share price stayed below the strike price as expiration approached), you can buy back the call option for less money than you sold it for. This buying back is called a Buy-To-Close, or BTC. Once you Buy-To-Close the contract, you are no longer obligated to sell him your shares anymore[3], and you get to keep whatever premium is left over after you paid to buy the call back.

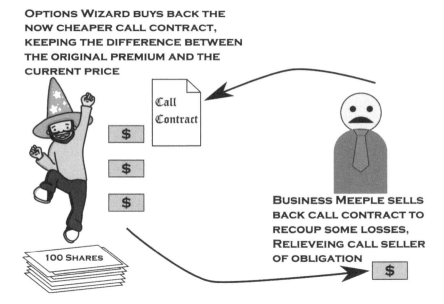

OPTIONS WIZARD BUYS BACK THE NOW CHEAPER CALL CONTRACT, KEEPING THE DIFFERENCE BETWEEN THE ORIGINAL PREMIUM AND THE CURRENT PRICE

Call Contract

100 Shares

BUSINESS MEEPLE SELLS BACK CALL CONTRACT TO RECOUP SOME LOSSES, RELIEVEING CALL SELLER OF OBLIGATION

Notice in the picture that only one of the four symbolic dollars was required to buy the call contract back and relieve the wizard of his obligation to sell shares. This was done intentionally to illustrate the call's decline in value relative to when it was sold, due to the

---

[3]The contract is closed, done, kaput, etc.

underlying shares never reaching and/or surpassing the strike price.

CHAPTER 9

Reading Option Chains

He main tool you use to sell calls is the options chain. This chapter is a key/legend/cipher to decoding and understanding it. Although they look intimidating, they actually allow you to find the information you need rather quickly by virtue of their arrangement and graphic design. As a quick note— I apologize if some of the images are difficult to read, but each section is highlighted and explained. It is recommended you pull up a live options chain on your favorite brokerage or free financial website and follow along whilst reading this chapter.

Firstly, there are two main ways you will see an option chain displayed: as a list or straddle. I personally prefer the straddle view— it's a more condensed visual display of quantitative information[1] and

---

[1] The book of the same name written by Edward Tufte is a fantastic read, even

allows for quicker, parallel comparison of the calls and puts.

Below is the options chain for Wal-Mart (WMT).[2] How did I find this? I searched "wal-mart options chain" in Google. If you are trading options, you will use the chain your brokerage provides— it really doesn't matter where you find the information, as long as you know how to use it.

I grabbed this info offline during the middle of the day on 11/21/19 (the February 21st expiration was 92 days in the future), when the stock price was $119.39 per share.

9.1   Straddle and List View

This is the "List" view, presenting calls on top and puts on the bottom:

This is the "Straddle" view, presenting corresponding calls and

---

if you aren't a graphic designer.

[2]Remember! I don't give investment advice or recommend any specific securities in this book. I only used Wal-Mart as an example because I assumed most readers would be familiar with it.

puts for each strike side-by-side:

Last Price	Change	% Change	Volume	Open interest	Strike ▲	Last Price	Change	% Change	Volume	Open interest
		Calls			February 21 2020			Puts		
10.84	-0.80	-6.87%	-	-	110.00	1.66	+0.15	+9.93%	-	-
7.15	-0.65	-8.33%	-	-	115.00	2.99	+0.34	+12.82%	-	-
4.20	-0.45	-9.68%	-	-	120.00	5.03	+0.40	+9.38%	-	-
2.15	-0.31	-12.60%	-	-	125.00	8.00	+0.53	+7.38%	-	-
0.97	-0.19	-16.38%	-	-	130.00	-	-	-	-	-

And this is the same chain from one broker I trade options on:

WMT Feb 21 2020 — 92 Days to Expiration — Settings

Calls	Bid	Ask	Last	Change	Vol	Op Int	Strike	Puts	Bid	Ask	Last	Change	Vol	Op Int
105.0 Call	15.25	15.45	0.00	0.00	0	0	105.00	105.0 Put	0.87	0.88	0.87	-0.05	20	77
110.0 Call	11.05	11.15	11.10	0.24	11	25	110.00	110.0 Put	1.59	1.60	1.66	0.13	0	75
115.0 Call	7.39	7.45	7.35	0.19	18	54	115.00	115.0 Put	2.84	2.86	2.85	-0.10	31	252
120.0 Call	4.35	4.45	4.51	0.31	322	441	120.00	120.0 Put	4.85	4.90	5.03	0.41	0	211
125.0 Call	2.32	2.34	2.34	0.19	76	387	125.00	125.0 Put	7.75	7.85	7.85	-0.15	13	15
130.0 Call	1.07	1.09	1.09	0.13	11	431	130.00	130.0 Put	11.96	11.79	11.70	-0.19	3	90

I wanted to present both views, but also include a chain that had bids and asks. The prices are a bit different— this is because I snipped the second chain later in the day, and the price of WMT shares had risen a bit. For right now, the specific numbers aren't important— we are only trying to figure out where everything is and what everything means. We will get to the applications of the values later.

9.2   Key

9.2.1   Calls/Puts(circled on the following chart)

Tells you whether you're looking at a call or a put.

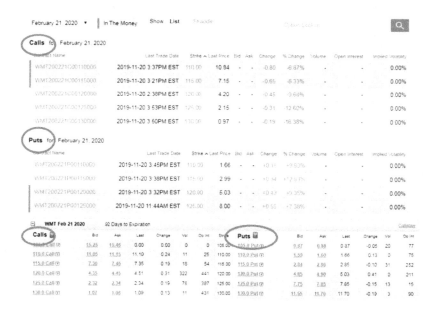

9.2.2 Expiration Date

This is when the option contract expires. The owner of the contract can exercise it at any point up to and including that expiration date. The more days until expiration, the more time value (extrinsic value) a contract will have "built into" it. This chain has 92 days until expiration, so there's quite a lot of "time value" in the options— a concept that will be explained and expanded upon in chapters on extrinsic and intrinsic value.

WMT Feb 21 2020		92 Days to Expiration											
Calls	Bid	Ask	Last	Change	Vol	Op Int	Strike	Puts	Bid	Ask	Last	Change	Vol	Op Int
105.0 Call	15.25	15.45	0.00	0.00	0	0	105.00	105.0 Put	0.87	0.88	0.87	-0.05	20	77
110.0 Call	11.05	11.15	11.10	0.24	11	25	110.00	110.0 Put	1.59	1.60	1.66	0.13	0	75
115.0 Call	7.30	7.45	7.35	0.19	18	54	115.00	115.0 Put	2.84	2.86	2.85	-0.10	31	253
120.0 Call	4.35	4.45	4.51	0.31	322	441	120.00	120.0 Put	4.85	4.90	5.03	0.41	0	211
125.0 Call	2.32	2.34	2.34	0.19	78	387	125.00	125.0 Put	7.75	7.85	7.85	-0.15	13	15
130.0 Call	1.07	1.08	1.09	0.13	11	431	130.00	130.0 Put	11.55	11.70	11.70	-0.19	3	90

February 21, 2020 ▾ | In The Money Show List Straddle

Calls for February 21, 2020

Contract Name	Last Trade Date	Strike ▲	Last Price	Bid	Ask	Change	% Change	Volume	Open Interest	Implied Volatility
WMT200221C00110000	2019-11-20 3:37PM EST	110.00	10.84	-	-	-0.80	-6.87%	-	-	0.00%
WMT200221C00115000	2019-11-20 3:21PM EST	115.00	7.15	-	-	-0.65	-8.33%	-	-	0.00%
WMT200221C00120000	2019-11-20 2:38PM EST	120.00	4.20	-	-	-0.45	-9.68%	-	-	0.00%
WMT200221C00125000	2019-11-20 3:53PM EST	125.00	2.15	-	-	-0.31	-12.60%	-	-	0.00%
WMT200221C00130000	2019-11-20 3:50PM EST	130.00	0.97	-	-	-0.19	-16.38%	-	-	0.00%

Puts for February 21, 2020

Contract Name	Last Trade Date	Strike ▲	Last Price	Bid	Ask	Change	% Change	Volume	Open Interest	Implied Volatility
WMT200221P00110000	2019-11-20 3:45PM EST	110.00	1.66	-	-	+0.15	+9.93%	-	-	0.00%
WMT200221P00115000	2019-11-20 3:38PM EST	115.00	2.99	-	-	+0.14	+12.83%	-	-	0.00%
WMT200221P00120000	2019-11-20 3:32PM EST	120.00	5.03	-	-	+0.43	+9.35%	-	-	0.00%
WMT200221P00125000	2019-11-20 11:44AM EST	125.00	8.00	-	-	+0.55	+7.38%	-	-	0.00%

And a zoomed in expiration date for the calls only:

WMT Feb 21 2020	92 Days to Expiration						
Calls	Bid	Ask	Last	Change	Vol	Op Int	Strike
105.0 Call	15.25	15.45	0.00	0.00	0	0	105.00
110.0 Call	11.05	11.15	11.10	0.24	11	25	110.00
115.0 Call	7.30	7.45	7.35	0.19	18	54	115.00
120.0 Call	4.35	4.45	4.51	0.31	322	441	120.00
125.0 Call	2.32	2.34	2.34	0.19	78	387	125.00
130.0 Call	1.07	1.08	1.09	0.13	11	431	130.00

9.2.3 "In The Money"

This is not a standard feature of every option chain, but the shading behind the words "In The Money" corresponds to the shading on the chain for all contracts that are currently "In the Money[3] (ITM)". This lets you visualize with a quick glance what contracts are ITM.

A couple things to notice here— firstly, the calls and puts[4] are reversed in terms of "moneyness". Secondly, the split happens between the 115.00 strike and the 120.00 strike— this is because the stock price was 119.39 when these option chains were pulled.

---

[3]We cover ITM, and the general concept of "moneyness" in the next chapter.

[4]We do not cover puts in depth in this book, but they exist on the chain so I should be acknowledging them, rather than ignoring them and leaving half the chain a mystery.

A zoomed in view of "In The Money" and associated shading for the calls only:

9.2.4 Contract Name

Not important, but nice to know what this means. Notice this isn't even present on the straddle view. Option tickers follow the format XYZyymmddC/Pxxxxxxxx where XYZ is the ticker, yy is the year, mm is the month, dd is the date and all the xxxxxxxx is the strike price. C/P refers to call or put. I never have any practical use for this nomenclature.

9.2.5   Last Price

The last price, per share (remember options are traded in quantities of 100 shares), that the option in question traded for. This is not necessarily the price you will get.

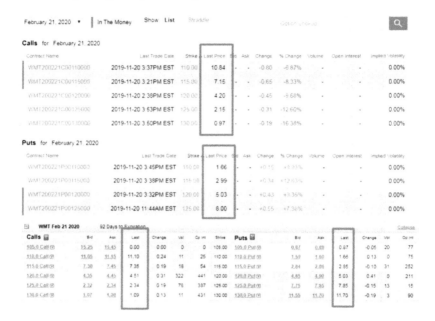

A Zoomed in picture of the straddle view to reference for **Last Price**, as well as the next few points— **Change, Bid–Ask, Volume** and **Open Interest:**

Calls	Bid	Ask	Last	Change	Vol	Op Int	Strike
105.0 Call	15.25	15.45	0.00	0.00	0	0	105.00
110.0 Call	11.05	11.15	11.10	0.24	11	25	110.00
115.0 Call	7.30	7.45	7.35	0.19	18	54	115.00
120.0 Call	4.35	4.45	4.51	0.31	322	441	120.00
125.0 Call	2.32	2.34	2.34	0.19	78	387	125.00
130.0 Call	1.07	1.08	1.09	0.13	11	431	130.00

WMT Feb 21 2020   92 Days to Expiration

9.2.6   Change

The amount the last price changed from the previous last price executed

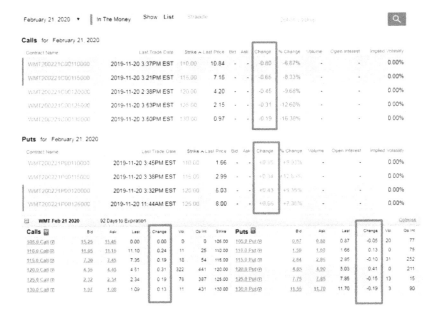

9.2.7 Bid

This is what buyers are offering for the contract. **If you sell a call, you will likely get paid a premium closer to this price.**

9.2.8 Ask

This is what sellers are asking for a contract. If you buy a contract, you will pay closer to this price. Of note, the difference between the bid and the ask is the "bid-ask spread". Sometimes these spreads are huge. This tells me, in a very high-level sense of how markets work, that there are inefficiencies in pricing, and therefore opportunities for profit.[5]

---

[5] Basically, options are predictions about future prices— how likely a price is to deviate from today's price, and how far it might deviate. When there is a wide gap between the bid and ask (aka "have a wide spread") for an option, it indicates that there is less consensus on the expected price move and magnitude. This, like any situation with disagreement on pricing, is an opportunity for arbitrage if you as the option trader can parse out the "true" value.

As portfolio overwriters we are **not** trying to do this. I only mention it because it is interesting.

9.2.9   Volume ("Vol")

How many contracts traded today. [6]

9.2.10   Open interest ("Op Int")

How many open contracts there are out there.

Hopefully this is a good cipher for your future option chain reading.

Now that you can read the chain, we are going to break down the shaded and unshaded sections, and what they mean.

---

[6]To add some confusion, "Vol" is sometimes an abbreviation for volatility in options-land.

CHAPTER 10

Moneyness and Intrinsic Value

Oneyness": a totally real word in finance. The most general definition is as follows:

Moneyness is a term that describes whether or not an option contract has intrinsic value.

To start, just remember In The Money (ITM) means an option has intrinsic value. Out of The Money (OTM) means the option has no intrinsic value. At The Money (ATM) is when the price of the stock is the same as the strike price of the option in question.

Hearing that, you may think that a contract with no intrinsic value is worthless, but far from it. The price of any option contract, known as the **premium**, is made up of 2 things: "intrinsic value" and "extrinsic value." [1]

> Option premium = The price, usually expressed in dol-
> lars per share, of an option contract. It is composed of
> intrinsic and extrinsic value.

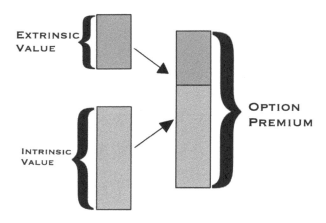

10.1   Where the Strike Falls

Another way to say this would be "Moneyness describes the relationship between an option strike price and the underlying asset price",
but this is much less relatable than the first definition. A simple illustration is that if a stock is trading for $50 a share, and you want
to buy the right to purchase the stock for $45 a share, that right will
cost you *at least $5 per share.*

Simply put, no one is going to let you buy something worth $50
for $45 and just forfeit the difference— it would be a losing deal!

---

[1]Extrinsic value is also sometimes referred to as "time value". It truly includes
time value and volatility, but I think the term time value is inclusive enough—
you'll see why in the chapter on time value.

10.2   Intrinsic Value

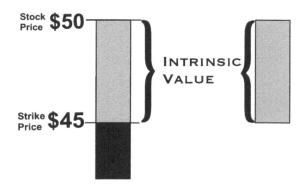

So what is intrinsic value? Arithmetically:

[Intrinsic Value] = [Stock Price – Option Strike Price]

If this number is negative, the option contract has no intrinsic value.

So let's look at this option chain for a $119.39 stock (this is the same chain we used in the last chapter) and try to figure out the intrinsic and extrinsic values of an OTM and an ITM strike price option:

Calls	Bid	Ask	Last	Change	Vol	Op Int	Strike	Puts	Bid	Ask	Last	Change	Vol	Op Int
105.0 Call	15.25	15.45	0.00	0.00	0	0	105.00	105.0 Put	0.87	0.88	0.87	-0.05	20	77
110.0 Call	11.05	11.15	11.10	0.24	11	25	110.00	110.0 Put	1.59	1.59	1.66	0.13	0	75
115.0 Call	7.30	7.45	7.35	0.19	18	54	115.00	115.0 Put	2.84	2.86	2.85	-0.10	31	252
120.0 Call	4.35	4.45	4.51	0.31	322	441	120.00	120.0 Put	4.85	4.90	5.03	0.41	0	211
125.0 Call	2.32	2.34	2.34	0.19	78	387	125.00	125.0 Put	7.75	7.85	7.85	-0.15	13	15
130.0 Call	1.07	1.08	1.09	0.13	11	431	130.00	130.0 Put	11.56	11.70	11.70	-0.19	3	90

WMT Feb 21 2020   92 Days to Expiration

To reiterate, when I took this data, the price of the underlying stock was $119.39. In this chain, all the options that are ITM (In The

Money) have a colored background. Calls are on the left, and puts are on the right.[2]

10.3   OTM Moneyness Example

We will zoom in and look at the $120.00 OTM (out-of-the-money) call. It's worth about $4.40 (I'm taking the midpoint of the bid-ask spread).

WMT Feb 21 2020		92 Days to Expiration					
Calls	Bid	Ask	Last	Change	Vol	Op Int	Strike
105.0 Call	15.25	15.45	0.00	0.00	0	0	105.00
110.0 Call	11.05	11.15	11.10	0.24	11	25	110.00
115.0 Call	7.30	7.45	7.35	0.19	18	54	115.00
120.0 Call	4.35	4.45	4.51	0.31	322	441	120.00
125.0 Call	2.32	2.34	2.34	0.19	78	387	125.00
130.0 Call	1.07	1.08	1.09	0.13	11	431	130.00

How much intrinsic value does it have?

The quick answer is none, because the strike price is above the current price of the security. This option premium is composed entirely of extrinsic value.

---

[2]For our purposes we only need to focus on the calls.

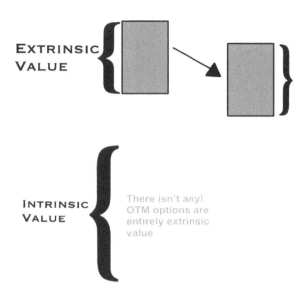

EXTRINSIC VALUE

INTRINSIC VALUE

There isn't any! OTM options are entirely extrinsic value

The longer answer is:

[**Stock Price − Option Strike Price**] = [**Intrinsic Value**]

so

[**$119.39 − $120.00**] = [**$ −0.61**]

...so it's a negative number...but because that doesn't exist in this realm, it simply has no intrinsic value! In the case of this OTM strike, all $4.40 per share is entirely "extrinsic value" aka "time value".

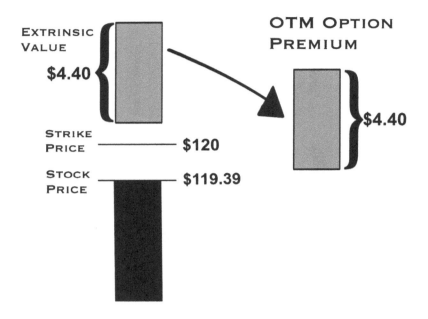

10.4   ITM Moneyness Example

What about the $115 strike price call?

Calls	Bid	Ask	Last	Change	Vol	Op Int	Strike
WMT Feb 21 2020			92 Days to Expiration				
105.0 Call	15.25	15.45	0.00	0.00	0	0	105.00
110.0 Call	11.05	11.15	11.10	0.24	11	25	110.00
115.0 Call	7.30	7.45	7.35	0.19	18	54	115.00
120.0 Call	4.35	4.45	4.51	0.31	322	441	120.00
125.0 Call	2.32	2.34	2.34	0.19	78	387	125.00
130.0 Call	1.07	1.08	1.09	0.13	11	431	130.00

It looks like it last traded at $7.35— how much of that is intrinsic value?

As you may recall:

[Stock Price – Option Strike Price] = [Intrinsic Value]

So, inputting our stock price of $119.39, a strike price of $115 we get:

[$119.39 – $115] = [$4.39]

So of the $7.35 premium, $4.39 is intrinsic value. To find the extrinsic value explicitly, we can start with the very first fact illustrated in this chapter, namely:

[Option Premium] = [Intrinsic Value + Extrinsic Value]

Rearranging, we have:

[Option Premium – Intrinsic Value] = [Extrinsic Value]

And substituting in the values from our example, we find:

[$7.35 – $4.39] = [$2.96]

In summary, for a stock trading at $119.39 per share the ITM $115 strike, selling for $7.35 per share, has an intrinsic value of $4.39 and an extrinsic value of $2.96

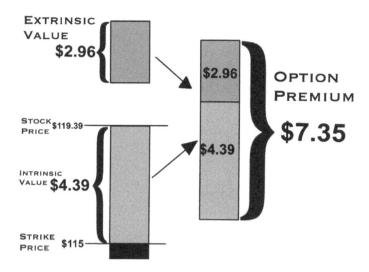

10.5   You Sell Time

As a seller of options, that **$2.96 time value is the value you should be paying attention to first and foremost.** This is the call seller's "bread and butter". It can be thought of as the extra commission you are paid to hold a stock for some amount of time. You could always sell the stock right now and make the intrinsic value; the extrinsic value is all value beyond that amount. If you like actuarial science or the abstraction of reality, then you might think of it as the cost of uncertainty, or a concrete value assigned to the market's best guess of price of risk over time (why I like to call it time value).

Intrinsic value and moneyness are easy. They are both well defined, and simple arithmetic gets you where you need to be, but extrinsic value is not the same "ting." We cover it in the next (few) chapters, starting with the option's Delta.

CHAPTER 11

Delta Δ

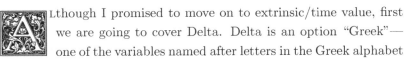Lthough I promised to move on to extrinsic/time value, first we are going to cover Delta. Delta is an option "Greek"— one of the variables named after letters in the Greek alphabet that defines an option's behavior. Delta is closely related to moneyness, and is one of the most important options "Greeks" for selling calls, next to theta.

Learning how "the Greeks" function mathematically isn't necessary for trading in a retail account, but the general dynamics of how things move and why they move is invaluable. Although it is somewhat complex at first glance, delta is useful as a concept because it allows you to understand how the price of your sold call changes as the price of the shares you sold it against changes.

Delta will show up in the options chain on your broker's website,

so I snipped this data from 11/22/19 for a preclinical biotech company
trading at $9.81 a share.

Last	Change	Bid	Ask	Volume	Open Int	Imp Vol	Delta	Action	Strike ▲	Action	Last	Change	Bid	Ask	Volume	Open Int	Imp Vol	Delta
—				CALLS					Dec 20 '19 (26 days)						PUTS			
0.00	0.00	4.50	5.00	0	0		0.9451	▾	5	▾	0.05	0.00	0.00	0.05	0	10	127.16 %	-0.0182
3.08	0.00	3.78	4.00	0	3	77.77 %	0.9959	▾	6	▾	0.00	0.00	0.00	0.10	0	0	109.84 %	-0.0382
2.35	0.00	2.70	3.00	0	25	53.55 %	0.9952	▾	7	▾	0.10	0.00	0.00	0.15	0	3	88.45 %	-0.0659
2.00	0.00	1.80	2.06	0	131	60.87 %	0.9089	▾	8	▾	0.11	0.00	0.10	0.15	0	187	70.12 %	-0.1234
1.15	0.00	1.00	1.20	0	422	55.80 %	0.7479	▾	9	▾	0.35	0.00	0.25	0.35	0	426	61.14 %	-0.2717
0.60	0.00	0.50	0.65	0	1,411	59.13 %	0.4957	▾	10	▾	0.75	0.00	0.65	0.75	0	531	56.47 %	-0.5127
0.28	0.00	0.25	0.30	0	534	61.44 %	0.2896	▾	11	▾	1.40	0.00	1.35	1.50	0	14	60.61 %	-0.7249
0.10	0.00	0.10	0.15	0	420	63.52 %	0.1531	▾	12	▾	2.47	0.00	2.20	2.40	0	6	65.35 %	-0.8525
0.05	0.00	0.00	0.10	0	255	63.97 %	0.0714	▾	13	▾	3.47	0.00	3.10	3.40	0	19	71.58 %	-0.9163
0.05	0.00	0.00	0.05	0	61	67.43 %	0.0378	▾	14	▾	0.00	0.00	4.08	4.40	0	0	—	-0.8377

Figure 11.1: *Right now the tiny numbers aren't important— I'm simply
showing you delta exists.*

11.1   So What is Delta?

> **Delta represents how much the price of an option's
> premium will change if the underlying stock
> appreciates $1.**

To get your confidence up, just start by knowing that the absolute
value of delta will only ever be between zero and one. Its range is
limited to 0–1. Easy, right? Since an option price would never move
more than the price of the underlying moved, delta is never going to
be more than 1.

For Example: If the delta of a long call option is 0.5 and the
underlying investment rises $1 in price, the price of a long call would
go up $0.50 (50 cents per share). If the delta of a long call is 0.3[1]

---

[1]To add some confusion, often a delta is referred to as it's actual value multiplied
by 100, so a 0.5 delta may be called the "fifty delta" or a 0.30 delta call referred
to as the "30 delta call". It's just easier to say than "point five zero."

and the price of the underlying drops $1, the price of the long call would be expected to decrease 30 cents. To reinforce this concept via comparison, stocks have delta = 1 (because if the price of a stock moves $1...the price of the stock moves $1).[2]

11.2 Delta as an Option's "Responsiveness"

Another way to think of Delta is as a value that tells you how "sensitive" an option price is to the movement of the underlying stock—the higher the delta, the more the option "responds" to the stock's price moves.[3] Put another way, options with a high delta move a lot whenever the stock moves. Low delta options don't really give a damn what the stock is doing, and barely budge in price when the underlying changes.

So why is Delta high or low in the first place? What determines whether the option price cares when the price of the underlying moves?

11.3 Moneyness and Implied Volatility

First, we can think about Moneyness. How deep ITM (In-The-Money) or OTM the option is makes the biggest impact on Delta. The easiest way to start understanding is with an example of the farthest OTM option in the chain from before. Zoom in!

---

[2]Tautology, Ahoy!

[3]For the mathematically inclined, delta is a first-order derivative of stock price (just like acceleration is a derivative of velocity, if you're into physics).

Last	Change	Bid	Ask	Volume	Open Int	Imp Vol	Delta	Action	Strike ▲	Actic
—					CALLS				Dec 20 '19 (26 days)	
0.00	0.00	4.50	5.00	0	0	—	0.9451	▼	5	▼
3.08	0.00	3.70	4.00	0	3	77.77 %	0.9959	▼	6	▼
2.35	0.00	2.70	3.00	0	25	53.55 %	0.9952	▼	7	▼
2.00	0.00	1.80	2.05	0	131	60.87 %	0.9089	▼	8	▼
1.15	0.00	1.00	1.20	0	422	55.80 %	0.7479	▼	9	▼
0.60	0.00	0.50	0.65	0	1,411	59.13 %	0.4987	▼	10	▼
0.28	0.00	0.25	0.30	0	834	61.44 %	0.2896	▼	11	▼
0.10	0.00	0.10	0.15	0	420	63.52 %	0.1531	▼	12	▼
0.05	0.00	0.00	0.10	0	255	63.97 %	0.0714	▼	13	▼
0.05	0.00	0.00	0.05	0	81	67.43 %	0.0378	▼	14	▼

Looking at the previous chain, the delta for the $14 strike call is 0.0378. So for every dollar the stock moves, the price of the $14 call will increase only 3.78 cents. For example, we bought a $14 strike call for $0.05 and the price of the stock increased from $9.81 to $10.81, our option premium would theoretically increase by 3.78 cents, from 0.05 to 0.08 cents.

I have to stop right here and say that you need to take this with a huge grain of salt— this understanding is correct in principle, but it doesn't actually work that way. Delta is more dynamic in practice— you'll immediately see why in the next chapter: Delta, A Moving Target.

SETUP		AFTER $1/SHARE APPRECIATION	
STOCK PRICE:	$9.81	STOCK PRICE:	$10.81 ($1 INCREASE IN SHARE PRICE)
CALL PRICE:	$0.05	CALL PRICE:	$0.08 ($0.0378 INCREASE PER $1 INCREASE IN SHARE PRICE)
DELTA:	0.0378		

But what about a higher delta? If you look at the $10 strike and $9 strike options, there is a pretty big jump in delta— it goes from 0.4987 to 0.7479:

Last	Change	Bid	Ask	Volume	Open Int	Imp Vol	Delta	Action	Strike ▲	Actio
—				CALLS					Dec 20 '19 (26 days)	
0.00	0.00	4.50	5.00	0	0	--	0.9451	▼	5	▼
3.08	0.00	3.70	4.00	0	3	77.77 %	0.9959	▼	6	▼
2.35	0.00	2.70	3.00	0	25	53.55 %	0.9952	▼	7	▼
2.00	0.00	1.80	2.05	0	131	60.87 %	0.9089	▼	8	▼
1.15	0.00	1.00	1.20	0	422	55.80 %	0.7479	▼	9	▼
0.60	0.00	0.50	0.65	0	1,411	59.13 %	0.4987	▼	10	▼
0.28	0.00	0.25	0.30	0	834	61.44 %	0.2896	▼	11	▼
0.10	0.00	0.10	0.15	0	420	63.52 %	0.1531	▼	12	▼
0.05	0.00	0.00	0.10	0	255	63.97 %	0.0714	▼	13	▼
0.05	0.00	0.00	0.05	0	81	67.43 %	0.0378	▼	14	▼

Why the big jump? For that matter, why do the lower strike calls have a delta that gets closer and closer to 1? Again, the reason is the moneyness, aka the intrinsic value. The $9 call is selling for $1.15, and since the stock is $9.81, you know that call has an intrinsic value of $0.81 cents per share.

Put another way, if you spent $1.15 for that call, it is worth at least $0.81 based on the stock price alone. If the stock goes up $1 to $10.81, your call is going to be worth more as well...not one dollar more, but theoretically 74.79 cents more based on the *current* delta (again, take this with a huge grain of salt— you'll see why in the next chapter).

SETUP		**AFTER $1/SHARE APPRECIATION**
STOCK PRICE:	**$9.81**	STOCK PRICE: **$10.81** ($1 INCREASE IN SHARE PRICE)
CALL PRICE:	**$1.15**	CALL PRICE: **$1.89** ($0.7479 INCREASE PER $1 INCREASE IN SHARE PRICE)
DELTA:	**0.7479**	

We should be able to generalize from these two examples that further OTM options have low deltas, and further ITM options have higher deltas. You can roughly graph the relationship of delta to moneyness, if it helps you understand better:

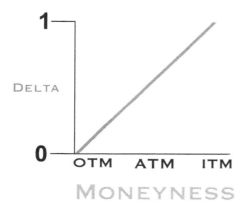

More precisely, it moves more like an "S" curve because delta increases exponentially as the call option becomes closer to ATM and levels off near 1 as delta goes further ITM.

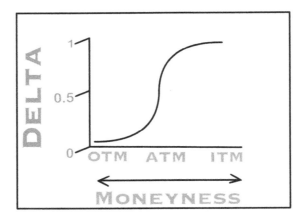

Even better, you can pull up an options chain on your broker's website and watch the delta change throughout the day in tandem with the stock price changes. It's riveting.[4]

---

[4]This is serious if you find options as interesting as I do, sarcastic if you do not.

11.4 Bigger Uncertainty Leads to Bigger Moves (and Even Bigger Returns)

The other factor influencing delta is extrinsic value/implied volatility. Right now that $14 strike call is only trading at 5 cents because the stock is sitting at $9.81. The chances it is going to bump up to $14, a 42.7% increase, in the next 26 days are probably pretty slim.[5] To put it another way, someone wanting to pay you for the right to buy a stock for $14 a share might seem a bit silly, especially with the stock currently trading at $9.81. They aren't going to pay much for that right— only 5 cents per share now, and only 3.78 more cents[6] if the stock goes to $10.81. The option has a low delta; it doesn't care much.

But, if that stock regularly moved up and down $6 at a time, hitting $14 would be more probable, and someone in their right mind would pay you more than 5 cents for the right to buy it for $14 in 26 days. Such a wildly vacillating stock price would have more implied volatility (because it is more volatile, and the increased extrinsic value would result in the price of the option premium being higher).

---

[5]Note: if that person knows something we don't or expects the stock to sky-rocket in the meantime due to some good news, then that 5 cent option might seem like a great deal.

[6]An increase of 5 cents to 8.78 cents *is a 60+% increase.* This should raise eyebrows for investors thinking about % returns.

11.5 Extrinsic Value can be The Lion's Share

Before we wrap it up, you have to be aware that although intrinsic value has a more concrete effect on delta, extrinsic value can represent a very significant percentage of the underlying stock's price. This is especially true of longer-dated calls, which have more time, and therefore more time value. To illustrate this, it is helpful to compare next month's delta on the same option with the delta 789 days from now.[7]

First let's look at the chain 54 days from now (recall that we were looking at a chain with expiration dates 26 days in the future previously).

	CALLS				Jan 17 '20 (54 days)					PUTS				
4.87	0.00 4.60 5.10	0	139	88.01 % 0.9653	▼	5	▼	0.05	0.00	0.00	0.10	0 1.069	101.75 %	-0.0293
4.32	0.00 3.70 4.10	0	20	63.16 % 0.9549	▼	6	▼	0.40	0.00	0.00	0.20	0 110	90.70 %	-0.0589
3.07	0.00 2.80 3.18	0	90	70.08 % 0.9169	▼	7	▼	0.10	0.00	0.10	0.20	0 99	75.47 %	-0.0979
2.05	0.00 2.05 2.20	0	1,409	87.52 % 0.8208	▼	8	▼	0.30	0.00	0.25	0.35	0 1,396	68.64 %	-0.1842
1.50	0.00 1.35 1.55	0	1,534	66.49 % 0.6834	▼	9	▼	0.60	0.00	0.55	0.70	0 304	67.47 %	-0.3206
0.95	0.00 0.85 1.05	0	3,141	66.57 % 0.5297	▼	10	▼	1.15	0.00	1.00	1.10	0 2,161	62.64 %	-0.4788
0.60	0.00 0.55 0.65	0	1,216	66.78 % 0.3869	▼	11	▼	1.71	0.00	1.65	1.85	0 477	68.10 %	-0.6201
0.34	0.00 0.30 0.45	0	3,036	67.56 % 0.2716	▼	12	▼	2.58	0.00	2.40	2.90	0 529	76.39 %	-0.6982
0.25	0.00 0.15 0.25	0	377	65.15 % 0.1704	▼	13	▼	3.60	0.00	3.20	3.60	0 160	68.94 %	-0.8195
0.11	0.00 0.05 0.30	0	613	73.10 % 0.1409	▼	14	▼	4.70	0.00	4.10	4.80	0 85	74.51 %	-0.8613

---

[7]This longer term option is a LEAPS— a Long term Equity AnticiPation Security. LEAPS function just like regular options, but they have an expiry date 1–2 years in the future.

Zooming in and looking at the $10 strike Delta for 54 days from now, notice it went from 0.4987 in the previous chain to 0.5297— a bit of a bump (I intentionally didn't circle the value so you could practice finding it).

—				CALLS				Jan 17 '20 (54 d)
4.87	0.00	4.60	5.10	0	139	88.01 %	0.9853	▾ 5
4.32	0.00	3.70	4.10	0	20	83.16 %	0.9549	▾ 6
3.07	0.00	2.80	3.10	0	90	70.08 %	0.9169	▾ 7
2.05	0.00	2.05	2.20	0	1,409	67.52 %	0.8208	▾ 8
1.50	0.00	1.35	1.55	0	1,534	66.49 %	0.6834	▾ 9
0.95	0.00	0.85	1.05	0	3,141	66.57 %	0.5297	▾ 10
0.60	0.00	0.55	0.65	0	1,216	66.78 %	0.3869	▾ 11
0.34	0.00	0.30	0.45	0	3,036	67.56 %	0.2716	▾ 12
0.25	0.00	0.15	0.25	0	377	65.15 %	0.1704	▾ 13
0.11	0.00	0.05	0.30	0	613	73.10 %	0.1409	▾ 14

Now let's compare the 54-day call to the two-year LEAP...

—		CALLS				Jan 21 '22 (739 days)					PUTS				
6.00	0.00	4.90	9.50	0	5	--	1	▾	3	▾	0.40	0.00	0.00	1.15	0	9	89.96 %	-0.0553
6.00	0.00	5.60	8.40	0	94	92.59 %	0.9377	▾	5	▾	1.05	0.00	0.70	2.60	0	5	95.74 %	-0.1129
3.68	0.00	2.85	6.00	0	20	58.34 %	0.8173	▾	8	▾	2.30	0.00	0.50	4.20	0	150	68.27 %	-0.2299
3.40	0.00	3.20	5.70	0	24	74.05 %	0.7658	▾	10	▾	3.41	0.00	1.30	5.10	0	65	60.71 %	-0.3251
2.50	0.00	1.20	4.30	0	50	53.78 %	0.6295	▾	12	▾	0.00	0.00	2.80	8.70	0	0	62.32 %	-0.4004
2.00	0.00	0.40	4.70	0	24	62.23 %	0.5842	▾	15	▾	0.00	0.00	5.08	8.70	0	0	66.19 %	-0.4832
1.50	0.00	0.10	4.70	0	20	65.63 %	0.529	▾	17	▾	0.00	0.00	6.20	10.40	0	0	57.78 %	-0.6045
0.95	0.00	0.25	4.90	0	43	75.60 %	0.526	▾	20	▾	0.00	0.00	9.70	12.80	0	0	64.64 %	-0.6315
0.00	0.00	8.30	4.10	0	0	73.28 %	0.4746	▾	22	▾	0.00	0.00	11.70	14.70	0	0	68.08 %	-0.6482

Looking at the $10 strike Delta for 789 days from now, notice it is 0.7658— a big bump from 0.4987.

				CALLS				Jan 21 '22 (789 days)	
6.00	0.00	4.90	9.50	0	5	--	1	▾ 3	▾
6.00	0.00	5.60	8.40	0	94	92.59 %	0.9377	▾ 5	▾
3.68	0.00	2.85	6.00	0	20	58.34 %	0.8173	▾ 8	▾
3.40	0.00	3.20	5.70	0	24	74.05 %	0.7658	▾ 10	▾
2.50	0.00	1.20	4.30	0	50	53.78 %	0.6295	▾ 12	▾
2.00	0.00	0.40	4.70	0	24	62.23 %	0.5642	▾ 15	▾
1.50	0.00	0.10	4.70	0	20	65.63 %	0.529	▾ 17	▾
0.95	0.00	0.25	4.90	0	43	75.60 %	0.526	▾ 20	▾
0.00	0.00	0.30	4.10	0	0	73.28 %	0.4746	▾ 22	▾

This happened because delta is tied to option value, which is inherently composed of intrinsic and extrinsic value. A lot can happen in 2 years. **A LOT.** A company can go bankrupt or discover a cure for hemophilia— so that extra time translates to a lot of time value. Extrinsic value is, inherently, the value of the unknowns in play for any given stock.

11.6   34% Return in Two Years?

If you reflect on this a bit, it seems like a good idea to buy a stock for $9.81 a share, then sell someone the right to buy it from you for $10 a share. In the above chain, that right just sold for $3.40 a share, so you'd make 36% on your investment in 2 years if the price went up, and you'd break even if the price dropped to $6.4— protection of 34% to the downside! Seems like a good deal, this selling LEAPs thing. But as with most things in life, it's more complicated than that.

Do you know for sure you want to own any given stock for 2 years?[8] Can you stick to your plan for 2 years and not be wracked with regret if the stock jumps to $20 (or $50) a share? More on that later, but for now we need to clarify that delta is a moving target, and then go over some cool tricks with delta to help you understand it better if you want a deeper intuition. Then we'll finally get to the topic of time value.

---

[8]If you are a Boglehead, the answer is a resounding yes for your chosen indexes.

CHAPTER 12

Delta- A Moving Target

Efore you take the delta ball and run with it, the big thing you need to understand is that delta changes with the wind,

97

and as a retail investor you cannot use simple arithmetic to accurately extrapolate future option values from delta.

Although delta tells you the expected change in the value of an option's premium given an underlying stock's change in value, it never really predicts the dollar change in an option due to a move in the underlying security past a given instant. This is because delta is a moving target (a derivative of stock price describing an instantaneous value— the change in option price).

12.1   Delta Changes Constantly, Whenever the Price of the Underlying Security Changes

When the delta changes, the options premium accelerates faster as the underlying price changes, typically resulting in a larger move than predicted if the price action happened with a fixed delta. Delta is itself a variable derived from, and dependent on, the changes it describes.[1]

To illustrate, from our example with the stock sitting at \$9.81, and the delta of the \$14 call at 0.0378. You'd expect the price of the call to go up 3.78 cents per dollar move in the underlying— That's our definition. Right???

Yes, but if the price of the stock raises \$5 to \$14.81, there's no way the price of the \$14 strike call is only going to go up 15.12 cents![2]

---

[1]The derivative of delta that describes how fast delta changes is gamma, covered in the next chapter.

[2]I warned you in the last chapter that it wasn't so simple.

		AFTER $5/SHARE APPRECIATION	
STOCK PRICE:	$9.81	STOCK PRICE:	$14.81
CALL PRICE:	$0.05 (26-DAY EXPIRY, $14 STRIKE)	CALL PRICE:	~~$0.18~~
DELTA:	0.0378		NO WAY!

That call is now in the money, it's going to be worth way more than 18 cents. Just think about it— with the stock price at $14.81, the $14-strike call is worth 81 cents in intrinsic value alone!

12.2 As Delta Increases, the Option Premium Increases Even Faster

So what happened? As the price of the underlying changed, the value of the option, and its delta, also changed. When the underlying rose, it approached, and then became ITM (in the money). In turn, delta rose closer to 1, which describes the price of the option increasing faster and faster.[3]

So what would the $14 call with the stock at $14.81 look like? I don't have the mathematical model to spit out an exact number, but I can tell you that it is going to look way more like a call that

---

[3]This is an example of what happens as you travel across the moneyness range and up the curve in the graph representing delta vs moneyness in the last chapter.

is currently 81 cents in the money— the $9 call. That call is going for $1.45 [1.35–1.55 bid-ask]. With $0.64 extrinsic value, you could ballpark with the stock at $14 that the $14-strike call would be going for $1.45[4] or more (most likely more because the big move up would cause implied volatility, and in turn call value, to spike), and now have a similar delta. It's not a perfect estimate, but it is an estimate with enough utility to serve our needs.

SETUP		AFTER $5/SHARE APPRECIATION	
STOCK PRICE:	$9.81	STOCK PRICE:	$14.81
CALL PRICE:	$0.05 (26-DAY EXPIRY, $16 STRIKE)	CALL PRICE:	>$1.45-ISH
DELTA:	0.0378	DELTA:	0.7479-ISH

Knowing this should prepare you for what happens when the underlying changes and the value of your sold calls changes, and keep you from being disappointed by incorrect expectations based on the Delta "snapshot" in time you may have based your strategy on. With all this in mind, it's time to talk about our good friend, gamma.

---

[4] Again, just for fun, notice $0.03 to $1.45 is a 2900% return if you were the buyer of the call. This is how call buying can leverage small initial investments into massive returns. The hardest part is finding out what stock, and perhaps more importantly when, to YOLO.

CHAPTER 13

Our Buddy Gamma γ

Ow that we know about delta, the first order derivative of price, we will cover the second order derivative, gamma.

The previous chapter, which described how delta itself changed as the underlying security price changed, was actually a clandestine description of gamma.

13.1 Gamma is the Rate of Change of Delta with Respect to Price.

When the price of a security changes, delta changes as well. Gamma measures how much delta changes relative to the change in the price of the underlying security.

> - Delta measures how much the price of an option changes when the price of the underlying changes
>
> - Gamma measures how much delta changes when the price of the underlying changes

Gamma has some interesting properties. Firstly, it is larger for strike prices that are closer to ATM (at the money). This is unlike delta, which rises steeply for ATM options and tapers off near 1 once ITM. The standard graph illustrating this difference looks something like the following:

GAMMA AND DELTA VS MONEYNESS

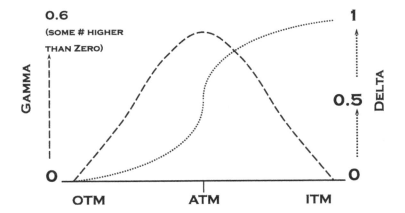

Gamma is also larger the closer a call is to expiry (expiration). This graphic shows the gamma curve for 3 different expiration calls. Each line represents a gamma with a different expiration. Notice the closest expiry gamma has the highest peak.

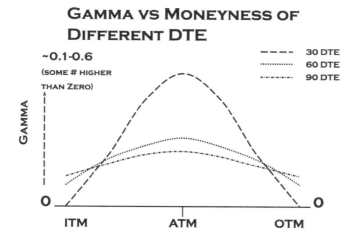

GAMMA VS MONEYNESS OF DIFFERENT DTE

The fact that gamma is larger as it moves closer to expiration can also be expressed graphically. There's an exponential increase in the gamma of an ATM call as expiry approaches (actually similar to the behavior of delta as it becomes ITM), all else being equal. You can visualize this with yet another graph!

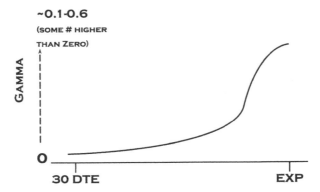

13.2 So How Does Any of This Apply to Portfolio Overwriting?

If you live in the covered call world for any amount of time, you're going to come across the phrase "gamma risk".[1] Put simply, as expiration approaches, close to ATM movements in a stock price will drastically affect the value of your short call, much more than they did earlier in the contract cycle.

---

[1]More importantly, if you're going to risk your hard-earned money, you should be well-versed in the arena you choose to risk it in.

This happens because the moves in a stock's price closer to expiration have much more impact on the probability of where a stock closes on expiration Friday than they did earlier in the contract cycle. It's difficult to visualize, but the best way I concocted to show it is as follows:

13.3   Gamma as a Wave

Pretend like you have a "probability spotlight" attached to the bow of a boat that you are trying to land at a dock at night in rough waters. We call it a probability spotlight because the light shines straight ahead, and whatever area it illuminates gives you a pretty good estimate of where you are going to hit the shore.

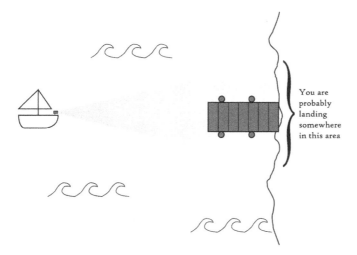

If you've ever spent any time on a boat, you'll know that it's pretty easy to head in a general direction and adjust as you go, but as you get closer and closer the little waves knocking your boat around matter more and more.

The spotlight is pointed directly forward off the front of the boat, and will give you a pretty good idea of where you are ending up if you keep it pointed at your destination. From far out, a pretty wide area is lit up, and you're likely to end up near the middle of that range if you keep chugging along and there aren't any major changes to the currents.

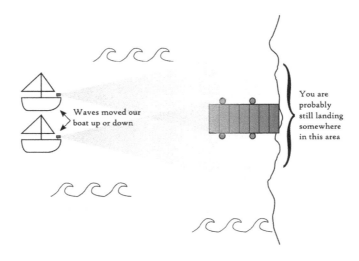

Waves moved our boat up or down

You are probably still landing somewhere in this area

But as you get closer and closer, you have to slow down and make more corrections as the shore approaches. The ebb and flow of the water makes a bigger difference the nearer you get to the dock. If you move too far off course, you'll know because the light is no longer shining on where you want to go.

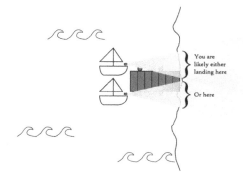

To explicitly break down the metaphor, the boat is your stock price. The shore is where the boat lands is where the stock closes at expiry, and the area the spotlight illuminates most is where you have the highest probability of landing— the price you end at on expiry. The waves are the random motions of the market; usually they are somewhat bounded, but every now and then tsunamis happen.

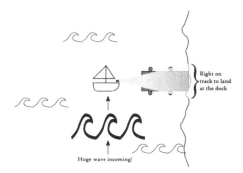

Finally, the motion of the ocean mattering more and more as you get closer to your destination is gamma risk. Farther out, waves aren't a big deal and you can pretty much feel confident you are going to land where you want to without much issue, even in rough weather. But when you get closer to mooring and the spotlight of possible futures narrows, things matter a lot more.

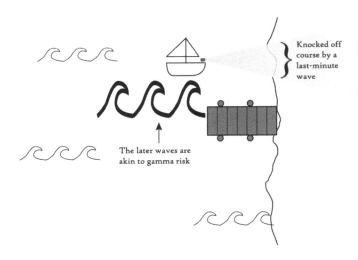

Knocked off course by a last-minute wave

The later waves are akin to gamma risk

CHAPTER **14**

Cool Delta Tricks

14.1 Cool Trick #1

Elta roughly represents the % probability that a given option will expire with some intrinsic value (ITM). I've read this a few places, but from what math I understand, this is a very rough estimate/derivation that results from the definition of delta.

Note that this does not directly imply profitability, just the chance that you will have your shares called at expiration if you do nothing. To illustrate, remember that a call will still be exercised if it only has $0.01 per share intrinsic value at expiration, regardless of what it was worth when you bought or sold it.

So, looking at the following chain[1] we can find the $10 strike call and see the corresponding delta is 0.4987.

Last	Change	Bid	Ask	Volume	Open Int	Imp Vol	Delta	Action	Strike ▲	Action	Last	Change	Bid	Ask	Volume	Open Int	Imp Vol	Delta
—					CALLS				Dec 20 '19 (26 days)							PUTS		
0.00	0.00	4.50	5.00	0	0	—	0.9451	▼	5	▼	0.05	0.00	0.00	0.05	0	10	127.16 %	-0.0182
3.08	0.00	3.70	4.00	0	3	77.77 %	0.9959	▼	6	▼	0.00	0.00	0.00	0.10	0	0	109.84 %	-0.0302
2.35	0.00	2.70	3.00	0	25	53.55 %	0.9952	▼	7	▼	0.10	0.00	0.00	0.15	0	3	98.45 %	-0.0659
2.00	0.00	1.80	2.05	0	131	60.87 %	0.9089	▼	8	▼	0.11	0.00	0.10	0.15	0	187	70.12 %	-0.1234
1.15	0.00	1.00	1.20	0	422	55.80 %	0.7479	▼	9	▼	0.35	0.00	0.25	0.35	0	436	61.14 %	-0.2717
0.60	0.00	0.50	0.65	0	1,411	59.13 %	0.4987	▼	10	▼	0.75	0.00	0.65	0.75	0	531	56.47 %	-0.5127
0.28	0.00	0.25	0.30	0	834	61.44 %	0.2896	▼	11	▼	1.40	0.00	1.35	1.50	0	14	60.61 %	-0.7249
0.10	0.00	0.10	0.15	0	420	63.52 %	0.1531	▼	12	▼	2.47	0.00	2.20	2.40	0	6	65.35 %	-0.8525
2.05	0.00	0.00	0.10	0	255	63.97 %	0.0714	▼	13	▼	3.47	0.00	3.10	3.40	0	15	71.58 %	-0.9163
0.05	0.00	0.00	0.05	0	81	67.43 %	0.0378	▼	14	▼	0.00	0.00	4.00	4.40	0	0	—	-0.8377

And a zoomed in view:

Last	Change	Bid	Ask	Volume	Open Int	Imp Vol	Delta	Action	Strike ▲	Actic
—					CALLS				Dec 20 '19 (26 days)	
0.00	0.00	4.50	5.00	0	0	—	0.9451	▼	5	▼
3.08	0.00	3.70	4.00	0	3	77.77 %	0.9959	▼	6	▼
2.35	0.00	2.70	3.00	0	25	53.55 %	0.9952	▼	7	▼
2.00	0.00	1.80	2.05	0	131	60.87 %	0.9089	▼	8	▼
1.15	0.00	1.00	1.20	0	422	55.80 %	0.7479	▼	9	▼
0.60	0.00	0.50	0.65	0	1,411	59.13 %	0.4987	▼	10	▼
0.28	0.00	0.25	0.30	0	834	61.44 %	0.2896	▼	11	▼
0.10	0.00	0.10	0.15	0	420	63.52 %	0.1531	▼	12	▼
0.05	0.00	0.00	0.10	0	255	63.97 %	0.0714	▼	13	▼
0.05	0.00	0.00	0.05	0	81	67.43 %	0.0378	▼	14	▼

With a Delta of 0.4987, the call has an implied chance of 49.87% to expire with intrinsic value (the shares are $10 or more at expiration). That's a pretty slick way to glean the whole option market's best guess about a future price in a couple of seconds.

---

[1]Snip was taken 11/22/19 for a preclinical biotech company trading at $9.81 a share

14.2 Delta Trick #1 Example:

Looking again at the above chain, I notice the delta for the 26–day $11 strike call is 0.2896

Last	Change	Bid	Ask	Volume	Open Int	Imp Vol	Delta	Action	Strike ▲	Actic
—			CALLS						Dec 20 '19 (26 days)	
0.00	0.00	4.50	5.00	0	0	—	0.9451	▼	5	▼
3.08	0.00	3.70	4.00	0	3	77.77 %	0.9959	▼	6	▼
2.35	0.00	2.70	3.00	0	25	53.55 %	0.9952	▼	7	▼
2.00	0.00	1.80	2.05	0	131	60.87 %	0.9089	▼	8	▼
1.15	0.00	1.00	1.20	0	422	55.80 %	0.7479	▼	9	▼
0.60	0.00	0.50	0.65	0	1,411	59.13 %	0.4987	▼	10	▼
0.28	0.00	0.25	0.30	0	834	61.44 %	0.2896	▼	11	▼
0.10	0.00	0.10	0.15	0	420	63.52 %	0.1531	▼	12	▼
0.05	0.00	0.00	0.10	0	255	63.97 %	0.0714	▼	13	▼
0.05	0.00	0.00	0.05	0	81	67.43 %	0.0378	▼	14	▼

- Me, thinking aloud: "What are the odds this stock closes above $11 on December 20, 2019?"

- Myself, answering me: "The options market says there is a 28.96% chance of that happening"

- Me: "Cool"

Although this delta = probability thing is neat, delta changes by the second, so don't think that it gives you a secret lens into the future. However, for some retail traders it does serve as a useful "reinforcing" number that fits into a larger system for entering and exiting trades.[2] If that works for you, great! Whatever works, works.

---

[2]FYI for the more mathematically inclined reader (not necessary for portfolio overwriting): Some trading systems use the delta-as-probability proxy to assume that a 16 delta call would represent a closing price on expiry within 1 standard deviation of stock price moves... if stock prices were in fact Gaussian random

14.3   Cool Trick #2

Delta represents the number of shares that each call represents, or acts as a surrogate for. Put another way, owning one $9 strike call from the chain above is equivalent to owning 74.79 shares (from a profit perspective).

Specifically, it equates the dollar amount of profit you get to participate in if the stock moves up and you own the call.[3] For instance, if you own a $9 call from the chain above, which has a delta of 0.7479, that means when the stock goes up $1 you, in theory, would make 74 cents per share— you participate in 74.79% of the profits that the holder of shares (delta = 1) would. Remember our infographic from before— let's update it with the long call profit:

---

walks (they aren't exactly). Other systems advocate only selling calls closer to the 35–40 delta to minimize chances of assignment. There is no perfect system, but understanding the logic behind these choices might, to some extent, help you choose a strike. I don't have enough faith in any specific rules-based trading methodology to advocate it, but you will likely come across this thinking if you research covered calls more on your own.

[3]Don't get confused! Portfolio overwriting is about selling calls, but in this example you own the call. This is only because delta as a proxy for share ownership is easier to understand from the call owner's perspective.

SETUP		AFTER $1/SHARE APPRECIATION	
STOCK PRICE:	$9.81	STOCK PRICE:	$10.81
CALL PRICE:	$1.15 (26-DAY EXPIRY, $9 STRIKE)	CALL PRICE:	$1.89
DELTA:	0.7479	CALL PROFIT:	$0.74/SH ($1.15->$1.89) WE KNOW THAT BECAUSE DELTA CHANGES AS IT MOVES THIS IS JUST AN ESTIMATE

Figure 14.1: *Note to reader: In this and other charts, "SH" means "Share". It is abbreviated simply to accommodate fitting enough information into each graphic.*

Pause and Ponder[4]— you could buy 100 shares at a cost of $981 and get $1/share profit on a $1 move, or you could spend $115 and get 74 cents/share profits on a $1 move. That's a much larger return on a much smaller initial outlay.

Explicitly, if you took your $981 and bought eight $9-strike calls

---

[4]You'll notice I use this phrase a few times throughout the book. It is a nod to Grant Sanderson, aka 3Blue1Brown on Youtube. He makes visually beautiful videos about math that make unintuitive concepts like calculus or linear algebra so clear that you feel like you could have discovered the field yourself. I would highly recommend checking him out. Not only is everything painstakingly and stylishly animated in Manim, Grant does well-thought-out narration in the smooth dulcet tones of his teaching voice— great for relaxing and learning math (or neural networks, or blockchain technology, or image processing— it's a wide range of interesting subjects), which is the opposite of the typical "math trauma" induced stress most people experience when they see an equation.

($981 ÷ $115 = $8.5, we'll round down) and the stock appreciated $1, you'd make $589 (0.7479 cents per share × 100 shares per call × 8 calls) instead of $100 ($1 per share × 100 shares × 1 call).[5]

This is the power of leverage; you can make almost eight times the profit on the same $981 investment. Although we are not covering that type of trading here, understanding the call **buyer's** perspective should help reinforce our role as call **sellers**.

14.4   Cool Delta Trick #3

FYI, this one's just a teaser with an important buried concept.

So far we have been talking about **buying** calls and positive deltas, but when we **sell** calls, that position has a negative delta. So how does a negative delta function? If you sold the rights to your shares and the shares rise in price, you are (in theory) losing money because you do not participate in those profits. On the flipside, your sold call makes money if the price of the underlying security falls, so it kind of "buffers" your portfolio by gaining when your shares lose.

Without getting too far in the weeds (intentional hedge pun), this negative delta "hedges" your portfolio. You may have heard of "hedge funds"— that's where the name comes from! Since shares you own always have a delta = 1, you could in theory use sold calls or short shares[6] to maintain a completely hedged (this is called "delta neu-

---

[5]This is call buying in a nutshell. If you ever see returns that are hundreds or thousands of percentage points, it is likely due to buying very cheap, very far OTM options that suddenly become very valuable when the underlying stock made a large move up.

Although an interesting topic, it is not the subject matter of this book, and it carries quite a lot of risk. Namely, shares do not expire, **but calls do. Any call you buy can go to zero**, and if that happened **you would lose your entire investment.** This is not to say that call buying isn't appropriate for some investors. Lotto tickets have their place, and it is possible to utilize buying ITM or ATM calls as part of safer strategies... it's just not the matter at hand.

[6]Recall that short shares are shares your account is "short". You borrow them

tral"[7]) portfolio, which would not change in value no matter what the market is doing. When shares gain, sold calls lose, and vice versa. Although this would be horrendously complicated and involve infinite trades to adjust to the second by second moves of the market (read: be impossible, especially for a retail investor), the overall concept can be used to understand how calls act as a hedge. Just know you will never truly be delta neutral.

That said, just know that you have to understand how negative delta affects the overall portfolio once you start selling covered calls. Once we sell a call, that negative delta in our account means that price rises will be a "loss" on our sold call— something to accept as fact now and have reinforced over and over later in the series. Also, remember that when our shares fall in price, our sold call shows "gains" in our account as its value decreases.

Now that we explored Delta a bit, we can move on to some funner stuff— time value and extrinsic value.

---

from your broker, and provide them by buying them on the market at a later date. If you are able to purchase them at a price lower than what you borrowed them for, you pocket the difference as a profit. As such, you make money when a stock that you have "shorted" decreases in value— basically the opposite of owning shares.

[7]In a "delta neutral" portfolio the positive delta of long positions and negative delta of short positions equals zero when summed. At that exact moment, moves of the underlying security in either direction would theoretically not matter, as the gains and losses from the different positive and negative deltas would offset one another. This is a concept that is good to understand, but not entirely possible for the average retail trader to begin to implement.

CHAPTER 15

Time Value/Extrinsic Value

o me, the idea of time value[1] is the most interesting part of an option. Basically, you are assigning a price to what could happen in the future, which is #1 impossible to do perfectly #2 really fun to think about. Imagine taking everything that could possibly happen in the next month to two years and distilling that universe of possibilities down to a very real, very concrete number. That's what time value really is. In fact, the raison d'etre for options in the first place is speculation about the future— guesses about what

---

[1] Disclaimer: Although Extrinsic Value is often considered to be made up of Time Value and Volatility, you might catch me referring to them all interchangeably. Time adds to volatility and uncertainty (the more time there is, the more time there is for things to happen), and it turns out that the concept occupies the same amorphous space in my brain because they are so inherently interrelated. An academic or institutional trader would take issue with this, but that level of understanding functions perfectly well for most retail traders.

is (or isn't) going to happen.

In terms of the simple but uncompelling technical definition, extrinsic value is "the value of the option premium above intrinsic value." We already know what intrinsic value is and how to find it with simple arithmetic. When we collect premiums from the sale of calls, extrinsic value is anything above that intrinsic value— the "icing" on the "call-premium-cake."

15.1   Time Value is Made Of...What?

So what goes into time value? And why do you care? We care because when we sell covered calls, premium from time value is a big source of profits. What goes into it is more complicated— underlying value, time to expiration, volatility (historical and implied aka uncertainty), interest rates (we don't care at the retail level), and dividends (we super care).

15.2   Time to Expiration

Time to expiration is easy— the more time there is until expiry, the more an option is worth. The more days that pass, the more chances there are for an option to be profitable.

15.3   Volatility— Historical

Volatility is a bit more complicated, and the term actually can be used to refer to two concepts: historical volatility and implied volatility. Historical volatility is technically the "standard deviation of log normal returns"— something I'm not actively computing. This is a statistical measure of the past prices and how much they vary. There are different ways to measure volatility mathematically, but for the purposes of understanding time value to sell covered calls, all you need to know is that stocks whose prices bounce around more are more volatile and have more time value.

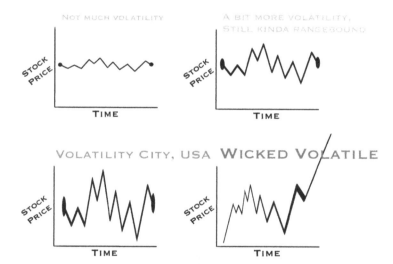

15.4   Volatility— Implied

Implied volatility is a bit more intense— if you want to really grasp it, you'd have to grock the Black-Scholes equation, the holy grail of options trading. The implied volatility is a variable that is backwards-derived from option price. In essence, it tells you the market's best guess of how much this stock is going to move given all the available information to buyers and sellers. It is one unknown variable that mathematicians solve for when trying to model options.

Figure 15.1: *The Black Scholes equation in a couple different forms on my blackboard at home.*

In my head it's the Thorp equation (After reading "A Man for All Markets"), but don't tell Myron.

Ever heard of Ed Thorp? He's the original options whiz, and author of Beat the Dealer. Even if you're not familiar with his name or the book, you've likely heard of the card counting strategy to win in blackjack that caused casinos to change the rules of the game and add more cards to each dealt deck. Ed Thorp invented it, along with a version of the Black-Scholes equation that he used at Princeton-Newport partners to generate 20%+ yearly returns for 10+ years, starting before Myron Scholes and Fischer Black published their paper.[2]

Do I understand Black Scholes? Kind of, on a surface level. Do I use it in practice? No. Would I like to understand it inside and out?

---

[2]Myron, a Nobel laureate, ran a hedge fund, too— Long Term Capital Management. For fun, look up how they are doing these days.

Yes, very much so. [3]

15.5   Anything Can Happen

There's some real magic (read: guesswork) here, because anything can happen. If you own shares of a drug company and they cure cancer, stock could go up an unlimited amount. Own a restaurant stock and they've been feeding people rats? That stock is going to tank. These are sometimes called binary events or black swans (see The Black Swan by Nassim Nicholas Taleb[4])— you won't know when they will happen, and sometimes the market will know before you know that they have happened.

It's a fun point to pause and ponder. An even funner point to pause and ponder would be the fact that maybe the market undervalues major moves in some stocks, and by extension the stock's options, and how you could make $ if that were true.

15.6   Other Factors in Extrinsic Value

Interest rates— don't care at this level of trading. They typically won't affect your decisions as a retail investor. Rho (the Greek representing interest rates) is up there in the Black-Scholes equation and I urge you to research it if you're curious and have a burning desire, but it can be set aside for now.

Dividends are important because they decrease the value of a stock by the amount of the dividend when they are paid, and therefore give set information about the future value of a security. The owner of the

---

[3]I do math in my free time. Understanding Black-Scholes better is one motivating goal.

[4]It's probably best to read all of his books in an effort to understand what we don't understand.

stock on the Ex-dividend date, not the owner of the option, gets paid the dividend. As such, you run the risk of getting assigned early if the dividend value is greater than the remaining value of the option.[5]

---

[5]This is more of an issue when it comes to stocks that pay a larger dividend, and less of a problem when it comes to index funds.

CHAPTER 16

Theta ⊖

F the 5 options Greeks (the variables that describe an option's value) theta is my favorite. As a covered call seller, theta is one of the big places you make your money.[1]

We already parsed out how every option premium consists of intrinsic and extrinsic value, and we saw that the more time until expiration, the more extrinsic value an option has. So what is happening as each day passes that makes the extrinsic value decrease as an option contract approaches expiration?

Theta decay, that's what!

As the clock ticks down to expiration, time value decreases. Theta is literally the amount, in dollars, that an option's value would decrease

---

[1]Note: Theta is a rate of decay, but "theta" and "theta decay" are often used interchangeably when discussing options. I'm sorry if this is confusing.

after one day if all else (stock price, volatility, etc) remained the same.

Theta decay (decreasing time value) is great if you sold an option, because the cost to buy your option back gets cheaper or drops to zero if it stays OTM. Conversely, it is the enemy of the option buyer, because the option they bought has a built-in decay over time. This built in decay is the biggest disadvantage to buying long calls instead of shares.

Figure 16.1: *I often say it in my head to the sing-songy startscreen tune of "Sega"*

What goes into theta? Primarily moneyness and volatility.

16.1   Moneyness

Moneyness is the first determinant— ATM options have the highest theta, with ITM and OTM options having a lower theta. This is related to the fact that ATM options also have the most extrinsic value. The more extrinsic value there is, the more extrinsic value there is to decay over time. Conversely, deep ITM or far OTM options have a low theta— they simply don't have as much extrinsic value to erode.

Knowing ATM strikes have the highest theta influences the strike price you choose to sell your call at. Mainly, theta tells you how much of the value of the call you sold will be "eaten away" by theta decay as one day passes. Remember— if we are portfolio overwriting and selling OTM options, then our entire option premium is made up of extrinsic value.

16.2   Volatility

Volatility is the second major influencer— more volatility results in a higher theta. Although this may seem counter-intuitive or be difficult to grasp, I like to think of it as follows: the more uncertainty that exists, the more another day that passes helps collapse the possibilities. I have also heard the rationale that higher volatility = more time value = more to erode, ergo higher theta, just like our reasoning with moneyness. Whatever the reason, more volatile = higher theta.

But we know one thing with the certainty that we know the sky is blue: theta is directional. Theta will always march forward with time.

As a result, option sellers often love watching theta decay in action. Every day that goes by, some theta erodes and creates a profit in the option seller's account, all other factors being equal. The colloquial term "theta farm" refers to the option seller who, instead of planting crops, sells calls. Rather than watching crops grow every day, they watch theta decay eat away at time value of short calls bit by bit and result in profits.

Figure 16.2: *Omnes vulnerant, ultima necat. If you haven't listened to the short podcast series S-town, it's worth your time.*

More interestingly, theta is **NOT** linear. Time decay ramps up as expiration approaches... which plays into the strategy of selling covered calls bigtime, but that requires its own chapter on theta decay. But before we tie that concept in, we can start to talk about overwriting and returns.

CHAPTER 17

Overwriting and Returns Part One

O you already own shares and you sell an OTM call against those shares. You collect the premium and make extra returns every month. Sounds cool. One of the neat things you can do is start to calculate an ROI on your investment as you make a small % back every month. Some people account for these premiums by subtracting them from the price they paid for a stock (the cost basis). If you paid $100 a share, and made $2 in call premiums this month, you could think of your cost basis as now being $98. Extrapolated over enough time, you might even pay off your original stock. . .

17.1 Making Money on a Stock That Doesn't Go Up

In theory, you could do this on a totally flat or range-bound stock and make a killing. To illustrate, consider this stock price over time with option position overlays below. The pictures below show the price of a stock over time, with entry and exit points and corresponding account values for the underlying and sold calls. In the case of this range bound stock[1], we sell calls, and buy them back when they are cheap (or let them expire worthless), then rinse and repeat. The stock is the same price as it was at the start of the graph, and we've made profits along the way.

Imagine you are looking at the graph of the following stock over the course of one month:

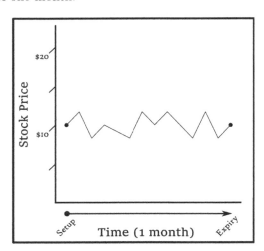

This moves around a bit, but kind of hovers at the $10 price point.

---

[1]The idea of a range bound stock is a bit spurious and time-sensitive, as most stocks only trade in a range for a limited period of time... until they don't.

You take your pencil and draw a line at the upper edge of how high the price gets— and it looks like \$12. In technical analysis[2] this would be called a "resistance" level.

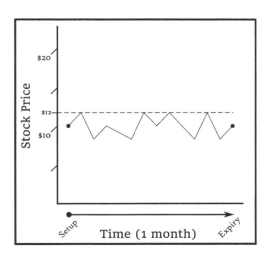

If you wanted to make money on this stock that hovered around \$10, you would sell a call for \$12 and collect the premium, as below:

---

[2]Which I am either too dumb to understand or don't believe in— I haven't decided. My thoughts on technical analysis are contained in a later chapter.

An Example of Overwriting a Flat Stock

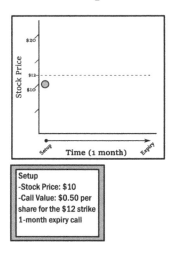

Share Price: $10.00

Call Value: $0.50 per share

Cash Balance: +$50

Account Value: (No Change)

Setup
-Stock Price: $10
-Call Value: $0.50 per
share for the $12 strike
1-month expiry call

To put some numbers to it, in this scenario the $12 strike call was selling for $0.50/share.

Notice 2 things— first, the cash available in your account increased by $50 ($0.50 cents per share × 100 shares per contract).

Second, the overall account value did not change, because even though you received $50 in liquid cash when you sold the call option, you are short a $50 call, so it evens it out the moment you initially make the trade.

Then, you'd let time pass until the option value dwindled to zero. If the underlying stock stayed flat and closed at $10 when the call expired, then that $12 strike call on a $10 stock ends up worthless. With the short call now worthless at the end of the month, you've made $50 on your $1,000 worth of stock.

Notice again: you immediately received $50 from the sale of your call, but didn't make money overall until the short position (the call you sold) decreased in value.

An Example of Overwriting a Flat Stock

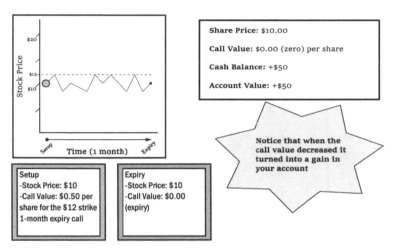

Share Price: $10.00

Call Value: $0.00 (zero) per share

Cash Balance: +$50

Account Value: +$50

Setup
-Stock Price: $10
-Call Value: $0.50 per share for the $12 strike
1-month expiry call

Expiry
-Stock Price: $10
-Call Value: $0.00 (expiry)

Notice that when the call value decreased it turned into a gain in your account

Over time, the extrinsic value of the call decreased to zero (due to theta decay) because the underlying did not approach or exceed our strike price.

So what's the ROI (Return on Investment)? If you invested $1,000 and made $50 on it, that's 5% in one month.

$$ROI = \frac{\$50}{\$1,000} = 0.05 = 5\%$$

Even better, you could do this every month and add it up, you'd have a 60% return. If you didn't just add it, but compounded twelve times over the course of a year, it would make you 79%. That's 79% you wouldn't have otherwise made if you just held a stock that waffled in that $9–12 range. 79% is pretty good compared to a return of 0% if you had just held the stock.

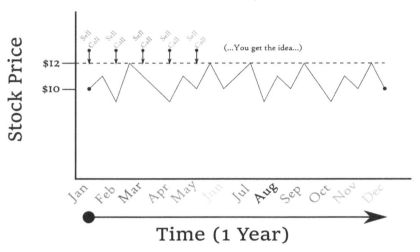

17.2   But the Market Isn't Flat— We Expect Our Index Funds To Go Up Over Time

But with overwriting, we expect our underlying to rise in value, especially if we are holding a Boglehead-style index. So let's adjust the graph a bit to show a slight upward trend.

The Ideal Scenario for Selling Covered Calls on an Appreciating Boglehead Index, Visualized

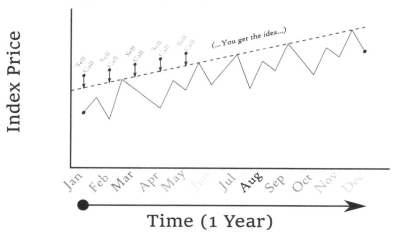

In this case, identifying an upward trend (if it even exists/is possible) would theoretically allow you to participate in all the share appreciation and all the call premiums. Ok, cool. So to recap, we own shares, and now our shares make money without us having to sell them. It's so easy that it's basically free money, right?

17.3   Time for a Reality Check

Not so fast. Slow your roll.

I had that thought too, but learning more and actually trading with your own money makes the Dunning-Kruger Effect hit you like a brick wall...fast. It's not that easy (although lots of people try to make it sound that way). I've included a lovely graphical representation of the Dunning-Kruger Effect below to illustrate that the "I know everything" peak is a sub-optimal place to be.[3]

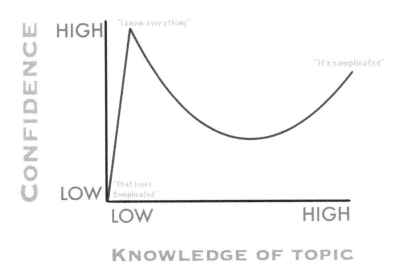

In reality, the price of your shares is going to move— sometimes up and sometimes down, sometimes way up and sometimes way down. There will be times when the underlying goes past your strike and you are forced to adjust your position at expiration.

---

[3]It is largely the realm of arrogant imbeciles. Say what you will about me, but at least I'm either smart enough or humble enough to know that I'm an idiot ☺

The *Reality* of Selling Covered Calls on an Appreciating Boglehead Index, Visualized

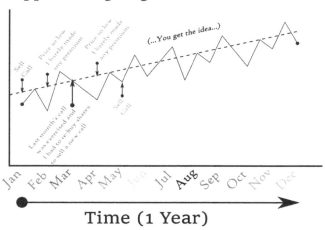

17.4   You Need to be Prepared

Whatever happens, you need to know what to do. If you don't, you're going to experience lost profits, executed calls and tax penalties if you aren't trading in an IRA, or find yourself locked into a deep in-the-money (ITM) position. For covered calls with FIRE, I often suspect the simplest answer is to just let shares be called and re-enter the position entirely, but we will get into that and all the other moves we can make later in this book.

The point is, don't count on your trendline and everything working out perfectly.

The second point is that's totally ok.

But before we cover how to manage the stock you own and the calls you sold over the life of an option, we have to figure out which call to sell in the first place.

CHAPTER 18

Price Time-Series Legend

Efore moving into the nitty-gritty position management chapters, we need to explain what the time-series[1] graphs found in each chapter describing position management are, and how they work. They are essential to visualizing what happens when you sell a covered call.

---

[1] A time series is just a fancy term for a type of graph with time on the x (horizontal) axis.

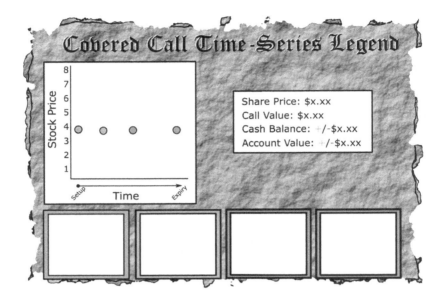

18.1 Why are There So Many Examples of These "Time-Series"?

The reason is simple— when you sell a call, how the underlying moves throughout the contract period will determine what your available courses of action are. From a high-level perspective, the stock moves and corresponding choices are as follows:

- No matter how the underlying price moves, we can always do nothing, letting our calls expire and shares get called if they are ITM

- If the price of the underlying stays the same, and remains below the strike price we can buy-to-close (BTC), roll up, roll out, or roll up & out (all explained later in this book)

- If the price of the underlying drops, we can BTC, roll out, or (god forbid) roll down

This is the essence of trading covered calls. Anyone can learn the general idea and sell a call from a short article or video. The profit and loss calculations are easy, and the concepts aren't rocket science. Beyond that, it gets complicated.

Position management is where the real skill and understanding resides. So, after a few more preparatory chapters, we will grind through all the possible scenarios to create a solid understanding of the endeavor. And you will emerge on the other side with a real understanding of covered calls.

The time-series show what happens over a contract period, typically a month.[2] They start at the beginning of the month, when you theoretically purchased a stock and sold a call.

---

[2]These are actually just a nicer version of what I would draw for myself when I started to learn how to trade covered calls.

18.2   Highlighting the Parts

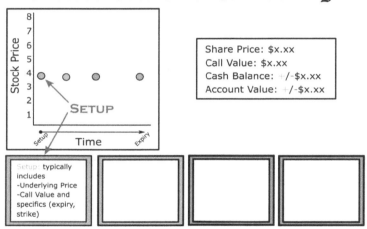

Each point in time on the graph is a price, and there is a corresponding "caption" box at the bottom explaining what happens at each time point.

Covered Call Time-Series Legend

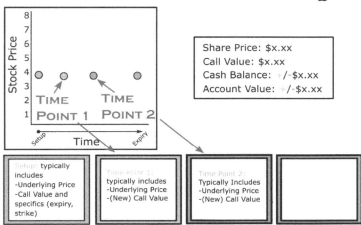

As the underlying price moves, the value of the call changes, and is updated in the boxes corresponding to each time point on the graph. There will also be times when a position is adjusted (a call is bought or sold); these points will not have new points on the graph or caption boxes— they will have the same price point and an updated caption box.

Here's an example of a position prior to adjustment, at the second time point (this example is directly from a future chapter):

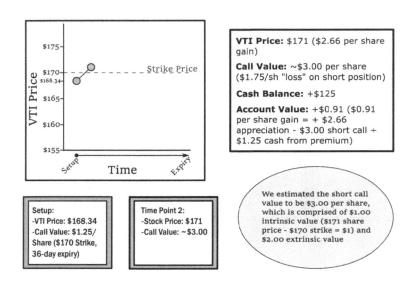

VTI Price: $171 ($2.66 per share gain)

Call Value: ~$3.00 per share ($1.75/sh "loss" on short position)

Cash Balance: +$125

Account Value: +$0.91 ($0.91 per share gain = + $2.66 appreciation - $3.00 short call + $1.25 cash from premium)

Setup:
-VTI Price: $168.34
-Call Value: $1.25/
Share ($170 Strike,
36-day expiry)

Time Point 2:
-Stock Price: $171
-Call Value: ~$3.00

We estimated the short call value to be $3.00 per share, which is comprised of $1.00 intrinsic value ($171 share price - $170 strike = $1) and $2.00 extrinsic value

And after adjustment:

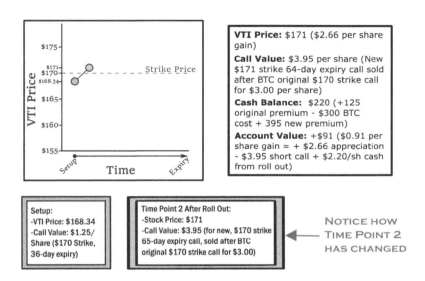

Figure 18.1: *Here we performed a "roll"— buying to close one call and simultaneously selling another, which will be covered in detail in a later chapter.*

In the upper right corner is always a separate box which shows a running tally of the value of all the open account positions, and most importantly the overall account value. I added this to make it easier to tell where we are, and how our decisions have affected our account value.

Of note, the overall account value often stays the same at the moment we adjust a position. Although we may receive a cash premium when we sell a call, we are simply changing long and short allocations (in the example of selling a call, we are we are creating a short call position in exchange for premium). Profit and loss do not occur when we adjust positions— rather, it happens over time as the price of the underlying security and the price of the option changes, and results from the effects of those changes on the position we created when we set up the trade.

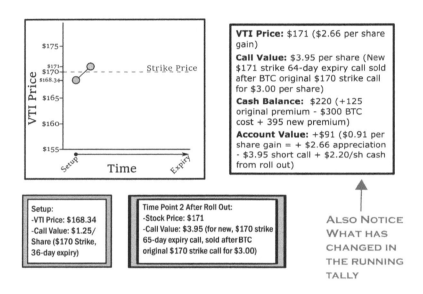

Although this can become a dense image by the end of a contract period, it really allows you to follow along and keep track of what happened without having to reference previous pictures. With just a quick glance you can understand the "life" of a covered call trade. It should also simulate what will happen when you are looking at your brokerage account and buying/selling calls, adjusting positions, and calculating profits/losses.

CHAPTER 19

Strike Price Selection Part One

O you own 100 shares, you're going to sell a call— but which call to sell? Not an easy answer, but you should always start with this question— how much are you expecting to make? It's time to look at returns, and all the fun stuff you can do with those numbers.

19.1   Example Portfolio Overwriting Returns

We'll use VTI for these calculations, with a chain taken on 12/13/19 when the share price was $161.27

VTI   VANGUARD TOTAL STOCK MARKET ETF   **$161.27** ↓ -0.06 (-0.04%)   AS OF 12:36:00PM ET 12/13/2019   More Quote Information

Last	Change	Bid	Ask	Volume	Open Int	Imp Vol	Delta	Action	Strike ▲	Action	Last	Change	Bid	Ask	Volume	Open Int	Imp Vol	Delta
—			CALLS						Jan 17 '20 (35 days)				PUTS					
5.45	0.00	4.90	5.20	0	9	13.44%	0.7626	▼	157	▼	1.28	0.00	1.15	1.30	0	9	13.71%	-0.2845
4.65	0.00	4.10	4.30	0	10	12.66%	0.7137	▼	158	▼	1.59	-0.01	1.35	1.50	3	30	13.02%	-0.33
3.70	+0.50	3.30	3.50	2	21	11.89%	0.6557	▼	159	▼	1.90	0.00	1.55	1.75	0	59	12.24%	-0.3826
2.20	-0.71	2.55	2.75	3	54	11.12%	0.5865	▼	160	▼	2.35	0.00	1.80	2.00	0	7	11.34%	-0.4444
1.97	-0.43	1.90	2.10	1	33	10.51%	0.5058	▼	161	▼	2.65	0.00	2.15	2.35	0	3	10.61%	-0.5182
1.47	-0.33	1.35	1.50	8	13	9.86%	0.418	▼	162	▼	4.03	0.00	2.55	2.80	0	22	9.86%	-0.6027
1.10	0.00	0.85	1.00	0	37	9.10%	0.3239	▼	163	▼	3.30	0.00	3.10	3.40	0	1	9.41%	-0.6902
0.71	0.00	0.50	0.65	0	2	8.60%	0.2357	▼	164	▼	4.60	0.00	3.70	4.00	0	1	8.49%	-0.7912
0.50	0.00	0.30	0.45	0	14	8.55%	0.1694	▼	165	▼	0.00	0.00	4.50	4.90	0	0	8.61%	-0.8544
0.35	0.00	0.15	0.30	0	18	8.40%	0.1139	▼	166	▼	0.00	0.00	5.30	6.80	0	0	12.72%	-0.7983

Say you are (like most Mustachians) a diligent Boglehead, and have worked hard to accumulate 100 shares of VTI. Looking at your account there's $16,127 worth of VTI sitting there growing like a gorgeous lophophora williamsii button.

Figure 19.1: *Artist's representation of aforementioned horticultural delight.*

You know to weather the storm, sit tight, and over time the market is going to go up, and up, and up. But for whatever the reason you want extra cash, and don't want to sell your shares.

Conundrum? Not really. Taking a look at the chain, you see that the $162 strike price call has a bid-ask of $1.35-$1.50

Last	Change	Bid	Ask	Volume	Open Int	Imp Vol	Delta	Action	Strike ▲	Acti
—				CALLS					Jan 17 '20 (35 days)	
5.45	0.00	4.90	5.20	0	9	13.44 %	0.7626	▼	157	▼
4.65	0.00	4.10	4.30	0	10	12.66 %	0.7137	▼	158	▼
3.70	+0.50	3.30	3.50	2	21	11.89 %	0.6557	▼	159	▼
2.20	-0.71	2.55	2.75	3	54	11.12 %	0.5865	▼	160	▼
1.97	-0.43	1.90	2.10	1	33	10.51 %	0.5058	▼	161	▼
1.47	-0	1.35	1.50	8	13	9.86 %	0.418	▼	162	▼
1.10	0.00	0.85	1.00	0	37	9.10 %	0.3239	▼	163	▼
0.71	0.00	0.50	0.65	0	2	8.60 %	0.2357	▼	164	▼
0.50	0.00	0.30	0.45	0	14	8.55 %	0.1694	▼	165	▼
0.35	0.00	0.15	0.30	0	16	8.40 %	0.1139	▼	166	▼

VTI Q VANGUARD TOTAL STOCK MARKET ETF $161.27 ▼ -0.06 (-0.04%) AS OF 12 36 00PM ET 12/13 More Quote Information

So you'll probably get $140 ($1.40 a share) for selling someone the right to buy 100 shares of VTI from you for $162 a share.

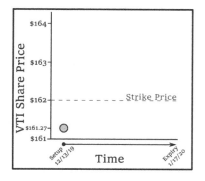

Underlying (VTI) Price: $161.27

Call Value: $1.40 per share

Cash Balance: +$140

Account Value: (no change)

Setup:
-VTI Price: $161.27
-Call Value: $1.40/
Share ($162 Strike,
35-day expiry)

Firstly, what's the return on the option premium? If you bought 100 shares of VTI today for $161.27, then the option premium alone would be a return of 0.868% (= $140 ÷ $16,127 × 100%).

$$\text{ROI} = \frac{\$140}{\$16{,}127} = 0.00868 = 0.868\%$$

19.2   Compound It

If you just rolled your eyes and shut your brain off, you need to re-think in terms of yearly compounding. That option expires 35 days from now, and there are 365 days in a year. If you could make 0.868%, and compound it 10 times over the course of a year, **you'd have made 9.02% off options premiums alone.**

1. That's better than the average long-term total market return of 7%.

2. That 9.02% is the return from options premium alone, not accounting for the potential additional profits if VTI happened to appreciate to your strike price.

You can use this method to calculate a theoretical annual return for your options— if you were going to make something in one month, multiply it by 12 (or compound it twelve times assuming reinvestment if you are very optimistic). Look at the number and marvel at how high it is for a yearly return...**and then immediately throw the number away,** realizing life happens and you rarely actually make that. I have found it to be more of a feel-good number than a realistic goal, which is why it is called a *theoretical* return. Life happens, stocks move, and it's rarely that simple.

19.3   Not Just Premiums— Returns from Share Appreciation, Too!

But those returns we just figured didn't even include potential appreciation! Back to our example— to recap: you're in it to win it at $16,127 and sold the Jan' 20 $162 strike call for $140 ($1.40 per share). All the sudden some good news happens— trade deal or blah blah or whatever— and the VTI shoots up to $164 and stays there until expiration.

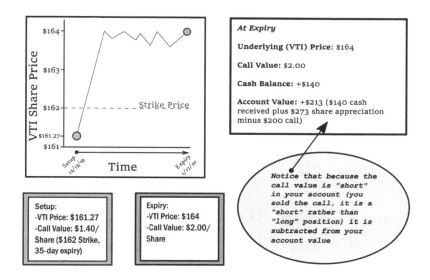

If you are trading in an IRA and don't care about capital gains, you could just let the 100 shares of VTI get "called" from you. In that case, you'd be selling them at the strike of the contract— $162 a share. So in addition to the premium you received, you're making the difference between your purchase price and the strike price, $73 [($162 − $161.27) × 100 shares]. Add that $73 to your $140 and you're at $213. $213 is a 1.32% return [($213 ÷ $16127) × 100%], better than the premium-only return of 0.868%.

$$\text{ROI} = \frac{\overset{\text{Call Premium}}{\$140} + \overset{\text{Share Appreciation}}{\$73}}{\$16,127} = 0.0132 = 1.32\%$$

Sounds good— you bought some stuff, and someone paid you

money for the right to buy the stuff from you for a higher price than you bought it.

Additionally, the annual return of making 1.32% ten times (it was a 35-day call, not 28 day) is 14%...

19.4   A Better ROI Awaits— Selling Calls Against Shares That Already Appreciated

Alternatively, if you got lucky and initially bought those VTI shares on Feb 12th, 2016 when VTI had a dip to $94.36, and have been holding ever since, your $140 premium alone would be getting you a 1.48% return on your investment ($140 ÷ $9436). One neat thing to realize is that if you sell calls on your already-appreciated shares, your premiums will account for a higher % of the original cost. Although this isn't really amazingly insightful, it would be nice to have a double-bagger[1] that could start to pay itself off while you still let the shares ride.

---

[1]A double-bagger is the trading term for a stock that doubled since the time you bought it, representing a 100% return.

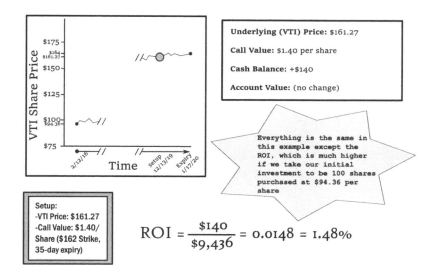

Setup:
-VTI Price: $161.27
-Call Value: $1.40/
Share ($162 Strike,
35-day expiry)

$$ROI = \frac{\$140}{\$9,436} = 0.0148 = 1.48\%$$

This is all well and good, but you have to keep in mind that if you let those shares get called, you will have to pay taxes on the gains VTI accumulated and the premium you were paid (unless you are trading in an IRA, which I'd recommend at least to start).

19.5 LEAP Calls and Their (Deceptively?) High Premiums

Just as a teaser— if you look at the options chain for March, which is 98 days away from when I took the data, the premiums go up a lot. And they increase for all the strikes, even the ones that are way out of the money.

Last	Change	Bid	Ask	Volume	Open Int	Imp Vol	Delta	Action	Strike ▲	Actiol

VTI   Q   VANGUARD TOTAL STOCK MARKET ETF   **$161.27** ↓ -0.06 (-0.04%)   AS OF 12 36 00PM ET 12/13/2   More Quote Information

Last	Change	Bid	Ask	Volume	Open Int	Imp Vol	Delta	Action	Strike ▲	Actiol
—					CALLS				Mar 20 '20 (98 days)	
7.20	0.00	7.10	7.40	0	220	14.90 %	0.6471	▼	1.07	▼
6.29	-0.01	6.40	6.60	28	34	14.43 %	0.6191	▼	158	▼
5.30	0.00	5.60	5.90	0	416	13.88 %	0.5891	▼	159	▼
5.30	+0.30	5.00	5.20	6	201	13.55 %	0.5558	▼	160	▼
4.42	+0.01	4.40	4.50	6	34	13.12 %	0.5207	▼	161	▼
3.70	-0.57	3.70	3.90	1	60	12.59 %	0.4829	▼	162	▼
3.60	0.00	3.10	3.30	0	38	12.09 %	0.4424	▼	163	▼
2.39	0.00	2.60	2.80	0	48	11.77 %	0.4013	▼	164	▼
2.60	0.00	2.15	2.35	0	155	11.47 %	0.3595	▼	165	▼
1.88	0.00	1.80	1.90	0	127	11.19 %	0.3179	▼	166	▼

Instead of $140 for a $162 strike, you could get $260 for a $164 strike call— substantially more premium AND more than $200 of potential share appreciation [($161.27 to $164) ×100 shares] before your stock hits the strike price and gets called at expiration.

19.6 Time Value Inequality

But before you let that tempting premium entice you into only selling farther-dated calls, take a closer look at the $162 strike for 98 days out. It's got a bid-ask of $3.70–$3.90, so you'll probably get $3.80 for it. Compare that to the roughly one month return of $1.40.

There's an inequality! This 3-month call does *not* trade for 3 times the value of $1.40 ($4.20), it trades for about 10% less than that. And if you went farther out, that time value inequality would be even starker.

As an exercise to reinforce this time-value inequality, pick any stock with LEAPS (2 year call expiration dates). Then figure out the premium **per day** you get on the one month call versus the premium per day on the 2 year call...I'd bet dollars to donuts it's less dollars per day. Just remember, the premium received *per day* is always less for further-dated options contracts.

> **Time value inequality is the phenomenon that options with an expiration date farther in the future are worth less premium *per day* than shorter-dated options.**

Now that you understand all that, time to move on to more things to think about when selecting a strike.

CHAPTER **20**

Overwriting and Returns Part Deux

E are aiming to make 0.5% per month from premiums.[1]

That said, some months we might have to wait for the price of our index to come back to cost basis before selling a call. And if you have more funds to sell calls against and don't need to generate income immediately, you may want to sell a further OTM call at a higher strike price in order to prevent capping your upside.

Although I just stated a specific % return, that's a general guideline for all portfolio overwriting. The good news is, FIRE adherents

---

[1] I really wanted to get to the point on that one, no sense burying the lead.

Of note, we are *aiming* for 0.5% per month. But if we are overwriting responsibly, which includes waiting for underlying prices to recover so we only sell above cost basis, I personally have found it is more along the lines of 0.1–0.25% over longer-term periods. Compounding is still compounding.

have relatively fixed costs of living, and a fixed SWR.[2] Mustachians aren't playing the same game as quantitative traders, hedge funds, and investment managers looking to maximize alpha[3] and make quarterly returns. We never were, and that's a distinct advantage. If you only want to cover your 4% SWR, it would make sense to aim for an even lower return of 0.33% per month.

Even though 0.5% a month isn't a massive ROI, I'm going to assume anyone reading this knows the power of compounding earnings over time. To reinforce— consider the following thought experiment.

20.1   How to Beat the Market Long-Term:

- Buy 100 shares of SPY.

- Sell the furthest OTM call you can get paid a premium for. Call prices bottom out around 5 cents a share, or $5 total. For example, some time ago when SPY was at $420 a share, there was a 36-day $460-strike call that paid 3 cents a share, or $3.

- As long as your index doesn't hulk out and jump 9.5% in the next 5 weeks (might happen, not likely) take your $3 and invest it in a fractional SPY share

- You will have beaten the market in perpetuity by $3 plus appreciation. Congrats.

---

[2]SWR is a common acronym for "Safe Withdrawal Rate" in the FIRE community. It is the theoretical amount (expressed as a percentage) that you could withdraw from a total market index portfolio yearly without ever completely exhausting your funds. SWR is based on historical market data. https://firecalc.com/ is a fantastic user-friendly tool available online for free if you'd like to "backtest" your own SWRs.

[3]Alpha is the fancy term for "excess returns". Said conversationally, your alpha is how much (what %) more you make than the total stock market each year, and "seeking alpha" implies trying to beat the market. It's very hard to do, which is why FIRE investors (wisely) stick to total market index funds.

Actionable? Maybe not. Illustrative? Yep.

> **Making premiums from shares can be used to increase returns via reinvestment in the underlying, or in uncorrelated assets (different securities, real estate, food trucks, etc)**

I didn't even posit what would happen if you waited to invest the $3 on a dip,[4] or invested it in something with even better returns. But they are thought experiments I encourage you to indulge in.

20.2 Covered Calls Don't Always Win— and the Algorithmic Covered Call Funds "Prove" It (But Only for Algorithmic Funds)

Many people, even if they are beyond the "options are risky"' phase, will cite that selling covered calls doesn't outperform buy and hold. Firstly, they are probably looking at the CBOE (Chicago Board Options Exchange) buy write index (or the tradeable version of that index, BXM), which follows a "dumb"[5] algorithm.

Over certain time-series, the buy-write index does underperform the S&P, and that's no surprise. The strategy the fund applies is to sell the one month call that is slightly out of the money (the next strike up) and wait to get assigned, or sell another call if it expires OTM. I couldn't imagine a more simplistic buy-write algorithm.[6] Here's some areas in the strategy that could likely be improved:

---

[4]Timing the market is hard, and usually not worth your time.

[5]I say dumb not as a value judgement, but as a commentary on the simplicity of the index and its associated trading strategy.

[6]Despite this, the BXM index was awarded the "Most Innovative Benchmark Index Award" at the 2004 Super Bowl of Indexing Conference. Pretty amazing,

- When the S&P tanks, it doesn't wait for recovery, it sells calls at depressed prices (a portfolio overwriter would ***never*** sell calls at a strike price below cost basis- it's a great way to lose money).

- It sells calls against all of its holdings (someone portfolio overwriting for FIRE would never cap the entire upside potential of a something they had an ironclad bullish bias on, specifically the S&P/overall US market).

- It only sells calls slightly above at-the-money, rather than titrating to market sentiment, upside risk tolerance and desired returns (A portfolio overwriter would choose strikes and returns that match their risk tolerance and temperament[7], and likely ladder[8] their calls across different expiry dates and strikes).

Really want to find out if portfolio overwriting beats buy and hold? Spoiler— a question that is so general is generally impossible to answer. Say that I wanted to improve the CBOE buy-write index strategy. I'd try a few things. Firstly, I'd probably sell multiple calls at different strike prices and different expirations.[9]

There is a really important point to be made here about backtesting[10] with regards to this line of reasoning. Given enough time, mental effort and computing power to build a set of trading rules, you could design a system that is theoretically able to beat the market for

---

especially when you consider that if you invest in the BXM, you're also paying a 0.49% expense ratio, which makes it underperform the index it is meant to replicate quite noticeably. This seems odd to me, because although my coding skills are nonexistent, my guess is that it is probably algorithmic trading 101, and handled in a few lines of Python. I'm sure it's more complicated than that, but I can't help but wonder if there is some scaling inefficiency present.

[7]I discuss this in-depth in a later chapter.

[8]I also cover this in a later chapter.

[9]This is called "laddering" and is covered in a later chapter.

[10]Backtesting is using data analysis to derive trading strategies that would have worked given the information you have about the past price behavior of a security.

all the price history you have available, layering on rules and exceptions for every anomaly in your given price history. And unfortunately your perfectly-tuned system could be invalidated today, tomorrow, 3 months from now, whenever— because history doesn't repeat itself.

So more appropriate questions than "Does selling covered calls beat buy and hold investing?" would be "Can selling covered calls beat buy and hold investing with some strategies in some timelines? And will it lose in others?"— the answers to which would be "Yes" and "Yes."

20.3 A Word on Other Actively Managed and Algorithmic Derivatives Funds

I would like to point out that there are other covered call funds available to the retail investor. Although some follow a similar strategy to BXM for different indexes, there are some that employ a more active use of derivatives via a proprietary strategy to produce income. Notable examples would be QYLD, XYLD, and RYLD[11] on the simple covered call side, JEPI on the more opaque ETN derivatives end.

For the FIRE investor looking to generate income without the hassle of actually selling the calls themselves[12], these could be viable considerations in a portfolio given their high dividend outputs, and all of them pay dividends monthly. I make no specific endorsements of any investment or strategy, but would encourage the reader to ru-

---

[11]QYLD follows Nasdaq 100, XYLD the S&P 500, RYLD the Russel 2000

[12]I would encourage you to consider returns of the funds minus fees vs what you could accomplish by overwriting yourself. I don't endorse them or give investment advice.

More importantly, consider the repercussions of selling ATM calls against all your shares, and how it would hinder price recovery over time after a share price decline. This is covered more explicitly in a later chapter. People buying covered call funds that use algorithmic trading are exposed to this risk, Mustachians doing their own portfolio overwriting are not. They are not the same 'ting.

minate on the effect of utilizing those dividends for reinvestment into an uncorrelated asset, such as a more traditional FIRE-style index with higher expected growth, monthly bills, or some entrepreneurial venture.

20.4   You Don't Have to Be Perfect

Good news is you don't have be jealous that you aren't a quant at a hedge fund.[13] You don't have to toil endlessly to beat the market with novel strategies, or convince your investors it is still a good choice to keep their money invested with you when you have a bad year.

Take comfort in knowing you can develop an understanding of options and some heuristics that will enable you to sell calls and make some extra money. No matter what, the fact remains that when you sell a call, cash is deposited into your account that you wouldn't have had otherwise, and that's something worth pursuing in my book.[14]

The real goal is FIRE, and we have time on our side, which can let us adjust our trading to suit our needs. So we should leverage that advantage. When it comes to compound returns, "anything helps"

---

[13]Unfortunately, I very much am. Not for the salary reasons but because thinking about this is very fun for me.

[14]Pun intentional.

CHAPTER 21

Strike Price Selection Part Two

sing the same math from the last article that we used for returns, we can reinterpret the premium earned on our call as downside protection and breakeven.

Downside protection is straightforward— it's the amount that a stock can decline where the call premium you received will still cover your losses. Surprise! It's the same number as your % return on investment. In our previous example, taken from this VTI chain.

| VTI | | Q | VANGUARD TOTAL STOCK MARKET ETF $161.27 ⬇ -0.06 (-0.04%) | | AS OF 12 36 00PM ET 12/13/2019 ↻ More Quote Information | | | | | | | | | | |

Last	Change	Bid	Ask	Volume	Open Int	Imp Vol	Delta	Action	Strike ▲	Action	Last	Change	Bid	Ask	Volume	Open Int	Imp Vol	Delta
—				CALLS					Jan 17 '20 (35 days)							PUTS		
5.45	0.00	4.90	5.20	0	9	13.44 %	0.7626	▾	157	▾	1.28	0.00	1.15	1.30	0	9	13.71 %	-0.2845
4.85	0.00	4.10	4.30	0	10	12.86 %	0.7137	▾	158	▾	1.59	-0.01	1.35	1.50	3	30	13.02 %	-0.33
3.70	+0.50	3.30	3.50	2	21	11.89 %	0.6557	▾	159	▾	1.90	0.00	1.55	1.75	0	59	12.24 %	-0.3826
2.20	-0.71	2.55	2.75	3	54	11.12 %	0.5865	▾	160	▾	2.35	0.00	1.80	2.00	0	7	11.34 %	-0.4444
1.97	-0.43	1.90	2.16	1	33	10.51 %	0.5058	▾	161	▾	2.65	0.00	2.15	2.35	0	3	10.61 %	-0.5182
1.47	-0.33	1.35	1.50	8	13	9.86 %	0.418	▾	162	▾	4.03	0.00	2.55	2.80	0	22	9.86 %	-0.6027
1.10	0.00	0.85	1.00	0	37	9.10 %	0.3239	▾	163	▾	3.30	0.00	3.10	3.40	0	1	9.41 %	-0.6902
0.71	0.00	0.50	0.65	0	2	8.60 %	0.2357	▾	164	▾	4.60	0.00	3.70	4.00	0	1	8.49 %	-0.7912
0.50	0.00	0.30	0.45	0	14	8.55 %	0.1694	▾	165	▾	0.00	0.00	4.50	4.90	0	0	8.51 %	-0.8544
0.35	0.00	0.15	0.30	0	16	8.40 %	0.1139	▾	166	▾	0.00	0.00	5.30	6.80	0	0	12.72 %	-0.7983

Zoomed in on the $162 strike:

| VTI | | Q | VANGUARD TOTAL STOCK MARKET ETF $161.27 ⬇ -0.06 (-0.04%) | | AS OF 12 36 00PM ET 12/13. More Quote Information | | | |

Last	Change	Bid	Ask	Volume	Open Int	Imp Vol	Delta	Action	Strike ▲	Acti
—				CALLS					Jan 17 '20 (35 days)	
5.45	0.00	4.90	5.20	0	9	13.44 %	0.7626	▾	157	▾
4.65	0.00	4.10	4.30	0	10	12.66 %	0.7137	▾	158	▾
3.70	+0.50	3.30	3.50	2	21	11.89 %	0.6557	▾	159	▾
2.20	-0.71	2.55	2.75	3	54	11.12 %	0.5865	▾	160	▾
1.97	-0.43	1.90	2.10	1	33	10.51 %	0.5058	▾	161	▾
1.47	-0.3	1.35	1.50	8	13	9.86 %	0.418	▾	162	▾
1.10	0.00	0.85	1.00	0	37	9.10 %	0.3239	▾	163	▾
0.71	0.00	0.50	0.65	0	2	8.60 %	0.2357	▾	164	▾
0.50	0.00	0.30	0.45	0	14	8.55 %	0.1694	▾	165	▾
0.35	0.00	0.15	0.30	0	16	8.40 %	0.1139	▾	166	▾

If you sold the $162 strike call for $140 ($1.40 a share), you would be expecting to make 0.868% return $[(\$140 \div \$16,127) \times 100\%]$.

21.1 How Downside Protection Works

That $140 premium in a way protects you against a downward move. Because you are immediately paid the option premium into your account, you make $140. So, if the value of the shares decreases by $140, you've broken even— the premium provided 0.868% of "downside protection" and moves your "breakeven" price for the stock down to $159.87.

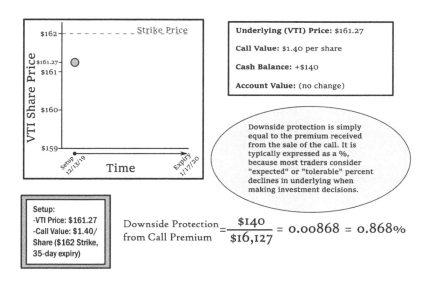

$$\text{Downside Protection from Call Premium} = \frac{\$140}{\$16,127} = 0.00868 = 0.868\%$$

Basically, if you sold a call for $1.40 and the price of VTI moved down to $159.87 by expiration, your total account value would be the same as if you had just sold the stock for $161.27.

Consider this fabricated example using the same setup as above, and the stock immediately falls by the exact amount of your call premium, right after you set up the trade:

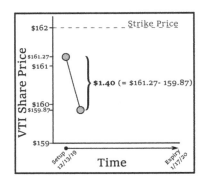

Underlying (VTI) Price: $159.87

Call Value: "<$1.40 per share"

Cash Balance: +$140

Account Value: (plus "whatever amount the call decreased by" minus the underlying drop of $1.40 per share")

Setup:
-VTI Price: $161.27
-Call Value: $1.40/ Share ($162 Strike, 35-day expiry)

Time Point 2:
-VTI Price: $159.87
-Call Value: "Less than $1.40 per share"

For illustrative purposes, the underlying price per share fell by the exact same amount as the call premium you received ($1.40 per share) in this example. What a masterfully contrived coincidence!

To keep things simple, we will simply say the call you initially sold for $1.40 is worth "less than $1.40" at this second time point where the underlying price falls early in the contract period (it involves estimation that we will use for future examples, but would complicate things too much at this point). We can however easily & definitively state that the call is worthless at expiration if the share price stays at $159.87, as shown below:

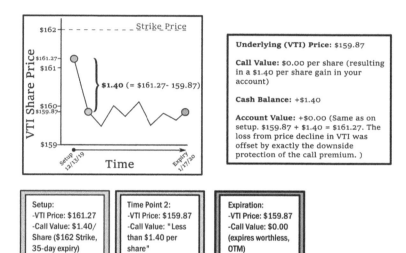

Underlying (VTI) Price: $159.87

Call Value: $0.00 per share (resulting in a $1.40 per share gain in your account)

Cash Balance: +$1.40

Account Value: +$0.00 (Same as on setup. $159.87 + $1.40 = $161.27. The loss from price decline in VTI was offset by exactly the downside protection of the call premium.)

Setup:
-VTI Price: $161.27
-Call Value: $1.40/ Share ($162 Strike, 35-day expiry)

Time Point 2:
-VTI Price: $159.87
-Call Value: "Less than $1.40 per share"

Expiration:
-VTI Price: $159.87
-Call Value: $0.00 (expires worthless, OTM)

Displayed differently, here is the accounting on setup and expiration:

SETUP		EXPIRATION	
STOCK PRICE:	$161.27	STOCK PRICE:	$159.87
CALL PRICE:	$1.40	CALL PRICE:	$0.00
CASH IN ACCOUNT:	$1.40	CASH IN ACCOUNT:	$1.40
TOTAL: $161.27		TOTAL: $161.27	

You'll notice that at the setup above on the left the $1.40 per share short call initially cancels out the call premium you received. The moment you sell the covered call, you do get money into your account, but the overall balance is still the same.

On the right after the short call value has dwindled to zero, you are still up $1.40 per share from the call premium, but here I had the stock decline by that exact same amount ($1.40 per share) to illustrate how the call premium compensated for it.

It's really just another way of categorizing profits in your head, but in a way that is useful if you anticipate a downward move in your underlying security.

21.2 Deep ITM Strikes Mean Deep Downside Protection

Those of you with wandering eyes and curious minds may have noticed that the call premiums increase even more the deeper into the money (ITM) you go. It's true! The $157 strike call has a bid–ask of $4.90–$5.20— you might be able to get a limit order filled for $5. In that case you would have 3.1% downside protection ($5 ÷ $161.27)

					VANGUARD TOTAL STOCK		AS OF 12 36 00PM ET 12/13		
	VTI	Q			MARKET ETF		More Quote Information		
					$161.27 ↓ -0.06 (-0.04%)				

Last	Change	Bid	Ask	Volume	Open Int	Imp Vol	Delta	Action	Strike ▲	Acti
--					CALLS				Jan 17 '20 (35 days)	
5.45	0.60	4.90	5.20	0	9	13 44 %	0.7626	▾	157	▾
4.65	0.00	4.10	4.30	0	10	12 66 %	0.7137	▾	158	▾
3.70	+0.50	3.30	3.50	2	21	11 89 %	0.6557	▾	159	▾
2.20	-0.71	2.55	2.75	3	54	11 12 %	0.5865	▾	160	▾
1.97	-0.43	1.90	2.10	1	33	10 51 %	0.5058	▾	161	▾
1.47	-0.33	1.35	1.50	8	13	9 86 %	0.418	▾	162	▾
1.10	0.00	0.85	1.00	0	37	9 10 %	0.3239	▾	163	▾
0.71	0.00	0.50	0.65	0	2	8 60 %	0.2357	▾	164	▾
0.50	0.00	0.30	0.45	0	14	8 55 %	0.1694	▾	165	▾
0.35	0.00	0.15	0.30	0	16	8 40 %	0.1139	▾	166	▾

Unfortunately, a $5 premium for a $157 strike call with the underlying trading at $161.27 only has $0.73 per share extrinsic value, and no chance of appreciation to the strike (the underlying has already appreciated past the strike).[1]

---

[1] If you prefer more downside protection and smaller premiums, this may suit you, but portfolio overwriting is traditionally selling OTM calls.

But what about this chain that shows all the strike prices for WMT (Walmart)? There are some waaaay deep-ITM calls available to trade on the chain shown below.

Last	Change	Bid	Ask	Volume	Open Int	Imp Vol	Delta	Action	Strike ▲	Action	Last	Change	Bid	Ask	Volume	Open Int	Imp Vol	Delta
—			CALLS						Jan 17 '20 (34 days)					PUTS				
73.20	0.00	73.75	77.20	0	6	114.91 %	0.9986	▼	45	▼	0.02	0.00	0.00	0.01	0	7,351	101.55 %	-0.0006
71.30	0.00	71.55	73.85	0	0	—	0.9724	▼	47.5	▼	0.01	0.00	0.00	0.03	0	2,479	105.58 %	-0.0013
67.98	0.00	69.80	71.35	0	11	—	0.971	▼	50	▼	0.01	0.00	0.00	0.04	0	844	102.80 %	-0.0018
63.00	0.00	63.20	67.50	0	16	—	0.9471	▼	55	▼	0.01	0.00	0.00	0.04	0	1,475	92.24 %	-0.002
58.80	0.00	58.40	62.50	0	35	—	0.9412	▼	60	▼	0.02	0.00	0.00	0.04	0	1,198	82.59 %	-0.0022
53.75	0.00	53.20	57.55	0	12	—	0.9343	▼	65	▼	0.01	0.00	0.00	0.04	0	1,710	73.70 %	-0.0024
50.01	0.00	49.10	51.70	0	29	—	0.9464	▼	70	▼	0.01	0.00	0.00	0.04	0	5,449	65.44 %	-0.0027
45.35	0.00	44.25	46.30	0	76	—	0.9538	▼	75	▼	0.01	0.00	0.00	0.04	0	4,655	57.72 %	-0.0031
40.56	0.00	40.90	44.80	0	7	—	0.9207	▼	77.5	▼	0.01	0.00	0.00	0.04	0	1,134	54.04 %	-0.0033
40.40	0.00	39.55	41.20	0	120	—	0.9521	▼	80	▼	0.01	0.00	0.00	0.01	0	7,496	44.28 %	-0.0011
37.60	0.00	37.20	38.70	0	37	—	0.9494	▼	82.5	▼	0.01	0.00	0.00	0.01	0	2,104	41.17 %	-0.0012
35.60	0.00	35.00	35.85	0	247	—	0.9665	▼	85	▼	0.01	0.00	0.00	0.01	0	5,309	38.15 %	-0.0013
32.53	0.00	32.20	33.70	0	65	—	0.9438	▼	87.5	▼	0.02	0.00	0.00	0.03	0	2,659	39.07 %	-0.0035
28.90	0.00	28.25	32.45	0	360	—	0.8892	▼	90	▼	0.02	0.00	0.00	0.01	0	3,455	32.32 %	-0.0015
25.55	0.00	26.50	30.00	0	90	47.15 %	0.9702	▼	92.5	▼	0.03	0.00	0.00	0.03	0	3,393	32.84 %	-0.0041
25.01	0.00	24.80	26.15	0	346	—	0.9335	▼	95	▼	0.02	0.00	0.00	0.02	0	5,104	28.59 %	-0.0032
22.90	0.00	21.70	23.85	0	240	—	0.9149	▼	97.5	▼	0.04	0.00	0.00	0.03	0	2,455	26.87 %	-0.0049
20.50	0.00	19.75	20.90	0	701	—	0.944	▼	100	▼	0.02	0.00	0.01	0.05	0	6,235	26.08 %	-0.0094
15.04	0.00	15.25	15.90	0	526	19.57 %	0.9896	▼	105	▼	0.06	0.00	0.04	0.07	0	19,736	21.75 %	-0.0199
10.98	0.00	10.35	10.95	0	4,163	16.76 %	0.9632	▼	110	▼	0.14	0.00	0.14	0.15	0	8,694	15.30 %	-0.051
6.14	0.00	5.80	6.10	0	5,192	14.34 %	0.8607	▼	115	▼	0.47	0.00	0.46	0.50	0	8,557	15.48 %	-0.1576
2.27	0.00	2.23	2.34	0	15,152	13.34 %	0.5556	▼	120	▼	1.67	0.00	1.68	1.77	0	3,078	13.46 %	-0.4501
0.44	0.00	0.41	0.45	0	14,943	12.26 %	0.1789	▼	125	▼	4.80	0.00	4.65	5.20	0	574	12.36 %	-0.8403
0.05	0.00	0.05	0.06	0	23,203	12.82 %	0.0311	▼	130	▼	11.38	0.00	8.10	11.60	0	58	20.67 %	-0.8846
0.03	0.00	0.02	0.03	0	3,976	16.14 %	0.0127	▼	135	▼	15.01	0.00	12.60	18.80	0	0	21.28 %	-0.9718

Looking closer:

Figure 21.1: *The $45 call has a bid–ask of $73.75–$77.20*

To illustrate, let's assume you could get the midpoint price (hard to do for deep ITM call) of the bid/ask spread and sell a call for $75.47 per share. You'd immediately get $7,547 ($75.47 × 100 shares) deposited into your account, as shown.

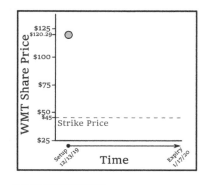

Underlying (WMT) Price: $120.29

Call Value: $75.47 per share

Cash Balance: +$7,547

Account Value: (No Change)

Setup:
-WMT Price: $120.29
-Call Value: $75.47/
Share ($45 Strike,
35-day expiry)

Then, let's say Walmart tanked for some reason to $45 a share... what would that mean for you? You wouldn't lose anything, because of the huge influx of cash you received in the form of your sold call's premium. In fact you'd feel pretty smart for
selling that call right before the drop. You effectively hedged your position with the sold call. Again, because sold calls have a
negative delta (mentioned earlier) it made money while your shares (owned shares always have a delta of +1) lost money.

So if WMT tanked and stayed at $45 for the next 35 days all the way up until expiration, you would have lost $7,529 ($120.29 per share −$45 per share) in underlying value. BUT you would have made $7,547 as the call you sold became worthless, for a grand total gain of $18.

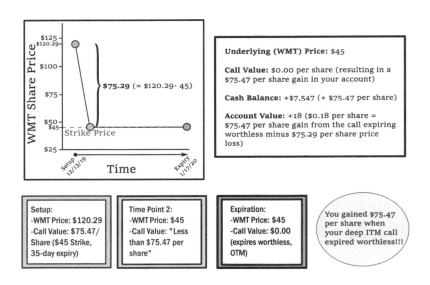

In this example, I skipped the middle step and just showed the full trade with setup, price drop, and expiration laid out to get you used to reading the time series graphs. I also replaced the standard "bouncing" up and down random stock price graph with a straight line, because that's all that is necessary to grasp the concept of what happens at expiry.[2]

---

[2]It's also much easier to illustrate with my limited graphic design skills.

SETUP	**EXPIRATION**
STOCK PRICE: **$120.29**	STOCK PRICE: **$45** ($75.29/SHARE LOSS)
CALL PRICE: **$75.47** (SHORT)	CALL PRICE: **$0.00** ($75.47/SHARE GAIN)
CASH IN ACCOUNT: **$75.47** (LONG)	CASH IN ACCOUNT: **$75.47**
TOTAL: $120.29	**TOTAL: $120.47**

Notice how your account total is roughly the same? Since we optimistically assumed you got the midpoint of the bid–ask, you actually made $18 overall on what would have otherwise been a $7,527 loss.[3]

Compare that to the guy who bought 100 shares of WMT and didn't sell a deep ITM call.

---

[3] For a fun thought experiment, imagine you set aside the $7,547 and then used it to buy shares of WMT when the price dipped at the new, discount price of $45 per share. And then imagine the price went back up to $120.29 eventually.

21.3   Why Not Just Sell Deep ITM Calls all the Dang Time?

Deeper ITM calls provide much greater downside protection, but unfortunately they don't provide much premium via extrinsic value. Sometimes they even trade at less than intrinsic value[4] if they aren't traded often enough to keep up with stock's price movements,[5] or if you pick a strike price way in the future which includes a discount for all the dividends expected to be paid from now until then.

Another point to be taken is that although you are making a huge premium, it's not a free taco from Rudy's Taco Stand[6]— you are almost definitely going to have to sell those shares unless the underlying stock experiences a precipitous drop. One useful way to think of deep in the money calls is "trading" your stock value for cash call value, or making the stock value a more liquid asset, because in theory you could use those call premiums to make other trades while still technically holding the shares. This is a more complicated form of leverage beyond this portfolio overwriting book.

Unfortunately, you can rarely make any money off the premium for deep ITM calls because the extrinsic value is so low, and the bid/ask is often very wide.[7]

---

[4]I've also seen this referred to as trading below "parity", when the market value of the option is less than intrinsic value.

[5]This would be referred to as a very "illiquid" option.

[6]https://www.youtube.com/c/AlphaInvestments69

[7]The call we used for our example was so deep in ITM that it was trading **below parity**, aka **below intrinsic value** (this shouldn't happen in theory). This is most likely because the trading volume hasn't kept the call value up to date with the current price and a discount for future expected dividends. Because of the small open interest, WMT has probably moved more frequently than this call trades, so $45 plus the premium of $73.75 =$118.75, which is actually **less** than the current stock value of $120.29 (you'd be losing money if you sold that call, because you'd be better off just selling the stock).

CHAPTER 22

The Ultra Hedger and the LEAPer

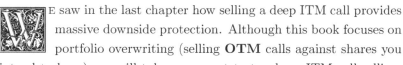E saw in the last chapter how selling a deep ITM call provides massive downside protection. Although this book focuses on portfolio overwriting (selling **OTM** calls against shares you intend to keep), we will take a moment to touch on ITM call selling, LEAPs, and the combination of the two.

You may have remembered the fallacious argument that selling OTM covered calls makes sense if you are "going to spend the money anyway." It doesn't hold up in all situations, especially ones where the underlying drops and you still need to pay someone.[1]

In the case of ITM calls, it does make a bit more sense because it mitigates a bit more downside risk. If you had 100 shares of SPY

---

[1] Holding underlying shares for any period of time has inherent downside risk, but index investors fully accept this risk as a given.

(and if its price was $420 a share) and you needed $2,000 right now, you could (based on prices at the time I wrote this) sell the 28-day, $400 strike call for $21.43 a share, giving you $2,143. Not only would you have your $2,000, you'd have an extra $143, and if the price of SPY fell to $398.57 in a month your account would have effectively "broke even" because of the downside protection.[2] Note this strategy still exposes you to upside risk, and caps your profits.

But let's think more critically for a moment— if you really needed $2,000 today, what price would S&P have to rise to in order to make selling shares outright and holding remaining shares superior to selling a call? The ITM call would net you an extra $1.43 in premium, but the true answer is *more* than $1.43 per share appreciation to $421.43.

Why? Because we sold 5 shares to cover our $2,000 need, so we have fewer shares left to appreciate. Specifically, selling 4.76 shares[3] leaves us with 95.24. So to make selling shares outright superior to selling a call, S&P would actually have to go up $1.49 per share. This is because 95.24 shares would have to rise $1.49 to get you the same appreciation that 100 shares rising $1.43 would.[4]

---

[2]For review, downside breakeven is underlying price minus premium received from the call. Here it would be $420 - $21.43 = $398.57

[3]$2,000 expense divided by $420 per share = 4.76 shares

[4]We still haven't considered benefits of reinvesting the extra $143 of extrinsic value in our example into shares of our index.

22.1 Selling More Shares Requires More of an Upward Move to Reach the True "Upside Breakeven" vs Selling ITM calls

The point is, the more you intend to withdraw immediately, the more the remaining shares would have to rise to make the additional premium you receive selling a call. A clever reader might note that by my logic, selling deep ITM calls would seem to make sense. If we had a $20,000 expense and sold half of our shares, the remaining shares would have to rise twice as much, $2.86 to make the $1.43 return, right?

In reality that is not the case. Fortunately, for indexes at least,[5] we will see the dilemma somewhat solves itself as you go deeper in the money and the extrinsic value dwindles, but you still leave yourself open to the possibility of profit on a downturn in the index.

But those big downward moves aren't common, and frankly they are impossible to predict[6], which is why most people don't sell ITM calls. In the case of indexes specifically, maybe an overall bearish market environment would make ITM call selling a more reasonable move. But at the end of the day it isn't very popular because it involves so much market timing.

---

[5]Sometimes deep ITM calls on higher volatility stocks do have a decent amount of extrinsic value in the premium, especially if they are LEAPS. For example, as I type this, a certain very popular, very volatile electric car maker sits at $677.35 per share. The two-year LEAP call for $550 is trading for $262 per share, which represents $134.65 extrinsic value— a full 19.87% of the underlying security's value. 20% return for 2 years isn't bad...

[6]Don't believe anyone who tells you that they can predict market moves, and then proceeds to sell you the secret.

22.2   ITM Calls Can Trade Below Intrinsic Value

Let's explore the $20,000 immediate expense more. If you examine an option chain for your favorite index, you will notice deep ITM calls offer little time value, and lack liquidity to the point that they will sometimes trade below parity. That is to say have a negative extrinsic value, or an intrinsic value below what the current price of the stock would imply. When I wrote this, the S&P price was at $420, and the one-month $220 call was going for $199.30, which is less than the expected intrinsic value of $200— you'd lose money[7] selling that call vs just selling your shares!

But that's just the one-month call. What if you piled on some time value by selling a LEAP? Bad news— it was even worse! The bid for the 1-year $220 call was $198.93!!! Even less than the one-month ITM call. How can that be??!??? Unfortunately, the deep ITM calls aren't as liquid, they include discounts for expected dividends, and people just aren't willing to offer much for them.

So why even show you this? There are two main reasons— first being, things don't always work the way they are "supposed to" in markets. There should be more time value for those longer dated calls, but going deep in the money destroys extrinsic value.

---

[7]Specifically $0.70 per share, or $70

22.3 The Impossible to Predict Case of Where Selling Deep ITM Calls Makes You Feel Like a Genius

Secondly, there actually is a time when these ITM calls would be a killer move. Selling a $220 call for $20,000 would be great if SPY dipped to $220 or less, you were able to buy-to-close (this is the first position management strategy we cover) your call for next to nothing or just let it expire, and SPY eventually went back up to $420. In that case, at the end of the day, you'd have the same amount of stock and an extra $20,000.

The problem is, you don't know the future. Some investors do have the belief that their overall view of the market[8] affords them a singular clairvoyance. I am not one of them.

But some investors also know they don't know the future, and are ok with the fact that if they sell a call S&P just might dip and allow them a smooth exit and some big downside protection and profits. This thinking would be something along the lines "I'd rather sell a call in the hopes SPY dips in the next year and have the chance of making some profitable moves than just sell my shares and have no chance of cashing in on downside protection."

The astute reader will note again that the "chance" of a dip and buy-to-close comes at a price— namely capping profits on the rest of your lot of shares you didn't cash out. As such, I wouldn't advocate this style of trading for most. But I want you to be aware that for every possible future price movement, there's an option strategy that would allow you to outperform buy and hold.[9] The problem is, we

---

[8]Or skills at charting, or technical analysis, or latest Tarot reading.

[9]This is way beyond the scope of this book, but I have to mention that employing different option strategies can, in a way, hedge bets across possible futures and

don't know the future. But I hope this sidebar chapter expanded your mind a bit.

22.4   One Final Note on when to Sell Deep ITM Calls

The only other reason it might make sense to sell a deep ITM call against an index would be to generate cash. If you needed \$ now for an investment (stock or otherwise) that you were absolutely positively sure would outperform your index shares between now and expiry.[10] If you reinvest in the markets, you're stock picking (risky), and if you invest in an alternative asset (real estate, widgets, small businesses), you're taking on a different kind of risk. I'll leave decisions of this kind up to the reader. Just remember— it's hard to beat the market.

---

allow for a lot more chances at profitability than simple buy-and-hold— its one of the major motivations for the multi-billion dollar industry surrounding derivatives that soaks up the best and brightest mathematical minds from our PhD programs.

[10]This is the whole idea behind investment, interest, and the time value of money. Borrow at X% then invest to get a return of Y%. Profit is $Y\% - X\% \times (investment)$

CHAPTER **23**

Strike Price Selection Part Three

Ast thing on strike price selection— Upside Breakeven/Best Case price. The concept here is a little hinky because we are selling calls, but the math is super easy.

Put simply, the upside breakeven is maximum underlying price **at expiration** that allows us to buy back our call using **only** the premium we received when we initially sold our call.

Starting with the easy stuff to keep your confidence up, the formula for upside breakeven when selling a covered call is as follows:

UPSIDE BREAKEVEN = (STRIKE PRICE) + (CALL PREMIUM RECEIVED)

*** **Important note** *** Don't get confused! This "Upside Breakeven" is not the same as the theoretical "max profit" for a cov-

ered call trade, which is potential appreciation plus the call premium
received. Nor is it downside breakeven. Upside breakeven is something
else entirely.

So what do we mean and what are we looking at with an "upside
breakeven," and why is it something we would want to think about?
With portfolio overwriting and selling covered calls in general, you
have two main sources of risk: underlying share price depreciation[1]
and upside risk, aka "lost profits."

23.1   Upside Risk/Lost Profits— Is Overwriting Worth It?

Upside risk, also referred to as "lost profits" or "opportunity loss", is
not being able to participate in share price appreciation. This other
source of risk is inherently different. It refers to all the gains you
don't get to cash in on because you sold someone else the right to call
your shares, and one of the goals with portfolio overwriting an index
is to keep lost profits to a minimum.[2] Ideally they will be outweighed
by the call premiums and, more importantly, the utility of the call
premiums that you generate.

---

[1] Underlying share price depreciation (downside risk) is just the risk of shares
decreasing in price, a risk that comes with owning anything. As an index investor,
you inherently accept this risk.

Interestingly, with selling covered calls downside risk is actually a bit less than
if you owned the shares outright. As we saw in previous chapters, the premium
from selling calls will provide a small hedge.

[2] Some months your underlying index will go past your strike price. It's in-
evitable if you do this long enough. The important thing is to not chase profits.
As long as you are content with your potential profit when you sell a call and able
to allow shares to be called, or patient enough to wait for the index to pull back,
or able to limit yourself to position management that does not "lock in" losses
or cause you to "pay into" positions, you will be fine. You may underperform
your index (upside risk) but you should not actively lose money to downside risk
in any magnitude greater than greater than your underlying index when portfolio
overwriting.

To this point, there are often opportunities to re-enter a lot of VTI shares following expiration at a lower or similar price, so unless VTI is moving steeply upwards you shouldn't drastically lag behind the total market.[3] Additionally, the whole goal of portfolio overwriting for FIRE investing is to generate some income on the FIRE journey, not to maximize profits. Because your expenses should be relatively fixed, there will come a time when small % returns from a portion of your portfolio outpaces them.

Would portfolio overwriting provide superior returns vs a simple VTI buy and hold? It matters who you ask, what data you look at, and your timing & trades. Will it provide similar returns, especially if you are only employing a portion of your portfolio in the strategy? Most likely— that's been my experience. Will the increase in quality of life (a few call premiums can make a huge impact on an otherwise frugal and Mustachian lifestyle) outweigh what would be a marginal loss of returns?

My experience is yes.

I fully realize that this "The rewards of overwriting, monetary and otherwise, outweigh lost profits" is an empirical claim, but I have personally found it to be true. Additionally, I strongly recommend laddering[4] and not overwriting all of your shares, so that you are always able to participate in some share appreciation.

23.2   Upside Breakeven in Action

Going back to the same example that we've been toying with for a bit (VTI is $161.27 a share, we bought 100 shares, and sold a $162 strike call for $1.40 a share):

---

[3] As they say, stocks take the stairs up and the elevator down.
[4] Covered in a later chapter.

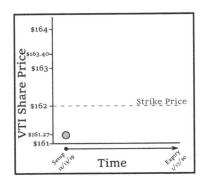

Setup:
-VTI Price: $161.27
-Call Value: $1.40/
Share ($162 Strike,
35-day expiry)

If we sell a $162 call for $1.40 per share, our upside breakeven is going to be $163.40.

Upside Breakeven = (Strike Price) + (Call Premium Received)

Upside Breakeven = ($162) + ($1.40) = $163.40

That means that if the stock goes to $163.40 at expiration, you will be able to buy back your call for what you bought it for and you get to keep your shares and their appreciation.

This is because on expiration day, only intrinsic call value remains. So with a stock at $162 on expiration day, a $162 call has zero intrinsic value. With a stock at $163 a $162 call has $1 intrinsic value. If the underlying is at $163.40, a $162 call has $1.40 per share intrinsic value.

If you decide to buy back your sold call, you are "buying into" the appreciation, paying to participate in appreciation. This appreciation was a loss since you sold the right to it, and as such it was a short call position in your account. When you are using exactly the call premium you initially received to buy back your short call, you are at the upside breakeven point.

Put another way, the call premium you received paid the cost for you to "buy into" the underlying appreciation, and you broke even.

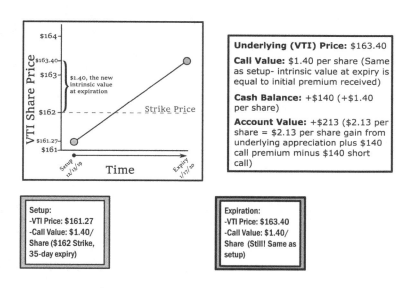

Underlying (VTI) Price: $163.40

Call Value: $1.40 per share (Same as setup- intrinsic value at expiry is equal to initial premium received)

Cash Balance: +$140 (+$1.40 per share)

Account Value: +$213 ($2.13 per share = $2.13 per share gain from underlying appreciation plus $140 call premium minus $140 short call)

Setup:
-VTI Price: $161.27
-Call Value: $1.40/
Share ($162 Strike,
35-day expiry)

Expiration:
-VTI Price: $163.40
-Call Value: $1.40/
Share (Still! Same as
setup)

Figure 23.1: *Here at the upside breakeven you can buy back your call at expiration using the call premium you received. Notice that since the call premium and appreciation above the strike are equivalent, the account value profit (+$213) is simply the share price at expiry ($163.40) minus cost basis ($161.27) of the underlying. Put another way, the sold call and appreciation past the strike price "cancel each other out" at expiration in this example.*

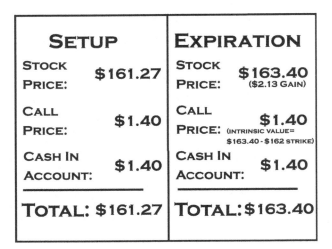

Figure 23.2: *Keep in mind the call price is short in this table, and as such it is subtracted from your stock price plus cash received from the call premium.*

To reiterate, upside breakeven is a bit more situation-specific because it relates the value of the premium received with relation to the cost to buy back your sold call. It is the point where our sold call is equivalent to the intrinsic value above the strike price at expiration. You can buy to close your short call here and still make the maximum profits via share appreciation.

Why do portfolio overwriters care about and consider upside breakeven specifically? It is the exact price point, at expiration, where they can retain share price appreciation and not incur any upside risk. It allows them the opportunity to break even with the buy & hold strategy without having to "pay into" the position.

23.3 Max Profits and the Profit and Loss (P&L) Graph

So let's discuss maximum profits a bit to close the loop. Whenever the underlying goes above the strike and the value of your sold call increases, standard accounting and your brokerage account will tell you that you hit max profits and are losing money on the sold call on any further upward move. Any amount that the underlying moves up, the short call will move up in tandem once that call is ITM.

Again, this is because you are missing out on profits[5] you could have made if you just owned the stock. When you sold your call, you effectively capped your profits. Visually you can see this with profit and loss graphs, which helped me conceptualize it a bit better. Here's a (not-to-scale) representation of this example. I drew the previous example ($161.27 share price, selling a $162 strike call with $1.40 premium) with a nice little dashed line running across the graph at the stock price to illustrate this.

---

[5] Upside Risk

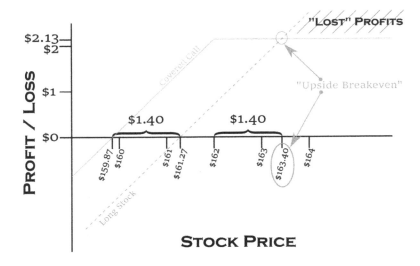

Figure 23.3: *This weird graph with the profit/loss on the Y axis, the stock price on the X axis, and lines representing long stock vs a covered call trade is a P & L graph. I really like them as a tool for learning but they are not necessary at this point for portfolio overwriting. They do aid in understanding of other options strategies, especially when combined, but I will not cover any of those in this book.*

Note that the standard P/L graph will show you what I call the "Upside Breakeven"— it is the intersection of the underlying price and the maximum profit.

23.4 Watching Our Underlying Index Rocket Past Our Short Strike

Imagine if VTI went way higher, to $170 or so. You would have made share appreciation from $161.27 to $162 = $73 ($0.73 per share x100 shares) and the $140 premium, which totals $213...but that's it. The rest of the appreciation (from $162 to $170) belongs to someone else— whoever bought the call contract from you. Your overall position would consist of a gain of $213, with the short call above $162 completely negating the share appreciation. You can see on the P/L graph for this covered call that no matter how far right you go on the X-axis (as the share price gets higher), your profits (the y axis) for the covered call never go above $2.13 per share.

Here's our more familiar breakdown of that scenario, with just the stock price and account balances:

SETUP		EXPIRATION	
STOCK PRICE:	$161.27	STOCK PRICE:	$170 ($8.73 GAIN)
CALL PRICE:	$1.40	CALL PRICE:	$8.00 ($6.60 "LOSS")
CASH IN ACCOUNT:	$1.40	CASH IN ACCOUNT:	$1.40
TOTAL: $161.27		TOTAL: $163.40 ($8.73 - $8 + $1.40 = STILL ONLY $2.13 PER SHARE TOTAL PROFIT)	

To reiterate for a 3rd time in this chapter, I have to say that in order to most effectively overwrite your portfolio by selling covered calls you should reframe your ideas surrounding the "loss" of appreciation if you are going to increase your chances of being successful.[6] Your account will show a loss on the short call in this situation, but your overall account value will be up from share appreciation and call premium.

Remember, your goal with the portion of shares you employ in portfolio overwriting is not maximum profits through appreciation. Rather, the goal is income generation using a portion of your long-term held shares and superior performance compared to buy-and-hold during months that are sideways, down, or have modest appreciation of underlying. We will talk more about the portfolio overwriting mindset we will need to use in later chapters. Although not technical, these insights on emotionally intelligent investing may be the most useful things I've put to paper.

BONUS EXAMPLE:

STOCK PRICE: $4.70

CALL PRICE FOR $5 STRIKE: $0.30

UPSIDE BREAKEVEN = $5.30

MAX PROFIT = $0.60

DOWNSIDE BREAKEVEN = $4.40

---

[6]You have to fully be aware of, understand, and accept upside risk from the outset when portfolio overwriting. It exists. If you incur it and in response attempt to "roll" your call or close your position irresponsibly, you will end up losing money. The ways this can happen and how to avoid it are covered explicitly in upcoming chapters and examples.

CHAPTER **24**

Theta Decay (Is Exponential)

E took a peek at theta earlier, and one of the things I teased getting into was how theta decay was not linear.

The graph on the next page shows extrinsic call value vs time. Remember intrinsic value is unaffected by time, but theta decay is always chipping away at extrinsic value. Also remember— if our call is OTM, it is comprised of entirely extrinsic value. Also, it is important to note that the option value decreasing faster represents theta decay increasing faster.

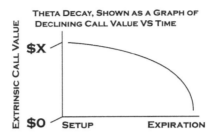

This is confusing for some, but remember that theta is the rate of decay of extrinsic value. One alternative way to illustrate the increase in theta decay would be theta as a % of call value remaining vs time, as below (FYI not to scale in any way):

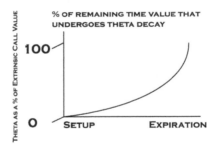

Practically, this means that as the expiration date of an option approaches, the time value of an option (in our case, the call we sold that is now short in our account) decreases faster and faster. Exponentially faster. This exponential decay kicks in when there are roughly two weeks or less to expiration.[1]

This dollar decrease in an option value is theta, typically expressed

---

[1]For example: If you sell a call with 30 days to expiry, over the first 15 days, about 50% of the original time value will erode. With only two days left until expiry, just one additional day may erode 50% (or more) of the remaining time value. The theta decay is a geometric process, not a linear one.

on a brokerage website for a sold call as a negative value. It corresponds to the dollar decrease in the option value as one day passes.

To see how theta decay is exponential you can track the theta of an option as expiration approaches. For example, one month to expiration, theta might be −0.50 (meaning option price decreases 50 cents each day that passes) for a stock. At two weeks from expiration theta might have increased to −0.75, then at 1 week from expiration to −0.90. All the while, the remaining time value gets smaller and smaller, so a larger portion of what remains is "eaten away" by this growing theta.

24.1   How Theta Helps Us

How is that going to be advantageous to us, as option sellers? If we sold a call, it is a short position in our account, ergo the value of the call decreasing is our profit! (We've seen this before in a previous chapter, so I'm just going use the same cartoony infographic here):

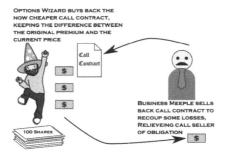

Being able to buy back a call for a cheaper price than the premium you received is how call sellers lock in profits before expiration (and is a preview of the upcoming chapters on position management). You can also let calls run until expiry, but in the case of overwriting we typically want to keep our shares.[2] Sidenote: given how low trading fees are now, I oftentimes won't let calls run until expiration. Instead, I buy back calls that have lost most of their value to theta decay before they expire, even if there is only a very small chance of a move in the underlying stock big enough to warrant assignment.

So if you know that the value of a call decreases faster as expiration approaches, and you want time on your side. . . what do you do with that information? How do you apply that to when to sell calls?

One school of thought advocates selling the shortest term call available so the time value chips away even faster! If you only sell calls with a month (or less) left before expiry, theta kicks in and makes you money in a big way when the decline becomes exponential the last 2 weeks of the contract. In fact, this is why most people who sell options for monthly income on individual stocks only sell monthly or (even better) weekly options. Although most whole market ETFs and index funds do not have weekly options, SPY does if you consider that security good enough for your index investing.[3]

24.2   When Theta Really Benefits Us

To apply this, looking at the graphs of theta decay vs time, as call sellers we want to be more towards the right of the graph, when extrinsic value decreases at a steeper rate and theta decay really kicks in. That steep decline in extrinsic value translates to losses quickly accumulating for the call holder and gains quickly accumulating for us.

---

[2]Especially in a taxable account because, as you may recall, assignment is a taxable event.

[3]This is also covered in a separate chapter. The only other potential problem with SPY is that it requires a lot of capital to buy 100 shares of.

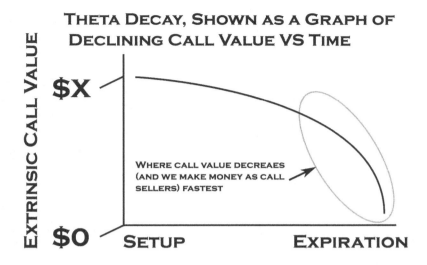

THETA DECAY, SHOWN AS A GRAPH OF DECLINING CALL VALUE VS TIME

EXTRINSIC CALL VALUE

$X

$0

WHERE CALL VALUE DECREAES
(AND WE MAKE MONEY AS CALL
SELLERS) FASTEST

SETUP

EXPIRATION

Personally, I have found that I prefer a lower–stress trading situation, so I employ another fact about theta that benefits me, at the potential loss of some profits. Namely, for farther OTM options, although premium, extrinsic value, and theta are initially smaller than ATM options, theta increases faster as expiration approaches. This is because a farther OTM option has less and less chance of expiring ITM with each day that passes, if it remains OTM.

24.3   But Not Every Options Wizard Sells The Shortest-Dated Calls

Combined with the fact that the further out you go with the expiration date, the higher the premium, I lean towards selling a 1.5–2 month OTM option at a slightly higher (more OTM) strike, if possible. It gives a better sense of control because the underlying has to climb a lot more before you risk it ending up ITM and having to adjust your position. Also, it gives you more room for added profits from share appreciation.[4]

Although I mentioned portfolio overwriters typically don't like to sell shares, I personally don't mind having shares called occasionally. I can just buy another lot and sell another call... but that's just a personally useful mental framework I apply to my shares set aside for portfolio overwriting, and may not apply to those trading in retail accounts with larger tax burdens.

For now let's preface diving deeper into what happens to shares and sold calls in the next chapter about underlying price moves and their effect on options.

24.4   Balancing Gamma Risk vs Theta Decay

A more astute reader may realize that although we experience an exponential increase in risk from gamma, we as call sellers also experience an exponential benefit from theta decay as expiration approaches.

---

[4]This is just my opinion, not trading advice or an endorsement of a specific expiry. 1–2 month call selling suits my temperament, but theoretically selling weekly or daily calls garners the most value from theta decay (offset by the most gamma risk). It's all a balancing act, and I describe different types of investors and what flavor of portfolio overwriting would likely fit them best in a later chapter.

Further, I am reticent to suggest any specific trading guidelines, for fear that someone without an appreciation for (or with an aversion to) nuance and a desire for simplicity will take this book as specific trading advice (it's not), lose money, and then come at me. I can describe every facet of how covered call selling works, but any application beyond that is up to the reader. There are lots of "systems" out there, which I encourage you to seek out if you feel a more rigorous strategy would benefit you. No matter what, I would encourage any new option trader to paper trade first. And don't buy any "secrets." There is no magic system that maximizes profits every time.

This concept can be shown with the following picture:

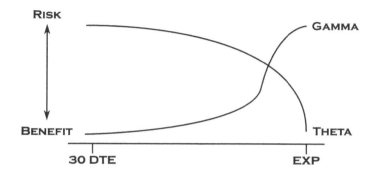

GAMMA RISK VS BENEFIT OF THETA DECAY OVER TIME

Although this graph has a Y-axis (vertical or up and down axis) with ridiculous units[5], it illustrates that as call sellers, gamma and theta decay are often competing forces at different points in time for us. As theta decay ramps up and turns OTM calls into gains, gamma risk carries the peril of assignment (being forced to sell your shares if your sold call finishes ITM).

Some traders inclined to abstract thinking will want to find the sweet spot where those two lines intersect— the time point where you get the most benefit out of theta decay before gamma risk takes over. The consensus[6] is that this magical date occurs around 21 days before expiration, and that the best way to mitigate the risk is to buy back your call around 21 DTE (days to expiration) and sell another one for

---

[5] Poor graph axis labels and general graph abuse is a pet peeve of mine, and yet I've committed that very sin here. You either die a hero or live long enough to become the villain, I guess.

[6] At least in the online community of retail options traders.

around 6 weeks out.

This strategy is very viable, and pretty low stress because you are collecting a larger premium, and have more time for good position management opportunities if they present themselves. You do lose some premium because of the time value inequality (multiple, shorter term calls are worth more in aggregate than fewer, longer term calls)[7] But, in the theta gang and wheeling community,[8] it is a popular guideline I wanted you to be aware of.

---

[7]This is mentioned elsewhere in the book multiple times, for it is an important concept.

[8]Theta gang is the moniker for the (primarily Reddit-based) community of traders that tries to make money from theta decay. They either sell covered calls, as described in this book, or perform a slightly more complicated strategy known as "wheeling". Wheeling consists of selling a put (not described in this book) rather than buying shares outright, and then selling a call if they are assigned shares. The process is circular— sell a put, sell a call, sell a put, sell a call etc— hence the name "wheel."

Although this book does not describe selling puts, doing so is the inverse of selling a call, and as such should be easy to grasp once you understand covered calls.

CHAPTER 25

SPY and Weeklies

Lthough most of the examples I've used so far are monthly options, we need to mention weeklies.

All optionable stocks have a minimum of four expiration months. The current month, the next month, and two others that are determined by that stock's particular calendar cycle.[1] Stocks that have LEAPs will include the next two January's expirations (up to 2 years in the future).

Some stocks also have weekly expirations. These are typically larger cap or heavily traded stocks. SPY is so popular that it actually has intra-weekly (Monday, Wednesday and Friday) expirations

---

[1]These cycles are referred to with the first initial of the relevant months, such as JAJO, FMAN, and MJSD. For example, JAJO is January, April, July, October.

available.[2]

25.1 MAXIMUM Premium per Day

Having covered the time value inequality, we know that longer dated calls pay less premium per day than shorter dated calls. By extension, ultra short dated calls will pay the most! So if you are looking to maximize premium per day, weeklies are where it's at!

25.2 MAXIMUM Theta Decay

We also know that theta decay is exponential near the end of an options contract— and these bad boys expire in a week (or less for the intra-week SPY strikes)! So if you're looking to maximize theta decay, look no further— the exponential decay is in full swing if you are trading short term options.

25.3 MAXIMUM Gamma Risk

Unfortunately, if you're looking to maximize gamma risk, also look no further! The price of these ultra short term options is highly suscep-tible to underlying moves in SPY.

Trading dailies or weeklies is really a preference of the call seller, which we will get into more deeply later. Until then, if you like more active trading, position management and quick expiration of calls, weeklies are probably for you. If you don't want to manage positions much and prefer something a bit farther OTM you can sit back and watch, waiting for the perfect time to BTC, or you are happier with

---

[2]This was true when I first wrote it. Now, in the midst of my (hopefully) final edit circa November 2022, there are daily options available.

Figure 25.1: *I've titled this composition "Cats on McMillan on Options." It exists here, in the chapter on weeklies, because we were facing a serious dearth of fun pictures.*

fewer/larger premiums, then monthlies are where you will probably land. I'd recommend you try them both!

As far as actually trading goes, there's nothing unique about how weeklies work compared to other options. All the same concepts apply, just in the extremes of some qualities. So as you forge on, remember the weeklies are always there to be traded.

CHAPTER 26

I Sold My Call, Now What? Part 1- OTM (and ATM)

o you bought 100 shares of a stock. You sold a covered call. What happens next?[1]

Short answer— a lot!

Up until their expiration date options can be traded just like stocks, and you can make unlimited moves in the interim to adjust your po-

---

[1]This chapter begins the nitty-gritty, dense and detailed work of position management. There's a few groundwork chapters then it gets real and the grind goes from chapters 30–37.

It's not that hard, but it takes some effort and can be tedious. So take your time and rest assured that when chapter 38 rolls around you will have more experience than most new covered call sellers. You will have seen a general example of every price movement and how you could manage it in your account, as well as the reasoning behind it all— and you will be prepared for some portfolio overwriting of your own!

sition... but the best way to learn is backwards. It's always easiest to start at the expiration date and go in reverse because the call price at expiration is always well-defined, with a known intrinsic value and no extrinsic value.

The reference example setup that we will use repeatedly is as follows:

You bought 100 shares of MJC corporation for $84 a share the third week in May (in this example MJC is a large-cap, slow moving pharma company with a ridiculously handsome CEO— a traditionally safe dividend stock).

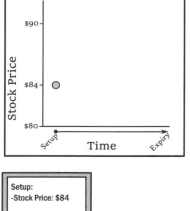

You look at the options chain and see that the $85 call for next June (next month) is selling for $2 a share— I made up this example so I don't have an actual options chain for you to look at. The idea of share price appreciation and a call premium sounds swell, so you sell that option.[2]

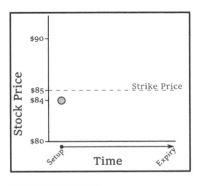

Stock Price: $84

Call Value: $2 per share

Cash Balance: +$200 (+$2.00 per share)

Account Value: No change

Setup:
-Stock Price: $84
-Call Value: $2.00/ Share ($85 Strike, 1- month expiry)

So at expiration, the price of the stock is going to be in one of three general places— below the strike price, at the strike price, or above the strike price.

---

[2]$2 a share $85 call for a safe, large cap dividend stock trading at $84 is a bit high, but we're working with that premium for the sake of easy math.

26.0.1 Brief Refresher 1: Options terminology (for calls you have sold)

- If the price of the stock is below the strike price of the call option = the option is Out of The Money (OTM)

- If the price of the stock is at the strike price of the call option = the option is At The Money (ATM)

- If the price of the stock is above the strike price of the call option = the option is In The Money (ITM)

- At expiration there will be no extrinsic value remaining.

26.0.2 Brief Refresher 2: Options Terminology, more generally and more technically:

- Out of the Money = No Intrinsic value

- At the Money = No Intrinsic value (underlying security's price is equal to the strike price)

- In the Money = Has Intrinsic Value

- Remember we defined intrinsic value as the component of the call premium that is equal to share value minus the strike price. If it is a negative number, there is no intrinsic value.

- Extrinsic value is the portion of the call premium not attributed to intrinsic value.

26.1 When a Call is Out of the Money (OTM) at Expiration

In our example, the strike price of the option we sold was $85. This means that, per our sold call contract, we are only obligated to sell our shares if the price of the stock is higher than the strike price of $85 at expiration.

If nothing happened with MJC corp and the share price stayed at a rock solid $84 all month, barely deviating from that price point, our option at expiration would end up being out of the money (OTM) at expiry. Because we are only obligated to sell at $85 or higher, and the stock is at $84, the option we sold is worthless! By worthless, I mean the call's value literally decreases from the $2 we sold it for all the way down to $0.

Put another way— who is going to buy shares from us at $85 when the market is offering them for $84? No one!!! They'd immediately lose $1 per share!

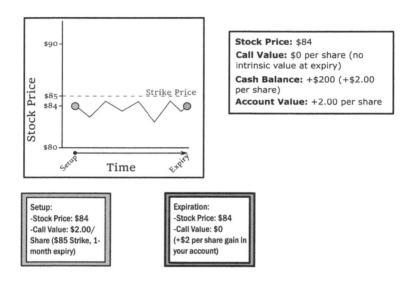

Stock Price: $84
Call Value: $0 per share (no intrinsic value at expiry)
Cash Balance: +$200 (+$2.00 per share)
Account Value: +2.00 per share

Setup:
-Stock Price: $84
-Call Value: $2.00/ Share ($85 Strike, 1-month expiry)

Expiration:
-Stock Price: $84
-Call Value: $0
(+$2 per share gain in your account)

26.2   When a Call Is At the Money (ATM) at Expiration

The same thing happens if the stock closes on the last day of the options contract exactly at $85— nothing happens because there is no intrinsic value, no profit within the contract that is gained by exercising it. The nice thing here is that you made $1 per share from appreciation (remember we bought it for $84, in this example it's $85 at expiry) in addition to the $2 premium.

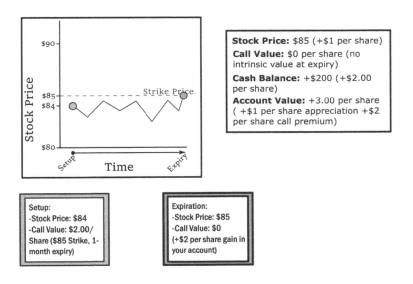

An option closing at exactly your sold strike price is, in a way, the best result you could hope for. Instead of just making $2 per share from the short call premium dwindling to nothing, you also made an extra $1 per share from price appreciation— a total of $3 per share!

26.3 ATM Expiration is Kind Of the Best

This is kind of great! In both situations, the $2 per share premium we sold the $85 strike call for dwindled down to $0 per share over the course of the month, and we don't have to do anything! Since the sold call was "short" in our account, any decrease in its value is a profit to us. The $2 per share call premium we initially received is ours to keep.

This dwindling of an option's value (specifically it's extrinsic value) is theta decay in action. For now just keep in mind that if a stock doesn't move much, the value of an OTM call exponentially decreases as the expiration date of the contract approaches.

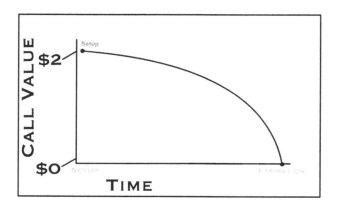

26.4   Most Option Sellers Buy to Close Early

In reality, we probably shouldn't be letting contracts expire or ride until expiration, as gaps up or down on market close can cause some nasty surprises.[3]   As such, most portfolio overwriters (in fact, most option sellers in general) typically buy back the option at some point[4]

---

[3]This is our buddy gamma in action.

[4]A popular rule of thumb is buy back at 50% profit and roll into the next month. Other covered call sellers will buy back any option which has surpassed the initial dollars per day of premium they received is exceeded. For example if they received a $300 premium for a 30-day call ($10 per day) and after only two days

for a gain.

But what about if the stock price is above \$85 when the contract expires?

---

the value of the sold call has decreased to \$100, the remaining call value is \$5 per day (\$100/20 days), so they would buy to close.

Further research will give you lots of ideas for these strategies, but nothing works all the time. As such, I am hesitant to recommend specific rules for if and when an option seller would buy-to-close. I encourage you to experiment and find what works for you. The market is random, your temperament is more consistent. Unfortunately there's no easy answer (and you should be highly suspicious of anyone who tells you that there is).

CHAPTER 27

I Sold My Call, Now What? Part 2- ITM

E will use the same setup from last time. We bought 100 shares of a stock for $84 a share, and sold a one-month, $85 call for a $2.00 premium.

The last situation you could find yourself in at expiration is with the price of your underlying above your strike price. To illustrate we'll start with the same setup as last chapter, but this time we'll have the share price of MJC jump to $90. Now you have an obligation to sell it for $85 a share to whatever anonymous person on the options exchange owns an $85 call.

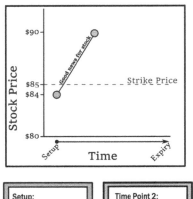

Stock Price: $90 ($6 per share price appreciation)

Call Value: ???

Cash Balance: +$200 (from call premium)

Account Value: ???

Setup:
-Stock Price: $84
-Call Value: $2.00/ Share ($85 Strike, 1-month expiry)

Time Point 2:
-Stock Price: $90
-Call Value: ???

27.1   Let The Shares Go?

You have a few choices— first choice is just to let this happen. You will get paid $85 a share, and you will get to keep the $2 premium you got paid, so you will have made a total of $3 a share. To reiterate, you bought them for $84 a share so you would make $1 selling them for $85, plus the $2 premium for the call you sold = $3 per share profit. Just letting it go is what I like to call "No-Action Overwriting", and although I haven't yet decided if it is the best or most profitable[1]

---

[1]There likely isn't a "BEST" strategy from a profits perspective. This may be impossible to ever definitively figure out given the random nature of markets and unlimited way to construct an algorithm, or "rules" for trading. It is possible for historical data, but the future is not like the past. And even then, every different time period for historical data will yield a different result.

But there is a "BEST" strategy for each individual investor, from a temperament perspective! Find what you are comfortable with and enjoy life.

course for FIRE portfolio overwriting, it definitely has its place and fits in well with the attitude of a (mostly) passive investor.

Letting your shares get called is good or bad, depending on how you look at it. On one hand, you made $300 on $8,400 in a month— 3.57% a month, or 52% annualized. This is great, most people would love this. Further, most "dividend stocks" barely pay 3.57% a year, so parking your $ in one of those vehicles won't yield much more unless there is share growth accompanying the payouts.

27.2   Did I Just Lose Money?

Looking at it another way, you just experienced some major "lost profits".[2] How exactly did you lose, when you made 3.57%? The astute reader will point out that you just sold a $90 stock for $85 a share plus $2 premium, when you could have sold it for $90 a share! In theory, you lost out on $200.[3]

In fact, when the price of the underlying initially rises your account will show red on the sold call (the call is now worth $7,[4] but since you are "short" the call it is negative $7 to you), but green on the share

---

[2] Yep. That's upside risk.

[3] You made $300 when you could have made $500

[4] Why $7? This is a rough estimate, but it is $5 intrinsic value plus $2 extrinsic value.

We know for a fact the intrinsic value is $5, because the strike is $85 and the stock value is $90.

The contract, when we sold, it had $2 extrinsic value, so that same contract will likely have at least that, plus some extra due to volatility. We have seen that as an option moves deeper in the money (our option is now slightly ITM), the extrinsic value will actually decrease. But our sold option is still close to ATM with share price at $90 and strike price at $85, so the effect of extrinsic value decreasing as options move further ITM would likely be offset by the volatility of the upward move.

For that reason, and simplicity's sake, we left extrinsic value at $2, leading to a total call value of $7, which is a very realistic estimate and easy number to work with for learning purposes.

price, as below:

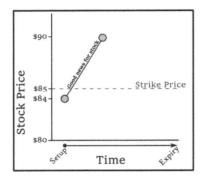

Stock Price: $90 ($6 per share price appreciation)

Call Value: $7 ($5 per share "loss" because the call is short in your account

Cash Balance: +$200 (from call premium)

Account Value: +$1 per share (+$6 share appreciation - $7 per share short call +$2 premium received)

Setup:
-Stock Price: $84
-Call Value: $2.00/
Share ($85 Strike, 1-
month expiry)

Time Point 2:
-Stock Price: $90
-Call Value: ~$7/sh
($5/share loss) as
call becomes ITM

Did you miss out and experience "lost profits"? In theory, yes, but maximizing profit is a different goal than making a somewhat consistent, liquid monthly percentage return, so I would argue that it all depends on your goals in the first place. If you want income from your index investments, then you met your goal.[5]

Of note, if you looked at your account at expiration, you'd only see a $3 loss on your short call position because there would no longer be any extrinsic value included in your short call price. Effectively, the $2 premium offsets the loss of the $5 call value at expiration. Put another way, you sold something for $2, and now that it is worth $5, you really only have to pay $3 from your starting cash balance if you

---

[5]One would care about upside risks in other types of options trading with different goals, but not as much when portfolio overwriting.

want to buy it back (buying to close, aka BTC, which we will discuss later in position management).

So the short call value is $5, but it's only a $3 loss to you in your account.

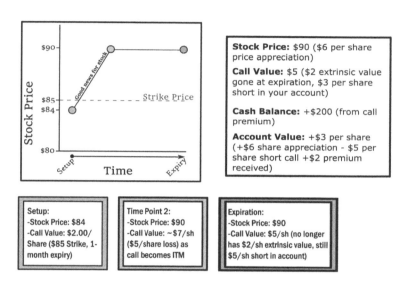

Stock Price: $90 ($6 per share price appreciation)

Call Value: $5 ($2 extrinsic value gone at expiration, $3 per share short in your account)

Cash Balance: +$200 (from call premium)

Account Value: +$3 per share (+$6 share appreciation - $5 per share short call +$2 premium received)

Setup:
-Stock Price: $84
-Call Value: $2.00/Share ($85 Strike, 1-month expiry)

Time Point 2:
-Stock Price: $90
-Call Value: ~$7/sh ($5/share loss) as call becomes ITM

Expiration:
-Stock Price: $90
-Call Value: $5/sh (no longer has $2/sh extrinsic value, still $5/sh short in account)

27.3 You Don't Have to Let Your Stock Get Called Away

You can still adjust your obligation by buying and selling that option contract all the way up until 3:59 pm Eastern Time before the market closes on the day of expiration. Want to hold it another month and make a little more money? You can "Roll Out". Want to not sell your stock and pay for the chance to hopefully sell it for a higher price? It's probably going to cost you, but you can "Roll Up". Have unlimited time and no qualms about holding your stock for a while, and are averse to spending money to adjust your position? You can "Roll Up and Out". The following chapters cover all these "options."

CHAPTER 28

Position Management Overview

Basically, one or more of three things happen over the life of a covered call— the underlying stays the same, declines, or rises in price. Usually, throughout the life of a contract, it's all three, and all the while time passes and extrinsic value erodes away. So, unless you are going to take a fully set it & forget it approach, you need to know how to handle each situation.

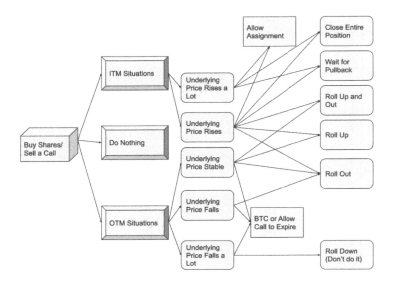

28.1   Death and...

This is especially important if you are selling covered calls in a taxable
account. Call premiums received and share appreciation are taxable if
you let your lot (100 shares) of stock get called.[1] I don't know exactly
how it's taxed, because I'm not a tax guy.[2] I also don't give tax advice,
and I mostly sell covered calls in my IRA, where taxes aren't an issue.

---

[1] If you allow the call to get assigned, you can actually re–enter your VTI position at a discount by selling puts to enter positions. Alternately selling cash
secured puts to enter positions and then covered calls on the stocks once you own
them is colloquially known as "wheeling". Put–selling tech is a bit outside of this
book's wheelhouse, but is still very important. As such, I may cover it in a future
edition of this book, or different book if anyone likes this one. In fact, I think it
fits in great with FIRE investing because it gets you a discount on an asset you
were going to buy anyway. It's another skill worth your time (read: money) as an
investor.

[2] I pay someone to do mine.

28.2 OTM Situations

The easiest situation to handle is when the underlying stays the same, rises a little (but does not exceed the strike price), or drops. In other words, when your sold call ends up OTM at expiration. Since you are selling OTM covered calls, the hope is that theta will eat away at the (entirely) extrinsic value. If this happens, then at the end of the month the call you sold will expire worthless. You can then move on to the next month having made the call premium as a profit.

> **Pause and Ponder: this is a great way to make good returns in years when the market is stagnant.**

We saw an idealized example of this in a previous chapter:

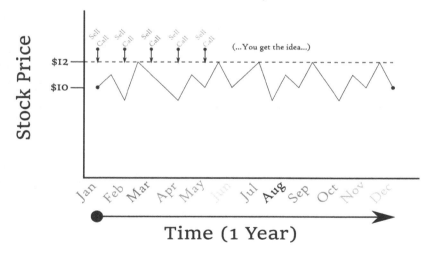

The Ideal Scenario for Selling Covered Calls on a Flat Stock, Visualized

These times when the call remains OTM, you can also adjust your position before it expires. This includes doing one of the following:

buying to close, or in certain cases, rolling up and/or out. If your sold call declined in value enough to show a meaningful[3] gain, I would typically recommend buying to close.

Although rolling out is not always the go–to choice, you should learn and understand it. It will make you a well–versed portfolio overwriter, and options trader in general.

If the price of the underlying drops, in addition to waiting until expiry or buying to close, there is also the option to do the dastardly deed of rolling down. I do not endorse rolling down in the context of portfolio overwriting. However, I will cover rolling down later so that you have a complete toolkit.

28.3   ITM Situations

If the price of the underlying rises past the strike, you can simply let shares get called as we will see in No-Action Overwriting, or you can adjust your position. Adjusting your position includes buying back the call and rolling up or rolling out, which we will cover. This is somewhat complicated, and it's actually possible to roll up & out at the same time... also covered later. But before we get into the weeds with rolling up and out, we can start with the stoic method of No-Action Overwriting.

---

[3] "Meaningful" here means meaningful to you, the call-selling Mustachian. It is not objectively defined as a fixed % or dollar amount.

CHAPTER 29

No-Action Overwriting

---

o you sold a covered call, and now you have X days of uncertainty to wait until expiration day. In the interim, the stock can go to the moon or to zero... so what does that mean to us? How would we deal with it?

Because we are overwriting index funds that we intend to buy and hold forever, we have the unique ability to do... nothing. I am presenting covered call selling in the context of index investing, which may be an overly rosy view, but it's fairly accurate given the presuppositions of buy–and–hold. It is possible to lose money overwriting, but we'll cover in-depth how that happens, and how to avoid it.

Disclaimers aside, our assumptions about you, the index investor, are as follows:

- Buy an index

- Let it ride

29.1   Flex On 'Em

Figure 29.1: *My man, Seneca the Younger*

The ability of the average index investor (FIRE or not) to hold index funds unwaveringly is a superpower. This stalwart attitude is baffling to most active traders! Withstanding vicissitudes (or just blatantly ignoring) the movements of the underlying security are Herculean feats of strength. In the simplest version of FIRE overwriting, which I will call No Action Overwriting[1], you:

- Sell a call against VTI (or your favorite index)

- Let the shares get called if stock rises, then buy back VTI and repeat

- Or let the call expire worthless and sell another call when VTI is at or above cost basis.[2]

29.2   What Happens ITM

When the stock rises, the value of stock you own increases. The value of the call you sold also increases— which is a "loss" for you (you are short the call). You'll see it when you look at your account. Whoever bought the call will see green and be happy because that investor owns (is long) the call.

---

[1]This moniker is my tip-of-the-cap to the Taoist principle of wu-wei.

[2]This can include discounts to cost basis from call premiums received, if you want to account for it that way

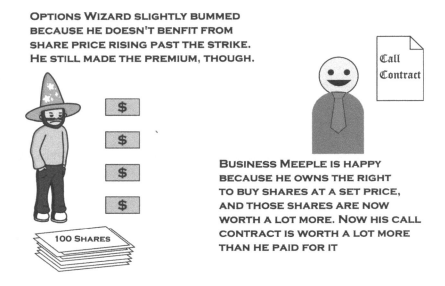

OPTIONS WIZARD SLIGHTLY BUMMED BECAUSE HE DOESN'T BENFIT FROM SHARE PRICE RISING PAST THE STRIKE. HE STILL MADE THE PREMIUM, THOUGH.

100 SHARES

Call Contract

BUSINESS MEEPLE IS HAPPY BECAUSE HE OWNS THE RIGHT TO BUY SHARES AT A SET PRICE, AND THOSE SHARES ARE NOW WORTH A LOT MORE. NOW HIS CALL CONTRACT IS WORTH A LOT MORE THAN HE PAID FOR IT

Figure 29.2: *Remember this?*

Remember this fact! Once the stock passes the strike price and the call becomes ITM, the amount it moves up is completely offset by the short call's gains in intrinsic value. Gains above the strike are a wash for you as the covered call seller.

29.3 The Short Call Offset, Visualized

At setup, share price has value X, and the call is comprised of intrinsic and extrinsic value

At Setup

Share Price **: X**

Call Value **: Extrinsic Value** **+** **Intrinsic Value**

For OTM calls, there is only extrinsic value, as shown here:

At Setup, *OTM Call*

**Share
Price** $\cdot$ **X**

Call $\cdot$ **Extrinsic** **+**   **Intrinsic**
Value $\cdot$ **Value**   **Value**

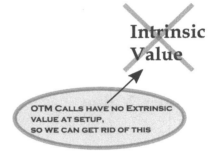

OTM CALLS HAVE NO EXTRINSIC
VALUE AT SETUP,
SO WE CAN GET RID OF THIS

Figure 29.3: *Since we are selling an OTM call when overwriting, we can just remove intrinsic value from our setup.*

At expiration, there is by definition no extrinsic value to the call, so if there was no underlying appreciation, the call value at expiration is zero, which has become a gain in your account.

At Expiration

OTM Call, *NO underlying appreciation* **during contract period**

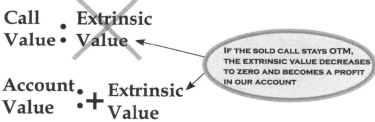

Figure 29.4: *At expiration, if there was no underlying appreciation past our strike, the extrinsic value the call had originally all disappears and becomes a profit in our account*

If the underlying does appreciate, the appreciation should be divided in the mind of the call seller into two distinct categories: appreciation up to the strike price, and appreciation past the strike price.

Mid-Contract Period
OTM Call, *underlying appreciation past*
strike price during contract period

Share Price **: X** **+** **Appreciation to Strike Price** **+** **Appreciation past Strike Price**

Call Value **: Extrinsic Value** **+** **+** **Intrinsic Value**

INTRINSIC VALUE IS THE SAME AS APPRECIATION PAST THE STRIKE PRICE FOR A SOLD CALL

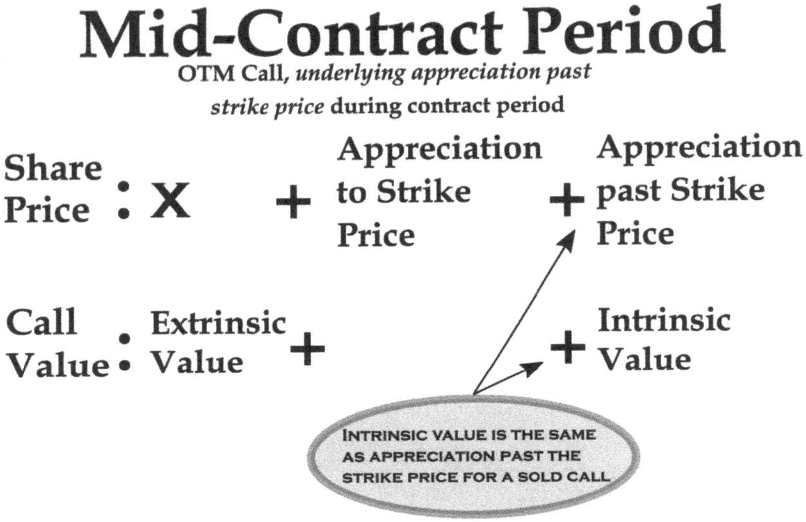

Figure 29.5: *In the middle of a contract, if there was appreciation past the strike price, our sold call now has intrinsic value equal to said appreciation past the strike price*

At expiration, share price includes all appreciation, the call includes intrinsic value (appreciation past strike price) and *the call has no remaining extrinsic value* (which has turned into a gain in your account).

At Expiration

OTM Call, *underlying appreciation past strike price* at expiration

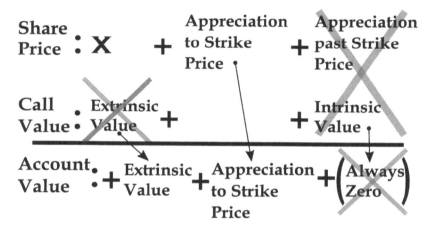

Figure 29.6: *If the underlying remains above the strike price at expiration, the extrinsic value is still a profit to us as the call seller, but the remaining intrinsic value (equal to appreciation past the strike) is still a loss to us.*

Put another way, the gain we make on share price appreciation past the strike is completely offset by the loss to our short call in the form of the call gaining intrinsic value. We still make the extrinsic value that eroded away over the life of the contract and the appreciation to the strike price.

Adding these short and long positions, you will see appreciation past the strike price on the stock (long) position will be completely offset by intrinsic value (by definition the difference between stock price and strike price) of the sold call (short) position.

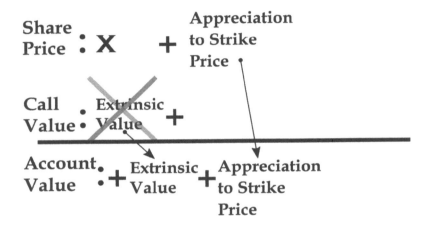

At Expiration

OTM Call, *underlying appreciation* TO STRIKE PRICE ONLY at expiration

Figure 29.7: *We can see that because appreciation past the strike is always offset (negated) by the short call's intrinsic value, we will make the same profit at expiry if the share price goes exactly to our strike (shown in this figure) or if the share price skyrockets past it (shown in the previous figure). This is the maximum profit of a covered call trade, visualized.*

29.4 The Only Way to Cash In is to Buy Out

You need to be aware of the offset, because it inherently prevents you from participating in share appreciation unless you relieve yourself of the call obligation. The only way to relieve yourself of the call obligation is by buying back the contract (buying to close)... which will cost you.[3]

If the stock stays above the strike price at expiration, and you don't buy back or roll your call (buying back and simultaneously selling another call), your underlying shares get called away.

29.5 You "Lost" Money While You Made Money

But always keep in mind— *you still make the call premium and the share appreciation up to that strike price.* The fact that you still make share appreciation and call premium is supremely important to how you view selling covered calls. In fact, it's the secret to No–Action Overwriting! If you know what you stand to make if the stock is called and are fine with that return, Hakunah Matata. Stick to the plan.

If VTI is $163/sh, and you sell a 3–month $165 call in an IRA for a $3.00/sh premium (this was all true on the date I wrote it, 12/19/19), you're still going to make 3%[4] if VTI flies past $165. If you do that 4 times this year, that's 12.5%. Compared with a long–term

---

[3]If you roll for a credit, which is covered in the upcoming chapters on rolling out and rolling up and out, you don't pay using just cash from your account, but rather are selling some more "time value" in the transaction.

[4]$2 appreciation plus $3 premium, divided by the initial $162 investment.

market average of 7%–10% per year (depending on how you account
taxes/inflation) jump for joy, take the returns, and be content.

29.6   Ohm

If you are super zen, you can even do this with long term calls or
LEAPS. LEAPS are just calls with expiration dates way in the future.
Trying to adjust and maximize profits can oftentimes be a losing game
(we will see how soon enough), and sometimes the simplest option
is to stick to the plan and ride it out. In a way you are capping
profits, but if you trade consistently with a concrete goal for yearly
returns, choosing strike prices to generate premiums adjusted to your
risk tolerance accordingly, then the profits you are making should be
"enough".

Figure 29.8: *A Very Zen Options Wizard*

But lots of portfolio overwriters adjust their position, and you
need to know how. We will start with the example of BTC (buying–to–close) when the underlying decreases in price in the next chap-

ter.

29.7 Regardless of Zen Status

Even if No-Action Overwriting sounds great, you still need to know how to manage your sold calls. It is part of the covered call seller's skill set, and it would be irresponsible not to understand it. Consider it part of your due diligence.

CHAPTER 30

A Steady Price

So the first thing we will consider about position management is what to do when the underlying goes...nowhere. When the price oscillates up and down a little bit the entire contract period and stays below the strike as expiration approaches, we can be happy because our short call value just erodes away to nothing due to theta decay. We saw an example of this already in our soft introduction:

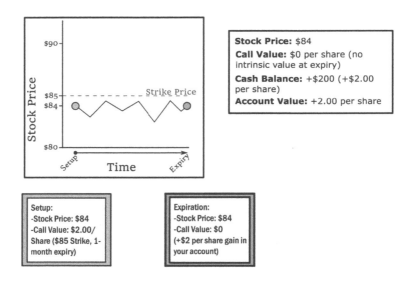

Figure 30.1: *Remember this?*

Just letting the sold call's extrinsic value dwindle to nothing and turn into a profit in our account is pretty nifty.

30.1   So Why Do Anything?

If you have a suspicion that the share price might jump up past the strike at some point in the contract (we are expecting our indexes to appreciate long-term, after all) then it would make sense to buy the call back (at a profit to you) after it has decreased in value some amount.[1] If you don't buy back your sold call and the share price rises suddenly past your strike before expiration, then you are going to be

---

[1]That specific amount is up to you. You can buy to close at any time if you are happy with the profits.

forced to sell your shares or adjust your position by buying back your call and selling (or not selling) a new one.

30.2 You Down With BTC? Ya' You Know Me...

When you purchase back a call you have sold, this is called "buying to close" or "BTC" and it relieves you of the obligation to sell your shares at a certain price— you effectively exit the option contract when you BTC. Additionally, if you sell a call and then buy it back later, at a lower price, it "locks in" profits from the call premium on your overall position.

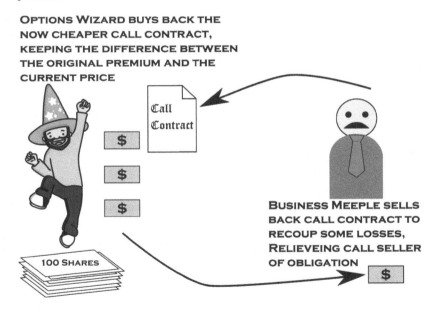

Figure 30.2: *Remember this?*

30.3 Uncapping the Gains

One other advantage of BTC is that you have more days with your shares "uncovered"— meaning that the shares do not have a covered call sold against them, and can appreciate without having profits capped at the strike. These uncovered shares can be very helpful because they offer you the chance to have the best of both worlds. By locking in some profits and buying to close, you can either leave shares uncovered and potentially participate in some underlying appreciation, or sell another call.[2]

30.4 Can I BTC and Sell Another Call Right Away to Get More Time Premium?

If you are happy with your strike price, potential share appreciation, and monthly call premiums, then you also have the option to just BTC and simultaneously sell the call with the same strike price for next month. This is called "rolling[3] out",[4] and allows you to adjust

---

[2]There is a strong argument here for buying to close and leaving shares uncovered for some portion of time. Capturing additional price appreciation isn't possible when calls are constantly rolled, as sold calls effectively "cap" your profits. In general, *you should never sell calls against all your shares for this reason— when the market is in bull mode and rises past your strike, portfolio overwriting **can and will** underperform buy and hold.* Unless you are in dire financial straits and would rather sell calls and hope for the possibility of a flat month/pullback than you would cash out any index funds shares, always leave most of the FIRE nest egg uncovered.

[3] "Roll" is a fancy way of saying closing one option contract and opening another. Although I presented it as buying to close and then selling to open another call, these two transactions are done simultaneously as one order with most brokers.

[4]Rolling "out" refers to a future date. Rolling up or down refers to higher or lower strike prices. This is covered in detail in later chapters.

your position in one trade, resulting in a net credit to your account.[5]

---

[5]You technically do "pay" to BTC with part of the premium of the new sold call (or the original call premium, depending on your accounting). We do lots of accounting examples of buying to close and rolling (with pictures!) in the coming chapters.

CHAPTER 31

Position Management- A Falling Price- BTC

O recap, you know that when you sell a call and your underlying shares decline, you actually make money on the sold call as it loses value. Because it is short in your account, when the negative value becomes smaller, it will display as a profit. Reason being, the call's extrinsic value decreases after the underlying's price falls because it is now much less likely that the underlying is going to climb back and reach the sold call's strike price by expiration.

This short call acts as a hedge, and interestingly enough, it gives you a small reason for a small celebration in the face of your index fund's share price decreasing.

But what to do with your now-cheaper short call?

Broadly, you have 2 options— you can:

- Do nothing

- You can buy it back (aka BTC) +/- roll down or out.

We will now cover BTC in detail.

31.1   Start with the Call's Value

Say you sold a call, and all of the sudden the price of the underlying falls out from under you...where is the value of that call going? To zero or near zero, that's where. Even though the underlying price dropped, this half of the coin is good for you as a call seller.

If you choose to do nothing, you can monitor your position until expiry, watching the call value go to zero as long as the underlying stock stays below your strike price. The Monday after expiration Friday, you keep the premium and nothing happens to your shares; the call will have disappeared from your account. But you can relieve yourself of the call sooner, if you choose...

31.2   Locking in Profits by Buying to Close

The more prudent move is often buying back (buy-to-close) the call you sold when it has very little value remaining.[1] This prevents having

---

[1]If you noticed— I didn't define "very little value". This is because there is unfortunately no exact time when one should BTC and take profits on a call. Some people buy back their calls with lots of value remaining, even as early as when half the value is gone (keeping 50% of the premium). Some people wait until only 30% of the original value remains (they made 70% of the premium as profits). Some people will close out when 25% of value remains with 2 weeks left in the contract, integrating a strict percentage and a timeline into their system... and on and on.

to deal with a sudden rise to (or above) your strike price[2], or the rare chance of assignment when someone exercises the right to their call and buys shares from you.[3]

As an overwriter, buying back calls that have decreased in value is a situation that's mostly gravy— you've made money above what your underlying would have returned anyway— so my advice is twofold: don't be greedy, and do what you are emotionally and mentally suited to.

Keep in mind, however, that when you buy-to-close you are spending some of the premium you received, decreasing whatever percentage return calculations you made at the outset. If you set out to make 0.5% per month in premiums, then closing at 50% profit only makes you 0.25% per month. This is still 3% returns per year, which is very

---

With a little reading and searching you can find different suggested guidelines for when to take profits on a call, but unfortunately this is a grey area that you will have to figure out for yourself. There is no magic bullet that maximizes profits every time.

[2] aka Gamma Risk

[3] This is always a risk, but rarely occurs unless there are dividends in play. If upcoming dividends are worth more than the extrinsic value of a call, and said call is far enough ITM, the likelihood of early assignment is greatly increased

As an example to reference: If in our previous MJC example you sold the $84-strike and the price of MJC went to $95, the call's delta would increase (approaching 1) and the call would lose extrinsic value as it moved ITM (recall that deeper ITM options have less extrinsic value), resulting in an overall call price closer to $11 .

With the $84-strike call now ITM and worth $11, if MJC corp declares a $2 per share dividend, the price of the stock will decrease by $2 on the dividend date, and that $2 will go to the holder of shares— which is you if you sold the call.

The call buyer will be facing an $11 profit that will immediately decrease to a $9 profit on the dividend payout date, because the $2 dividend will go to us and the shareholder. Knowing this, the call buyer could exercise the call, buy the shares, retain the share appreciation, and receive the dividend payment if they exercise before the ex-div date (the date of record for owning shares in order to be paid a dividend).

This does not always happen, however, because buying shares requires a much larger cash outlay, and the call buyer exposes himself to much more downside by owning shares versus a call.

Just remember that assignment is always a risk to be aware of as a call seller, more so with dividends in play.

meaningful when compounded, but lots of new call sellers who aren't carefully accounting end up wondering where all the profits went after they BTC and roll at every chance they get.[4]

One thing that influences the decision of when to BTC is that most OTM calls will lose the majority of their value in the last 2 weeks leading up to expiry, so lots of call sellers (myself included) typically buy to close or roll with a week or so before expiration, once theta has really kicked in.

---

[4]I foolishly went through this phase when I first started trading covered calls.

31.3 BTC in Action

So let's look at an example. We will use the easy share price of $100, and then once you are a bit familiar with what's going on, we will snap back to the real-life VTI chain you all know and love.

Setup: Investor buys stock XYZ at $100/share.

Investor sells next month (30 days to expiration) $102 strike call for $1.50 a share.

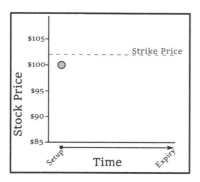

Stock Price: $100

Call Value: $1.50 per share

Cash Balance: +$150 (+$1.50 per share)

Account Value: No change

Setup:
-Stock Price: $100
-Call Value: $1.50/
Share ($102 Strike,
1-month expiry)

Stock drops to $90 the next day The $102 call is probably worth $0.20 per share now.[5]

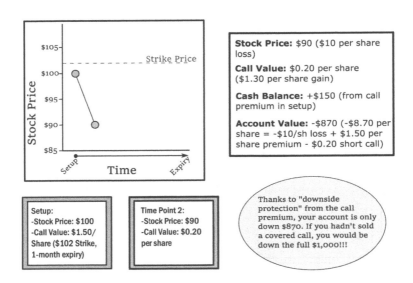

Stock Price: $90 ($10 per share loss)

Call Value: $0.20 per share ($1.30 per share gain)

Cash Balance: +$150 (from call premium in setup)

Account Value: -$870 (-$8.70 per share = -$10/sh loss + $1.50 per share premium - $0.20 short call)

Setup:
-Stock Price: $100
-Call Value: $1.50/
Share ($102 Strike,
1-month expiry)

Time Point 2:
-Stock Price: $90
-Call Value: $0.20
per share

Thanks to "downside protection" from the call premium, your account is only down $870. If you hadn't sold a covered call, you would be down the full $1,000!!!

---

[5] People who are more technically skilled than I am can mathematically model an exact expected call price after a drop in the underlying, even to the extent that such a drop is drastic enough to significantly alter volatility. I just use the heuristic of looking at the call premiums that are currently 13% above VTI's price, and the ones the same number of strikes away to concoct a theoretical premium as a % of price for our idealized $100 stock. A general heuristic like this (enhanced by experience) is usually all you need as a retail trader.

Investor buys back for $0.20 the call they sold for $1.50, locking in profits of $1.30 per share. The $1.30 per share premium they retained after BTC for $0.20 per share partly mitigates the $10 per share loss, resulting in only a $8.70 per share loss. The call premium mitigated downside risk just like it was supposed to!

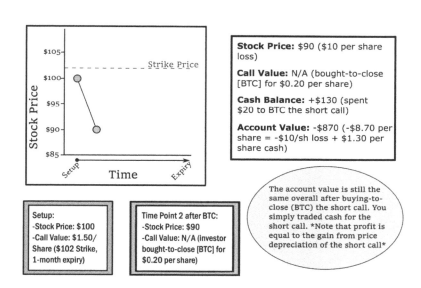

Stock Price: $90 ($10 per share loss)

Call Value: N/A (bought-to-close [BTC] for $0.20 per share)

Cash Balance: +$130 (spent $20 to BTC the short call)

Account Value: -$870 (-$8.70 per share = -$10/sh loss + $1.30 per share cash)

Setup:
-Stock Price: $100
-Call Value: $1.50/ Share ($102 Strike, 1-month expiry)

Time Point 2 after BTC:
-Stock Price: $90
-Call Value: N/A (investor bought-to-close [BTC] for $0.20 per share)

The account value is still the same overall after buying-to-close (BTC) the short call. You simply traded cash for the short call. *Note that profit is equal to the gain from price depreciation of the short call*

The investor, rather than buy back the call, could also wait. If the stock stayed at $90 the extrinsic value would erode quickly, allowing them to buy back for even less than $0.20... or they could simply let the contract expire worthless. The problem, as you probably recall, is that this investor would run the risk of the stock re-appreciating to the strike price or above it.

Consider the situation below where the investor does not buy back his/her call at a profit and shares re-appreciate:

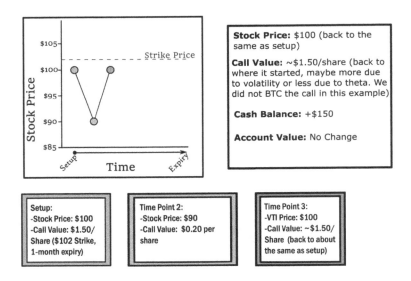

Stock Price: $100 (back to the same as setup)

Call Value: ~$1.50/share (back to where it started, maybe more due to volatility or less due to theta. We did not BTC the call in this example)

Cash Balance: +$150

Account Value: No Change

Setup:
-Stock Price: $100
-Call Value: $1.50/ Share ($102 Strike, 1-month expiry)

Time Point 2:
-Stock Price: $90
-Call Value: $0.20 per share

Time Point 3:
-VTI Price: $100
-Call Value: ~$1.50/ Share (back to about the same as setup)

This investor's account is pretty much the same as when the trade was established at setup.

One could say that this investor missed the opportunity to lock profits...

31.4   BTC Opens Up the Possibilities

However, if the investor did close out at a price of $0.20, it would open the door to the possibility of selling another call if the stock went back up in price, generating additional returns in the same contract period. Which leads us to...

31.5   2 for 1 aka The Dream

Same setup as above, but this time the investor does BTC for $0.20/Sh and locks in $130 of profits. Stock goes back up to $100 and investor sells another $102 strike call in the same contract month, and pockets another $150 premium!

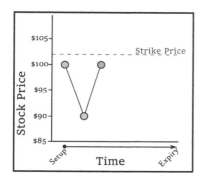

Stock Price: $100 (stock rebounded to setup price)

Call Value: ~$1.50/share (this is the second call we've sold this contract cycle)

Cash Balance: +$280 ($130 original call premium plus $150 new call premium)

Account Value: +130 (no change in stock price +280 cash -$150 [new] short call)

Setup:
-Stock Price: $100
-Call Value: $1.50/ Share ($102 Strike, 1-month expiry)

Time Point 2 after BTC:
-Stock Price: $90
-Call Value: N/A (investor bought-to-close [BTC] for $0.20 per share)

Time Point 3:
-VTI Price: $100
-Call Value: ~$1.50/ Share (back to about the same as setup)

Note that we have generated $280 in cash premiums, but our account value is only up $130 from the first call we sold and then decided to buy-to-close. This is because with the sale of the second $150 call, we immediately created another short position in our account that balanced out the new premium.[6]

---

[6] Just like when we sold our first call and generated cash— there was no initial profit because we sold a call, creating a short position in our account, and received equivalent cash in return. Simply selling the call doesn't make you money. It generates liquid funds in your account, but you don't see profit until theta decay erodes your short position.

If at the end of the contract period our $150 sold call expires OTM/ worthless, we will be left with $130 from the original premium and $150 from the second premium, totalling $280 in cash that is no longer offset by a $150 short call.

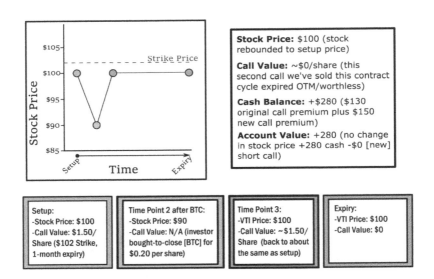

This investor makes 2.8% in one month if the second call expires worthless OTM. Compare that to the buy-and-hold investor not versed in the arcane arts of position management, who experienced two *wild* swings, first a 10% drop then a 10% gain,[7] and ended up with the same account value.

Although you won't always have this opportunity to make a premium twice in a contract period, it's really cool when it happens.

---

[7]Actually 11.1% from the price nadir

> Pause and ponder— someone only holding this stock
> would have the same account value at the beginning
> and end of this timeline. The call seller who sells one
> call makes profits once. The call seller who bought to
> close and then sold another call made profits twice.[a]
>
> ---
>
> [a]Seeing this, one might think if they could identify a trading range,
> they could make a killing over time, not even having to wait for a call to
> expire to make additional premiums.

This curated example showcases one of the most intriguing things
about covered calls to me— the ability to make money in a sideways
market.

Now that we know we can buy-to-close (and maybe get lucky and
sell another call) what if we buy-to-close and immediately sell another,
lower strike call?

CHAPTER 32

Position Management- Falling Price, Rolling Down

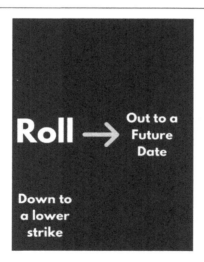

O the price of your underlying fell, and you know you can buy back your call or do nothing, and we briefly mentioned that you can do even more. This chapter ventures into the

255

territory of more risk-taking and profit-seeking than most portfolio overwriters (much less passive traders/Bogleheads) are comfortable with, so don't say I didn't warn you. Although rolling down doesn't apply well to overwriting, it has to be covered for completeness. More importantly, the more examples you see, and the more possibilities you are exposed to, the better your understanding and the better your trading. Knowledge is mycelial (synergistic).

Anyway, back to buying a stock at $100 per share, selling a $102 strike call for $1.50 per share, and the stock drops to $90. In the previous chapter, we covered different strategies including taking our profits and calling it a day.

You might, however, notice that after you buy back your call for $0.20 a share, the $92 call is now paying a $1.50 per share premium![1]

Seems pretty tempting, right? It is tempting! Unfortunately, making more premiums right away by chasing a falling stock price will often force you to end up selling an obligation that, in effect, locks in a loss for you.

---

[1] Don't get excited. It's a trap.

Imagine this example:

Same setup as in previous chapters.

You buy your $100 per share stock.

You sell $102 strike call for $1.50 per share.

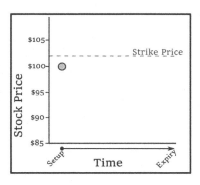

Stock Price: $100

Call Value: $1.50 per share

Cash Balance: +$150 (+$1.50 per share)

Account Value: No change

Setup:
-Stock Price: $100
-Call Value: $1.50/
Share ($102 Strike,
1-month expiry)

Share price drops to $90. You buy back the call for $0.20.

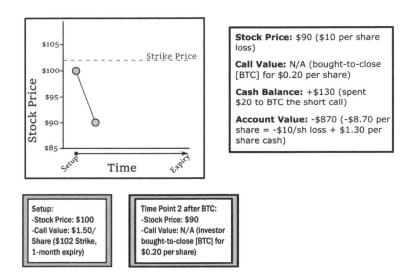

Stock Price: $90 ($10 per share loss)

Call Value: N/A (bought-to-close [BTC] for $0.20 per share)

Cash Balance: +$130 (spent $20 to BTC the short call)

Account Value: -$870 (-$8.70 per share = -$10/sh loss + $1.30 per share cash)

Setup:
-Stock Price: $100
-Call Value: $1.50/ Share ($102 Strike, 1-month expiry)

Time Point 2 after BTC:
-Stock Price: $90
-Call Value: N/A (investor bought-to-close [BTC] for $0.20 per share)

Cool, you made $130 to partly offset what would have been a $1000 loss otherwise.

Thanks to the downside protection the call premium gave you, you only lost $870 instead of $1,000...

32.1   The Forbidden Fruit

It can turn out, however, that you're too clever for your own good, and after buying to close your sold call, you take a peek at the options chain and see that now, after the price has dropped, the $92 call is now going for $1.50.

Unable to resist temptation, you now sell a $92 call for $1.50.

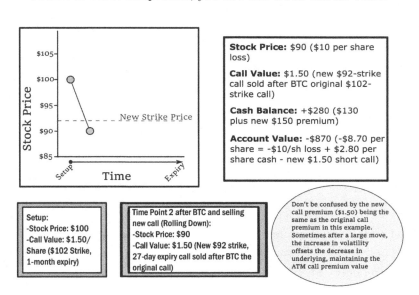

Stock Price: $90 ($10 per share loss)

Call Value: $1.50 (new $92-strike call sold after BTC original $102-strike call)

Cash Balance: +$280 ($130 plus new $150 premium)

Account Value: -$870 (-$8.70 per share = -$10/sh loss + $2.80 per share cash - new $1.50 short call)

Setup:
-Stock Price: $100
-Call Value: $1.50/ Share ($102 Strike, 1-month expiry)

Time Point 2 after BTC and selling new call (Rolling Down):
-Stock Price: $90
-Call Value: $1.50 (New $92 strike, 27-day expiry call sold after BTC the original call)

Don't be confused by the new call premium ($1.50) being the same as the original call premium in this example. Sometimes after a large move, the increase in volatility offsets the decrease in underlying, maintaining the ATM call premium value

Done together, this constitutes a "roll down" and would be reflected as a $2.80 gain in the cash balance in your account (the original $1.50 premium, minus $0.20 to buy back, plus the new $1.50 premium). Overall, at the time of transaction your account would only be up $1.30 total because the new $1.50 premium is offset by the equivalent short call price (a covered call is always "even" in your account when you set it up).

You let it ride and luckily the underlying stays at $90/share until expiration.

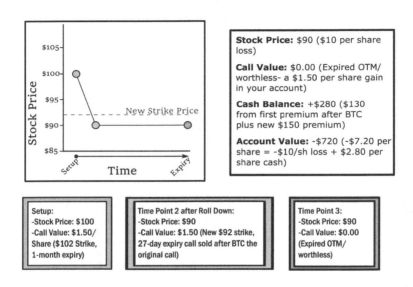

Setup:
-Stock Price: $100
-Call Value: $1.50/Share ($102 Strike, 1-month expiry)

Time Point 2 after Roll Down:
-Stock Price: $90
-Call Value: $1.50 (New $92 strike, 27-day expiry call sold after BTC the original call)

Time Point 3:
-Stock Price: $90
-Call Value: $0.00 (Expired OTM/worthless)

Theta causes your new $92 strike call to wither away to zero.

Cool! Because of your rolling down moves and the $280 in premiums, you only lost $720 ($7.20 per share) on what would have otherwise been a $1000 loss. Better than if you simply held the stock, and if you're index investing with FIRE you're holding this fund forever anyway. All good, right? It's just like the 2-for-1 in the last article, right?

32.2   The Problem Is, You're Picking Up Pennies in Front of a Steamroller

Let's consider the same example as above, except that this time after you sell the $92 call the stock flies back up to $100 and stays there until expiration. Also, let's assume you don't have enough $ to buy-to-close the call and are forced to sell.

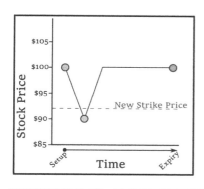

Stock Price: $100 (Share price rebounded, no gain or loss here)

Call Value: $8.00 (Entirely intrinsic value at expiry)

Cash Balance: +$280 ($130 from first premium after BTC plus new $150 premium)

Account Value: -$520 (-$5.20 per share = $0/sh loss - $8.00 short call + $2.80 per share cash)

Setup:
-Stock Price: $100
-Call Value: $1.50/
Share ($102 Strike,
1-month expiry)

Time Point 2 after Roll Down:
-Stock Price: $90
-Call Value: $1.50 (New $92 strike,
27-day expiry call sold after BTC the
original call)

Expiry:
-Stock Price: $100
-Call Value: $8.00
(entirely intrinsic
value at expiry)

32.3   Premiums... But at What Cost?

You made a couple premiums amounting to $280, but you sold your lot of $100 shares for $92 each, losing $800, so overall you lost $520! What was supposed to be a 1.5% gain is now a 5.2% loss!

This is the danger of rolling down.

32.4 Don't Sell Calls at a Strike Price Below Your Cost Basis!!!

This example should illustrate how important it is to #1 keep in mind your entry price/cost basis and #2 not chase the underlying in a way that could compromise your goals and lock you into a lower sale price below your cost basis, forcing you to sell at a loss. Our goal here is to at minimum keep pace with VTI appreciation— accruing losses is the last thing we want to do.

There definitely is a place for rolling down in more active forms of options trading. But for mostly passive investors engaging in portfolio overwriting, rolling down is not consistent with the desire to keep shares, or at minimum only sell them above cost basis. It's simply too risky.[2]

32.5 Less Paper Loss at the Cost of Less Possibilities

Now you may be scratching your head thinking "Hey, didn't the investor that rolled down only lose $520 or $720, instead of $870? And don't you constantly say not to worry about lost profits?" Yesssssssss, but you must realize that the deplorable roller-downers locked in the loss. If this was a stock you really weren't attached to and weren't banking your financial future on slow constant appreciation of, that might be a good move— getting out for a 5.2% loss.

But, the idea is that we are perma-long bullish on VTI, and the last thing we want to do is lock in losses since we can always hold until

---

[2]Unless you've been holding a long time and are able to roll down to a strike that is still above your cost basis... and even then you're capping appreciation you once had.

it goes back up to our cost basis,[3] or even sell a further dated strike at our cost basis. But we don't ever want to sell our shares below our cost basis. The goal here is to make an occasional small % return while buying and holding, selling OTM calls to allow for the possibility of some price appreciation and growth, with a full awareness of the potential for upside risk it entails.

Selling at a loss due to share price depreciation is not the same as unrealized gains— *it makes your account shrink!* This is entirely different than a small, capped appreciation that stops at the strike price in lieu of larger gains, and entirely at odds with the goals of portfolio overwriting.

Consider instead if our investor waited and was able to hit a 2-for-1 as described in the previous article. In that case, due to patience and the good position management of buying back the sold call, she'd be up 2.8% for the month, instead of down...

So when would one roll down? In portfolio overwriting for FIRE, *probably never* if the strike was below your cost basis. In some alternate strategies you constantly adjust positions...but that's thinking like a trader, and for FIRE we think like Bogleheads.

32.6   But Wait! Not All Rolls Are Bad!

If you assume since there is a roll down there must be a roll up, you'd be right! But since it doesn't have much use when the share price depreciates, we will first cover the option of rolling out when the price has fallen.

---

[3]Remember— time is on our side!

Figure 32.1: *This wizard Rolls Down all the time. Don't be like him. Socks and sandals are just one of his crimes against humanity.*

CHAPTER 33

Position Management— A Falling Price and Rolling
Out

E started with a stock price falling, and talked about how we
can BTC (Buy-To-Close) our option, and how we can roll
down (simultaneously buy back and sell a call at a lower

strike). But what else can we do?

As we know from the article on time value, longer dated options are worth more, so why not just close our position and roll to a future date that will pay us more? We totally can! It's called "rolling out", and when you do it you are, in effect, selling more time.

Rolling out gets you another option premium without having to roll down to a lower strike and possibly lock yourself into a loss. It also prevents you from having to pay into the position with money from your account balance, because part of the new, larger premium from the call you rolled out to pays the cost to BTC.

33.1   Call Sellers, Roll Out

So what would rolling out look like? We'll use the same setup from the past 2 articles:

- You buy your $100 per share stock.

- You sell $102 strike call for $1.50 per share.

- Share price drops to $90.

- You buy back the original call for $0.20

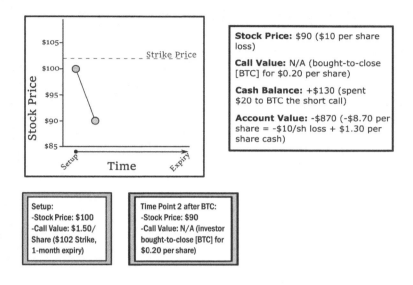

Figure 33.1: *I skipped the setup picture and went straight to the part where we were buying back our call.*

To perform the roll out, you buy back the original sold call for $0.20 and simultaneously sell a $102-strike call for 1, 2, 3, 4 or 5 months from now, netting profit from the higher premium of the further-dated $102 call. Let's say the 2-month expiry $102 call is going for $0.70, and the next available 3-month[1] expiry call has a premium of $1.35.

---

[1]VTI typically only has 3–4 different expiry months active, and always includes the current and next month, so the months available to sell calls change as time passes and new months become available. I believe VTI is on the MJSD calendar, but since I usually only sell calls 1–2 months in the future as a portfolio overwriter, this typically doesn't matter much to me.

AVAILABLE CALLS

NEXT MONTH: **~50 DAYS TO EXPIRY** **$102 STRIKE** **$0.70/ SHARE** **CALL PREMIUM**	**3 MONTH:** **~80 DAYS TO EXPIRY** **$102 STRIKE** **$1.35/ SHARE** **CALL PREMIUM**

To illustrate, we will roll out to the 3-month call for $1.35 per share:

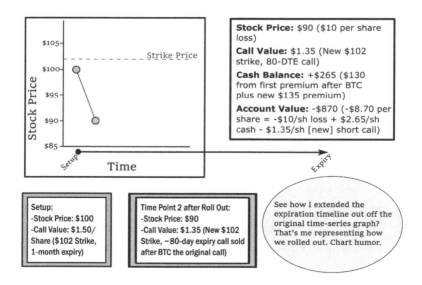

Stock Price: $90 ($10 per share loss)

Call Value: $1.35 (New $102 strike, 80-DTE call)

Cash Balance: +$265 ($130 from first premium after BTC plus new $135 premium)

Account Value: -$870 (-$8.70 per share = -$10/sh loss + $2.65/sh cash - $1.35/sh [new] short call)

Setup:
-Stock Price: $100
-Call Value: $1.50/ Share ($102 Strike, 1-month expiry)

Time Point 2 after Roll Out:
-Stock Price: $90
-Call Value: $1.35 (New $102 Strike, ~80-day expiry call sold after BTC the original call)

See how I extended the expiration timeline out off the original time-series graph? That's me representing how we rolled out. Chart humor.

In this example the price of the stock fell so that $100 strike is no longer at the money, and will probably not get you $1.50 per share for next month's call (unless the big drop created enough volatility to sufficiently increase next month's now OTM \$102-strike call). You'll probably have to go 3 or 4 months out to garner that premium, which is why the 3-month call has a value of \$1.35 in our example. If you are disciplined, don't like to manage positions, not chasing maximum returns, and just happy with the % return rolling out gets you, this might be suited for you, especially if you are trading in an IRA with no tax consequences if your shares get called.

33.2 What's the New Return?

In this case specifically, we can figure out our new expected return from premiums. Since we will be making \$2.65 per share, it will be 2.65% over 90 days if our option expires OTM. 2.65% isn't much, but it beats a 10% loss if the price remains low. It also retains the possibility of the share price re-appreciating and you not locking in a loss like rolling down would. Although you could roll out to a different strike, rolling out to the same strike will also make portfolio management easier because you know that the \$102 strike, regardless of the premium, still represents the same 2% potential underlying appreciation, and is above your cost basis.[2]

---

[2]Rolling out and down is not as bad as just rolling down if the new premium compensates for the new, lower strike price you potentially lock yourself into selling at. But for simplicity's sake most portfolio overwriters should never roll down to a strike below their cost basis.

By only ever selling OTM calls, you simplify your portfolio overwriting, knowing that any shares that may end up ITM and subsequently be called represent appreciation from cost basis. Compare this to constantly having to keep track of where your current strike is relative to cost like the deplorable roller-downers.

33.3   Rolling Versus Waiting

But rolling out might not be the best strategy for a stock you have an inherently long-term bullish bias on, which is exactly what index funds are to the FIRE investor. Chances are that, given time to do its thing, the market will re-appreciate and your call will end up in the money (ITM) before expiration. Most of the time, I've found that closing your call and waiting is the better choice. It also exercises your self-control and patience, keeping you rooted in the buy-and-hold mindset you worked so hard to develop.

Needing to sell calls all the time can be bad for the overwriter (trust me), and that depraved desire opens the door to the dark arts of rolling down, or god forbid, selling uncovered calls.[3]

33.4   Shorter Calls Add Up

The more important reason not to roll out is that selling a few long-term calls will net you less yearly than selling multiple, shorter-term calls because of extrinsic inequality.

33.5   So When Should You Roll Out?

So when is rolling out a good choice?

If you are portfolio overwriting, it's when you don't expect the underlying price to appreciate past the strike by the time your newer,

---

[3]I will NEVER describe the merits of this strategy, or any other strategy with unlimited risk. When I was a teenager and asked my bass teacher Cornell Wiley (RIP) to show me how to play pop-slap bass, he just frowned and told me to learn it from a friend. Then he proceeded to play the most painfully face-melting funky exhibition of riffs I'd ever seen, just to show that he could. I swear it was like Victor Wooten possessed him for 3 minutes. Anyway, same thing goes with margin trading— if you want a neat way to lose $, you'll have to learn it from someone else.

further-in-the-future call expires. Further, if you decide to roll out, it might be better sooner than later so you can capture the time value while it is high. Right after a share price drop, you have the most time until the next sold call, and the volatility is still high (from the drop). The longer the shares remain at a lower price, the more volatility will shrink (if the stock isn't moving back up it is less volatile and less likely to re-appreciate), and the less time value remaining. Both of these factors will decrease the extrinsic value you will receive when you sell a call.

Or it might be better to wait.[4]

If you are a disciplined investor, and rolling out would still meet your yearly ROI goals (even if the underlying went back above strike price and got called) it might be a good choice to go for it. But if you think that shares will re-appreciate after your call expires worthless but before the next month call expires, then maybe doing nothing is the best bet. Keep in mind that predicting the timing of stock price movements is easier said than done.

Thus concludes the options for managing our options when the share price drops. Now that you know about buying to close, rolling down, and rolling out, what can we do when the share price rises?

---

[4]Sorry to not provide you with one perfect, foolproof strategy— there isn't one. If anyone tries to sell you one, ask them if they will throw in the bridge for free.

CHAPTER 34

Position Management—A Rising Price and Buying to Close

Arning: this chapter is long

Anti-Warning: there's no rush here. Take your time to really digest what's going on, because it all fits together. The dynamic interplay between the price of stocks and calls is the essence of understanding options.

So far you're selling calls, and when the underlying price drops you buy them back or roll out (or down if you're a thrill seeker). But what about when the price of the underlying goes up? Welcome to the crazy world of hedging, where you do something other than rejoice when the price of your shares increases.

To reiterate ad nauseum, when the price of your underlying shares go up, so does the price of the call you sold... but that position in your account is negative (it's a short position, you sold it). Above the strike price someone else owns the call, and their gain is your loss![1]

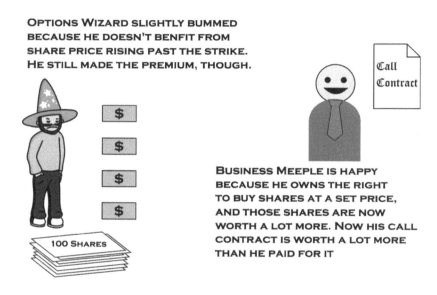

OPTIONS WIZARD SLIGHTLY BUMMED BECAUSE HE DOESN'T BENFIT FROM SHARE PRICE RISING PAST THE STRIKE. HE STILL MADE THE PREMIUM, THOUGH.

100 SHARES

Call Contract

BUSINESS MEEPLE IS HAPPY BECAUSE HE OWNS THE RIGHT TO BUY SHARES AT A SET PRICE, AND THOSE SHARES ARE NOW WORTH A LOT MORE. NOW HIS CALL CONTRACT IS WORTH A LOT MORE THAN HE PAID FOR IT

Although it's best to be stoic about lost profits, you don't want to deal with lost profits more than you have to (unless you are super zen).

Put simply, you would like to avoid having your calls in the money by the end of the contract period.[2] The first way to avoid assignment is to sell calls that are very far out of the money. Hopefully the share price won't rise enough to make them ITM, risking assignment.

---

[1] If you are sick of hearing this, it means you are learning— congrats!

[2] You may not want to be forced to sell your shares (the terminology is "be assigned" or "have your shares assigned") if you are trading in a taxable account, since having shares assigned is a taxable event like any other sale of stock.

34.1 Selling Farther OTM Calls in a Giant Account

The stated problem is that although these farther out of the money calls may have less chance of assignment, they unfortunately pay you less in premiums. But, if you have tons of shares to sell calls against, and are therefore willing to make less premium per call, you can sell calls with a pretty low chance of assignment and comfortably watch your account grow as theta decay chips away at your sold contract premiums. As a bonus— the father OTM your sold calls are, the more appreciation you get if they are assigned.

Let's do an example to illustrate:

Guess what? We are moving away from the fake XYZ $100 per share stock to the more complicated, real-world VTI chain now that we have some experience.

February 21 2020 ▼	In The Money	Show: List	Straddle	Option Lookup		🔍

Calls for February 21 2020

Contract Name	Last Trade Date	Strike ^	Last Price	Bid	Ask	Change	% Change	Volume	Open Interest	Implied Volatility
VTI200221C00154000	2019-12-23 10:44AM EST	154.00	11.08	10.10	10.80	0.00	-	-	1	20.95%
VTI200221C00156000	2019-12-23 10:50AM EST	156.00	9.10	8.30	9.10	0.00	-	-	1	19.82%
VTI200221C00161000	2019-12-23 2:58PM EST	161.00	5.00	4.30	5.00	0.00	-	-	5	16.05%
VTI200221C00163000	2020-01-03 9:48AM EST	163.00	3.78	3.00	3.60	0.00	-	3	11	14.71%
VTI200221C00164000	2020-01-03 3:48PM EST	164.00	3.12	2.35	2.90	0.00	-	3	55	13.78%
VTI200221C00165000	2020-01-06 9:30AM EST	165.00	2.20	0.00	0.00	-0.45	-16.98%	2	1,743	0.78%
VTI200221C00166000	2020-01-03 3:48PM EST	166.00	1.92	1.35	1.80	0.00	-	6	15	12.50%
VTI200221C00167000	2020-01-03 1:17PM EST	167.00	1.47	0.95	1.35	0.00	-	23	41	11.90%
VTI200221C00168000	2020-01-02 3:34PM EST	168.00	1.05	0.65	1.00	0.00	-	1	12	11.49%
VTI200221C00169000	2020-01-03 2:26PM EST	169.00	0.64	0.45	0.75	0.00	-	1	2	11.29%
VTI200221C00170000	2020-01-03 3:19PM EST	170.00	0.45	0.25	0.55	0.00	-	1	58	11.12%
VTI200221C00172000	2020-01-02 11:15AM EST	172.00	0.20	0.05	0.30	0.00	-	-	1	11.06%
VTI200221C00173000	2020-01-02 3:55PM EST	173.00	0.15	0.00	0.25	0.00	-	-	11	11.43%

For example, on 1/6/20, VTI was \$163.33 and the \$170 strike calls were at a bid–ask of 0.25–0.55, so you'd pry have gotten 0.40 a share, or \$40 premium per call contract. If you spend \$4,000 a month, and have 100 lots of VTI (aka 10,000 shares of VTI— \$1,633,300) set aside for portfolio overwriting, you could just sell the \$170 calls and sleep easy. The \$170 call is not very likely to get exercised; VTI probably won't jump that much. And even if the price of VTI does go to \$170 by expiration, you'll be banking \$66,700[3] in appreciation...

Unfortunately, if you're like most people, you don't have 1.6 million above and beyond 25× chilling in your investment account, so you have to titrate your strike price to your goals and risk tolerance. If you only have 10 lots (1000 shares, or \$163,300 worth), and can only sell 10 covered calls, maybe \$400 is enough for you. Alternatively, if you really want the money you can sell ten \$164 strike calls for \$250 each (based on a bid–ask of \$2.35–\$2.90 per share) and make \$2,500. Although this seems way better than \$400, read on to find out why it can get you in a lot of trouble quickly. Also note, the investor with \$1.6 million could sell 100 calls at \$250 and make \$25,000 a month— good motivation to accumulate a nest egg.

So, up until now, selling calls may seem pretty rosy, and I've admittedly presented it in a mostly positive light... but the time has come to explore how you lose when the underlying price goes above your sold call's strike and you BTC.

---

[3]\$6.67 in appreciation from \$163.33 to \$170, × 10,000 shares.

34.2 BTC After Share Appreciation with a Call Still OTM: Utilizing Upside Breakeven

So let's say you have 100 shares of VTI you bought today for $163.33 and you went ahead and sold that $164 call for $250.

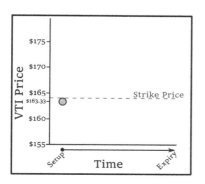

VTI Price: $163.33

Call Value: $2.50 per share

Cash Balance: +$250

Account Value: No change

Setup:
-VTI Price: $163.33
-Call Value: $2.50/
Share ($164 Strike,
1-month expiry)

Firstly, we should do the upside breakeven (at expiration) price calculation for a call that ends up ITM.[4] The upside breakeven on the total trade = strike price + premium, so in this case it is $164 (strike price) + $2.50 (premium received) = $166.50.

When you calculate upside breakeven, you are figuring out the highest the stock can go and still allow you to buy-to-close the call at expiration without a loss, retaining all the share appreciation. This is

---

[4]This is a review, I know.

important because it allows us to BTC and match the performance of underlying shares for a given contract period.

Example: if VTI is at $165 on expiration, it's $1 per share above the strike price (but still below our $166.50 breakeven). Because VTI went up $1 per share above the strike, your short call is still worth $1 per share extrinsic value. If you looked at your account on expiration day, you'd see the value of the short call would be only $1 (a decrease of $1.50 from the original call premium of $2.50 per share). This $1 is entirely intrinsic value,[5] because there is no extrinsic value at the end of expiration day.

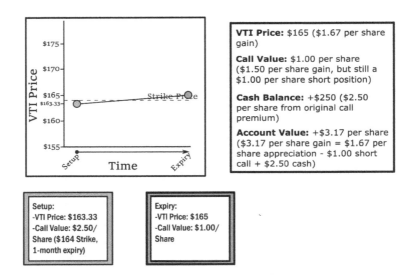

So although you made $1.50 as extrinsic value eroded away, there is still $1 intrinsic value in a $164 call for a stock trading at $165. As such, you'd have to buy back the call for $1 per share or it would

---

[5] Intrinsic value is share price minus strike price ($165 − $164) = $1.

get assigned and you'd be forced to sell your shares. So you did make $150 on the call premium, but not the original $250 from premium you anticipated if you use $1.00 per share to BTC. But, add that $1.50 per share to the $1.67 per share appreciation you get to keep now, and you have made $317 total.

To understand the dynamics a bit better, see below that you are still up $317 overall after you execute your BTC.[6]

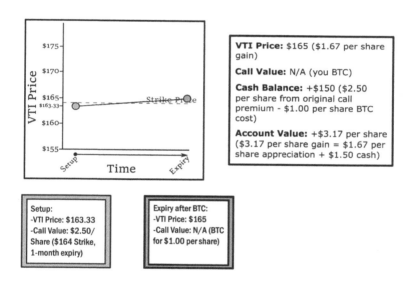

VTI Price: $165 ($1.67 per share gain)	
Call Value: N/A (you BTC)	
Cash Balance: +$150 ($2.50 per share from original call premium - $1.00 per share BTC cost)	
Account Value: +$3.17 per share ($3.17 per share gain = $1.67 per share appreciation + $1.50 cash)	

Setup:
-VTI Price: $163.33
-Call Value: $2.50/
Share ($164 Strike,
1-month expiry)

Expiry after BTC:
-VTI Price: $165
-Call Value: N/A (BTC
for $1.00 per share)

34.3   Upside Breakeven Buyback

So what if the stock went to the upside breakeven of $166.50? The call would be worth $2.50 per share at expiration because it has $2.50 of

---

[6]I am trying to reinforce the idea that buying and selling calls in and of itself doesn't make you money when you execute the trade. It is instead the theta decay of intrinsic value and underlying movements during the contract period that generate your returns.

intrinsic value, and *you'd have to use the whole premium you received if you wanted to buy to close, effectively breaking even on the call portion of the trade.* I used italics to emphasize that, because if you did use your premium to buy back the call, you've still made the appreciation on shares and get to keep that appreciation. So you break even on the call but still made $3.17 per share[7] ...not too shabby.

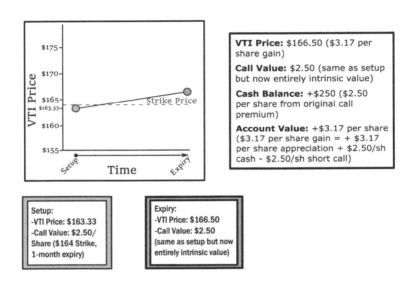

Also, did you notice it's the exact same number— $3.17? This really exemplifies the definition of the call and how it functionally caps profits. When you sold the $164 strike you are eligible for the call premium, the appreciation to $164, and nothing past that.

But why even care about buying back the call if you are making the same $3.17 per share? Because you can keep the appreciation and sell another call! Is there a difference between buying back your call when

---

[7]$166.50 − $163.33 (purchase price)

VTI is $165 and when $166.50? From an account value perspective, no. From a selling more calls perspective, yes. This is because if you sell another call, you are selling calls on $166.50 shares; they will garner a higher premium than if you sold calls vs $165 shares!

Lesson learned here is as follows: *buying back your call at the upside breakeven allows you to keep all the share price appreciation and still own the shares to sell a call against, without spending more money out of your account (**but at the expense of your call premium**).*[8]

34.4   ITM Call Buyback: The Risk

So far, this is all great, but when the stock ends up way above the strike, you are going to have to pay even more to keep it unless you make some moves. If VTI hits $170, at expiration you are going to be short a $164 call that's now worth $6 in your account.

---

[8]Also note- if you BTC at upside breakeven, then the month is a wash in terms of earning any call premium. You retain shares and share price appreciation, and your cash balance is the same as it was at the outset, effectively turning it back into a buy-and-hold month for you.

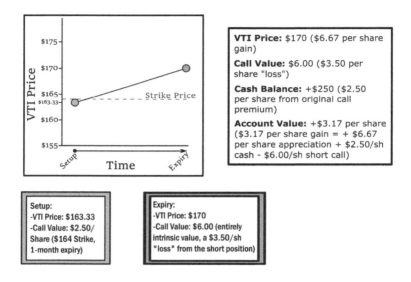

Sure, You can always let it get called and make your $3.17 ROI... but keep in mind it's a taxable event, and you'll miss out on the appreciation above your strike (the appreciation from $166.50 to $170 = $3.50) because you sold your right to attend appreciation party when you sold the call.

You can also BTC, but because you are short a call, *this incurs risk.* When you BTC an ITM call above upside breakeven, you are using money from the cash balance in your account and you are chasing profits. In the above example, same setup (buy 100 VTI at $163.33, sell a $164 strike call for $2.50), if VTI goes to $170, you're going to spend $6 per share buying back that call at expiration.

34.5 We Always Want to Avoid "Paying Into" Positions

Depending on your accounting methods, you really only spend $3.50 per share of your starting account value buying it back because you can use the original $2.50 call premium received, but make no mistake: *you still "paid into" the position.* This is not what we set out to do; as call sellers we should be making money selling premium, *not spending money buying it.*

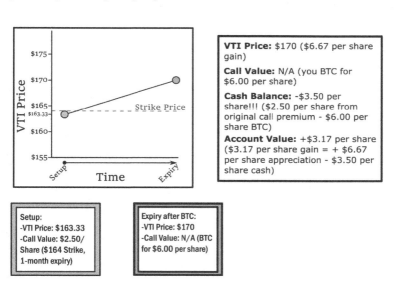

VTI Price: $170 ($6.67 per share gain)

Call Value: N/A (you BTC for $6.00 per share)

Cash Balance: -$3.50 per share!!! ($2.50 per share from original call premium - $6.00 per share BTC)

Account Value: +$3.17 per share ($3.17 per share gain = + $6.67 per share appreciation - $3.50 per share cash)

Setup:
-VTI Price: $163.33
-Call Value: $2.50/ Share ($164 Strike, 1-month expiry)

Expiry after BTC:
-VTI Price: $170
-Call Value: N/A (BTC for $6.00 per share)

So you might be looking at that scratching your head again and wondering "why does it matter? Account value still says $3.17 in green?

Academically, this is correct, but in the real world it only works if you sell your shares for the $6.67 gain at the same time. Your cash balance is liquid capital, unlike the $6.67 **unrealized** profits your VTI shares have now. And if you pay to BTC, you are adding money to your position that could immediately go away. The second the price of VTI shares drop, you are going to be losing $, and they will now only have to drop to $166.83 before you hit even (a price which is higher than the price you bought the shares for: $163.33).

Take a look at the cash balance: it is −$3.50 per share.

Consider it another way: In effect, **you paid $3.50 more for those shares.**[9] Your cost basis is now the original purchase price of $163.33 plus the $3.50 a share you paid in, for a grand total of $166.83 a share. *This is the opposite of using call premiums to reduce cost basis.*

34.6   The Risk of Paying Into Shares that Could Immediately Decrease in Value

To drive the point home, if you buy back your call on expiration Friday when VTI is $170, and the price of VTI plummets to $160 immediately after the trade clears, your $166.83 shares are now worth $160. You've effectively lost $683. Had you not "paid in" $3.50 per share, you'd only be down $3.33 per share.

---

[9]More precisely you added to the cost basis when you paid to relieve yourself of the obligation to sell the shares

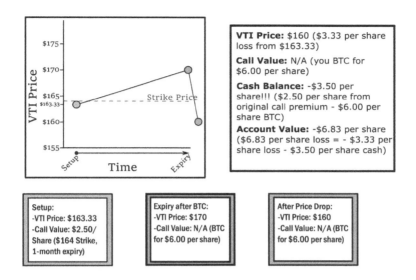

For these reasons, *I would not advocate a simple BTC in portfolio overwriting if the stock has moved past your upside breakeven. You typically want to roll so you aren't "paying into" your position.*

If you had sold a new call when you BTC, or left your original call in place, you would have gained something on this decline. One of the biggest benefits of portfolio overwriting is that small hedge you receive from the short call.

For those of you wanting an even easier rule to remember: just don't pay more into your position. You generally should be getting paid call premiums, and not paying more than you received (in premiums) to close those positions.

But buying back a call is just the first half of the story, because it is usually paired with simultaneously selling a new call to roll up...or out.

CHAPTER 35

Position Management– A Rising Price and Rolling UP

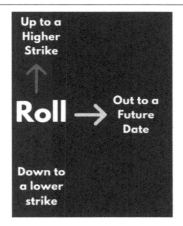

E already saw what happens with a rising price and buying to close, but what happens when we pair that with simultaneously selling another call? If the new call is at a higher

287

strike, it's a roll up!

Guess what? It's VTI chain time again! In this example, it looks like with a share price of $168.34, the 1-month $170-strike calls are going for $1.25 per share. If you buy 100 shares and sell a $170-strike call, and then the share price goes to $171, what is your account going to look like?

The Chain:

VTI		Q	VANGUARD TOTAL STOCK MARKET ETF $168.34 ↑ 1.43 (0.86%)				AS OF 4 10 00PM ET 01/16/2020 ↻ More Quote Information											
Last	Change	Bid	Ask	Volume	Open Int	Imp Vol	Delta	Action	Strike ▲	Action	Last	Change	Bid	Ask	Volume	Open Int	Imp Vol	Delta
...				CALLS					Feb 21 '20 (36 days)						PUTS			
4.86	0.00	5.40	5.80	0	75	13.31 %	0.7479	▾	164	▾	1.00	-0.30	0.95	1.10	1	19	13.00 %	-0.2478
4.38	+0.95	4.50	4.80	2	1,754	11.98 %	0.718	▾	165	▾	1.50	0.00	1.10	1.25	0	28	12.25 %	-0.2868
2.98	0.00	3.70	4.00	0	28	11.34 %	0.6698	▾	166	▾	2.01	0.00	1.30	1.45	0	8	11.60 %	-0.3347
2.90	+0.45	3.00	3.30	22	58	10.73 %	0.6124	▾	167	▾	1.64	-0.51	1.55	1.65	1	4	10.84 %	-0.3905
2.25	+0.58	2.30	2.50	11	37	10.08 %	0.5457	▾	168	▾	0.00	0.00	1.85	2.05	0	0	10.43 %	-0.4582
1.70	+0.28	1.75	1.90	15	18	9.70 %	0.4701	▾	169	▾	0.00	0.00	2.20	2.45	0	0	9.80 %	-0.5337
1.25	+0.35	1.20	1.35	72	79	9.06 %	0.3865	▾	170	▾	3.10	0.00	2.70	2.95	1	0	9.38 %	-0.6151
0.59	0.00	0.80	0.95	0	25	8.71 %	0.3038	▾	171	▾	0.00	0.00	3.10	3.60	0	0	8.62 %	-0.7072
0.55	+0.35	0.50	0.65	47	3	8.45 %	0.2271	▾	172	▾	0.00	0.00	3.60	4.30	0	0	7.58 %	-0.8141
0.30	+0.10	0.30	0.40	10	12	8.16 %	0.1584	▾	173	▾	0.00	0.00	4.70	5.10	0	0	8.43 %	-0.8484

The Setup:

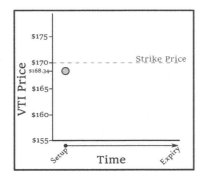

VTI Price: $168.34

Call Value: $1.25 per share

Cash Balance: +$125

Account Value: No change

Setup:
-VTI Price: $168.34
-Call Value: $1.25/
Share ($170 Strike,
36-day expiry)

Figure 35.1: *The Shade— orange for scale.*

After the Move:

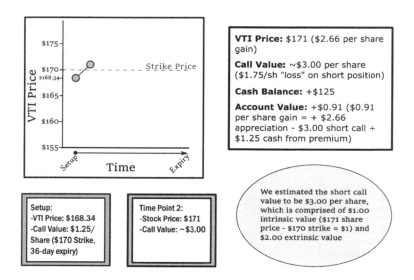

Setup:
-VTI Price: $168.34
-Call Value: $1.25/
Share ($170 Strike,
36-day expiry)

Time Point 2:
-Stock Price: $171
-Call Value: ~$3.00

We estimated the short call value to be $3.00 per share, which is comprised of $1.00 intrinsic value ($171 share price - $170 strike = $1) and $2.00 extrinsic value

VTI Price: $171 ($2.66 per share gain)

Call Value: ~$3.00 per share ($1.75/sh "loss" on short position)

Cash Balance: +$125

Account Value: +$0.91 ($0.91 per share gain = + $2.66 appreciation - $3.00 short call + $1.25 cash from premium)

Firstly, your sold call is now ITM. This is going to be a bit of a guess, but based on the extrinsic value in the first ITM call on the chain now, I'm going to *very roughly* ballpark that the $170 strike call you sold for $1.25 will now be worth about $3.00 per share.[1] Looking at the account, your VTI has a gain of $2.66 per share, but your sold call will show a loss of $1.75 per share.

---

[1]How did I do that? I took the first two ITM calls of $168 and $167 on the current chain and figured out that they each had about $2.00 extrinsic value. Ergo the $170 call in our scenario where VTI goes to $171 would probably also have about $2.00 extrinsic value, plus $1.00 intrinsic value (remember intrinsic value = share price of $171 minus strike price of $170 which is $1), which is $3.00. This is very back-of-the-napkin math, but it does the job.

35.1 Why Didn't We Make Our Max Profit?

But to keep things interesting, and layer on more real-world complexity, I made this price rise happen right away (instead of at expiration), and accordingly the call still has extrinsic value. As such, we show only a gain of $0.91, because that short call still has **a lot** of time value left, mitigating our gains from underlying appreciation.

That's way less than our expected maximum profit of $2.91[2]... but if we did wait until expiration and nothing changed, theta decay would remove the extrinsic value of the short call, leaving us with the max profit of $2.91 as below:

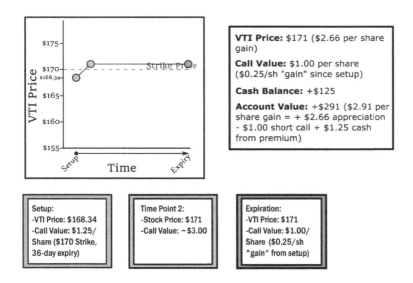

VTI Price: $171 ($2.66 per share gain)

Call Value: $1.00 per share ($0.25/sh "gain" since setup)

Cash Balance: +$125

Account Value: +$291 ($2.91 per share gain = + $2.66 appreciation - $1.00 short call + $1.25 cash from premium)

Setup:
-VTI Price: $168.34
-Call Value: $1.25/ Share ($170 Strike, 36-day expiry)

Time Point 2:
-Stock Price: $171
-Call Value: ~$3.00

Expiration:
-VTI Price: $171
-Call Value: $1.00/ Share ($0.25/sh "gain" from setup)

Notice how the extrinsic value decreased by $2 and we made $2 in

---

[2]$1.66 appreciation and $1.25 call premium

account value from that moment to expiration. One way to think of it is the extrinsic value "turned into" profit as we waited.[3]

But we aren't at expiration yet, we are still early in the contract period.[4]

If you wanna keep the shares, the only way to do that is to buy back (close) the call. The only question is, do you want to roll it **up**, effectively paying more to "reset" your covered call trade at a higher price? You totally can, and even though it is technically two separate options trades, it is usually best to do them simultaneously in case prices change between you closing one call and selling another one.[5]

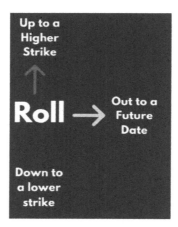

Before moving on, allow me to interject that this is also a form of chasing profits, thinking that your underlying will remain at the higher

---

[3]Intentionally repeating this concept here.

[4]I did this intentionally to show that unless you are at expiration, you may lose more money than anticipated when you BTC in the middle of the contract period. Too much volatility in the underlying could inflate extrinsic value to a level that is more than what you initially collected in premiums.

[5]This is if you want to roll. If your intent is to BTC and wait for some other underlying price move before selling another call, then simultaneous transactions would not apply.

price, and you are risking money by buying back the call to hold shares. Ergo, although I wouldn't normally recommend it for FIRE portfolio overwriting, I want to make sure anyone reading this knows what they are doing, and lay the groundwork for more intensive options strategy if you choose to journey beyond this book, or just desire a deeper understanding.

35.2   Brief Interlude

To keep our jargon straight, we need to remember the following:

- **Rolling up** is buying-to-close a call and simultaneously selling a call with a **higher strike** in the **same month**.

- When we **rolled down** we bought-to-close our call and sold another call at a **lower strike** in the **same month**.

- Rolling **out** implies a **later month**.

Figure 35.2: *Shade— eggplant for scale.*

35.3 A Rolling Up Example

Let's see a roll up in action. We guesstimated that with VTI at $171 the February $170-strike call is about $3.00 per share, so I'm also going to guesstimate that the $173-strike call is going to be worth about $2.15. So if you buy back the $170-strike call at $3.00 per share and simultaneously sell the $173-strike call for $2.15 per share, you'll end up paying $0.85 a share, or $85. That $85 will come out of your cash balance, and I find that the easiest way to track it mentally is some system of accounting similar to the diagrams I've drawn (I'm sorry, I myself never had a specific tracking spreadsheet or anything— I would share it if I did; it was always intuitive).[6] Below is what the account would look like after the roll:

---

[6]I'm not much for astrology, personality tests, or "Which DBZ character are you?" quizzes, but the Myers-Briggs INFJ (advocate) describes me perfectly, and my bent for intuition-based understanding.

Probably more Vegeta leaning when I was younger, kind of a Piccolo now (I'm probably deluding myself and would be described as a Yajirobe by people who know me).

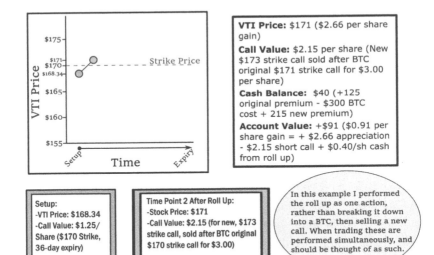

VTI Price: $171 ($2.66 per share gain)

Call Value: $2.15 per share (New $173 strike call sold after BTC original $171 strike call for $3.00 per share)

Cash Balance: $40 (+125 original premium - $300 BTC cost + 215 new premium)

Account Value: +$91 ($0.91 per share gain = + $2.66 appreciation - $2.15 short call + $0.40/sh cash from roll up)

Setup:
-VTI Price: $168.34
-Call Value: $1.25/ Share ($170 Strike, 36-day expiry)

Time Point 2 After Roll Up:
-Stock Price: $171
-Call Value: $2.15 (for new, $173 strike call, sold after BTC original $170 strike call for $3.00)

In this example I performed the roll up as one action, rather than breaking it down into a BTC, then selling a new call. When trading these are performed simultaneously, and should be thought of as such.

35.4   Was Rolling Up the Right Move?

Well, before we say yes or no, what exactly did we accomplish rolling up? The account value is still +$0.91 cents per share. The biggest thing we did for ourselves was raising our strike price to $173, which allows us the possibility of participating in more appreciation.

But raising the strike price to $173 wasn't free. We bought back that right using a combination of $0.85 of our cash balance and the new $215 premium from the $173-strike call. After spending $0.85 of our original $1.25 premium we only have $0.40 cash— that's the other big difference.

Note that suddenly we are buying the call, even though we were originally the call sellers. Most importantly, by converting cash to an asset (the call), we also assumed more exposure to the risk of the shares falling.

Yeah, so.... now that we know all that... was rolling up good?

Depends on what happens afterwards, really.

35.5   In the Case of the Share Price Remaining Elevated

If the price of the stock stays elevated but still below your new strike, then yes. You paid $85, but if the new call expires worthless, you get to keep the premium and the share appreciation becomes yours, because you are not obligated to sell the stock. Here's that scenario:

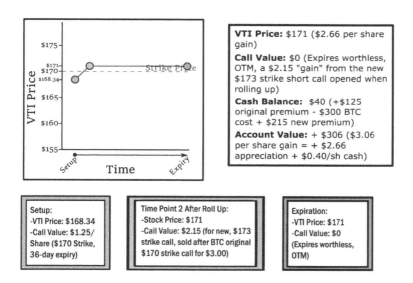

Seems pretty good right? Well, it would be even better if the shares went to $173, because you'd make another $2 appreciation, totaling

$5.06 for the month.[7]

But if the price falls right after you rolled up, or right after expiration, you paid $85 into something that quickly lost its value, which is no bueno. This should sound very familiar to the last article where we bought-to-close at a higher cost and the price dropped. This is because we did the same thing when we BTC as part of the roll up.

35.6   A Share Price Drop After Rolling Up

Let's explore a share price drop to $163 as an example:

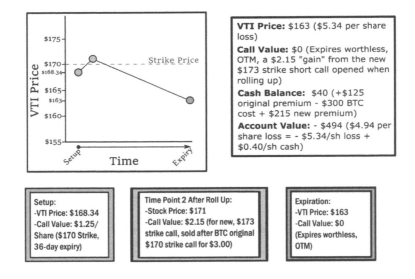

VTI Price: $163 ($5.34 per share loss)

Call Value: $0 (Expires worthless, OTM, a $2.15 "gain" from the new $173 strike short call opened when rolling up)

Cash Balance: $40 (+$125 original premium - $300 BTC cost + $215 new premium)

Account Value: - $494 ($4.94 per share loss = - $5.34/sh loss + $0.40/sh cash)

Setup:
-VTI Price: $168.34
-Call Value: $1.25/ Share ($170 Strike, 36-day expiry)

Time Point 2 After Roll Up:
-Stock Price: $171
-Call Value: $2.15 (for new, $173 strike call, sold after BTC original $170 strike call for $3.00)

Expiration:
-VTI Price: $163
-Call Value: $0
(Expires worthless, OTM)

Oh, gross. A $4.94 per share loss and barely any extra cash from where we started. If you hadn't rolled up, it would only have been a

---

[7]Practice calculating yourself! Hint: replace $2.66 per share gain in the above pic with $4.66. The call would still expire worthless if shares didn't exceed strike price.

$4.09 per share loss.[8]

Consider also, if the price rose again and you rolled up again. You'd keep paying in order to "buy into" share price appreciation, each time lowering your cash balance and adding to the cost basis of VTI shares, however you want to account for it. This could leave you with even more losses if/when VTI declines again.

Overall, this is why I don't like to only roll up much, but the good news is that you do have the option to roll out as well.

---

[8]This is because the full $1.25 per share premium would have been providing downside protection. Rolling up cost us some of that premium, and reduced its ability to hedge a downward price movement.

It is, however, still better than if we hadn't sold a call in the first place. Simply being long 100 shares of our index would have resulted in a $534 loss when the price went from $168.34 to $163.

CHAPTER **36**

Position Management— A Rising Price and Rolling

OUT

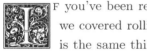F you've been reading along the path as intended, you know we covered rolling out after a price decrease— and yes, this is the same thing! But the math has different results when you pay into the BTC cost of the appreciated call to roll out. Hence, this is a different chapter with a different example.

Deja vu disclosure— I am copying the setup of the last chapter to illustrate that you always have multiple viable choices in the same scenario, and to allow you to compare and contrast what happens when you make different moves in the same context.

So let's say you really don't want to sell your shares. You love your shares, but you sold a call against your shares, and now it is ITM (In the Money). Maybe the account is taxable, or maybe you were gifted the shares and they have sentimental value. Maybe you think the shares are going to skyrocket soon, and you are hoping your option will expire right before they do. Whatever the reason, the only thing you can do at this point is to buy back the call or roll it. Last article we talked about the buying back (at a loss) to roll up, and now we'll talk about rolling out.

Guess what? Same setup as the last example! With a share price of $168.34, the 1-month $170 strike calls are going for $1.25 per share. If you sell one of those and then the share price goes to $171, what is your account going to look like?

VTI Chain:

VTI		Q	VANGUARD TOTAL STOCK MARKET ETF $168.34 ⬆ 1.43 (0.86%)			AS OF 4 10 00PM ET 01/18/2020 ⟳ More Quote Information											
Last	Change	Bid	Ask	Volume	Open Int	Imp Vol	Delta	Action	Strike ▲	Action	Last	Change	Bid	Ask	Volume	Open Int	Imp Vol	Delta
—				CALLS					Feb 21 '20 (36 days)						PUTS			
4.86	0.00	5.40	5.80	0	75	13 31 %	0.7479	▼	164	▼	1.00	-0 30	0.95	1.10	1	19	13 00 %	-0 2478
4.38	+0 95	4.50	4.80	2	1,754	11 98 %	0.718	▼	165	▼	1.50	0.00	1.10	1.25	0	28	12 25 %	-0 2868
2.98	0 00	3.70	4.00	0	28	11 34 %	0.6698	▼	166	▼	2.01	0.00	1.30	1.45	0	8	11 60 %	-0.3347
2.90	+0 45	3.00	3.30	22	58	10 73 %	0.6124	▼	167	▼	1.64	-0 51	1.55	1.65	1	4	10 84 %	-0.3905
2.25	+0 58	2.30	2.50	11	37	10 08 %	0.5457	▼	168	▼	0.00	0 00	1.85	2.05	0	0	10.43 %	-0 4582
1.70	-0 28	1.75	1.90	15	18	9 70 %	0.4701	▼	169	▼	0.00	0.00	2.20	2.45	0	0	9.80 %	-0.5337
1.25	-0 35	1.20	1.35	72	79	9 06 %	0.3865	▼	170	▼	3.10	0 00	2.70	2.95	1	0	9.38 %	-0.6151
0.59	0.00	0.80	0.95	0	25	8 71 %	0.3038	▼	171	▼	0.00	0.00	3.10	3.66	0	0	8.62 %	-0.7072
0.55	+0 35	0.50	0.65	47	3	8 45 %	0.2271	▼	172	▼	0.00	0.00	3.60	4.30	0	0	7.58 %	-0.8141
0.30	+0 10	0.30	0.40	10	12	8 16 %	0.1584	▼	173	▼	0.00	0.00	4.70	5.10	0	0	8 43 %	-0.8484

Setup:

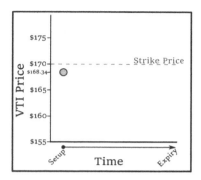

VTI Price: $168.34

Call Value: $1.25 per share

Cash Balance: +$125

Account Value: No change

Setup:
-VTI Price: $168.34
-Call Value: $1.25/
Share ($170 Strike,
36-day expiry)

After rise (still same as last chapter):

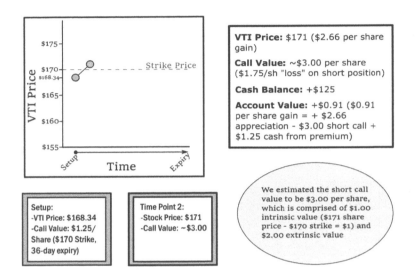

VTI Price: $171 ($2.66 per share gain)

Call Value: ~$3.00 per share ($1.75/sh "loss" on short position)

Cash Balance: +$125

Account Value: +$0.91 ($0.91 per share gain = + $2.66 appreciation - $3.00 short call + $1.25 cash from premium)

We estimated the short call value to be $3.00 per share, which is comprised of $1.00 intrinsic value ($171 share price - $170 strike = $1) and $2.00 extrinsic value

Setup:
-VTI Price: $168.34
-Call Value: $1.25/
Share ($170 Strike, 36-day expiry)

Time Point 2:
-Stock Price: $171
-Call Value: ~$3.00

Firstly, your sold call is now ITM. This is going to be a bit of a guess, but based on the extrinsic value in the first ITM call on the chain now, I'm going to ballpark the $170 strike call you sold for $1.25 will now be worth about $3.00 per share. Looking at the account, your VTI has a gain of $1.66 per share, but your call will show a loss of $1.75 per share.

But you don't want to get rid of your shares, and even better you think that VTI is going to drop back down in the next couple months— what's an options wizard to do? You're not big into paying more money to trade covered calls (they are supposed to make you money, not cost you money), so the roll up alone isn't appealing.

But what about a roll OUT?

36.1 Brief Interlude:

- Remember rolling **OUT** means buying back a call and then selling another call with the **same strike** at a **further out expiration date**.

- Rolling **UP** is buying-to-close a call then simultaneously selling a call with a **higher strike** in the **same month**.

- When we rolled **DOWN** we bought-to-close our call and sold another call at a **lower strike** in the **same month**.

36.2 Roll Out Dough

So what is a roll out, and how do I make money off of it? When you roll out, you are adjusting your strike price forward in time by buying-to-close your current option and selling the same strike option for next month. Since that option is farther out, it has more time-value, and is going to pay you more!

Whenever you roll out, you are collecting more premium by selling more time value.

36.3 Timing a Roll Out: Sooner is Often Better than Later

Sidenote— if your option is too deep ITM, it won't have a lot of extrinsic value, and rolling out is usually a breakeven proposition. Why? The bid-ask spreads get wider and less solvent, and deeper ITM and further OTM calls have less extrinsic value, so you barely make any more premium. This is why *if you are going to adjust your position, you usually have to do it while your strikes are close to the money for it to make sense.*

So we have our stock we bought for $168.34 that appreciated to $170, and our $170 strike call that we sold for $1.25 that is now worth $3.00 (a $1.75 loss to us). But hey, those $170 strike calls in March were going for a smooth $2.40 (lower midpoint of the $2.35–$2.50 bid-ask) when we set up our trade.

Last	Change	Bid	Ask	Volume	Open Int	Imp Vol	Delta	Action	Strike ▲	Action	Last	Change	Bid	Ask	Volume	Open Int	Imp Vol	Delta
—				CALLS					Mar 20 '20 (64 days)						PUTS			
6.30	-0.70	6.40	6.80	1	67	13.65 %	0.6992	▾	164	▾	1.85	-0.35	1.80	2.00	10	31	13.68 %	-0.3027
4.80	0.00	5.60	5.90	0	186	12.90 %	0.6691	▾	165	▾	2.80	0.00	1.90	2.20	0	19	13.23 %	-0.3363
4.82	+0.42	4.90	5.20	61	237	12.63 %	0.6302	▾	166	▾	3.00	0.00	2.25	2.45	0	15	12.67 %	-0.3727
4.10	+0.40	4.20	4.58	1	1	12.22 %	0.5891	▾	167	▾	3.20	0.00	2.50	2.70	0	5	12.07 %	-0.4135
3.05	0.00	3.50	3.80	0	6	11.66 %	0.5447	▾	168	▾	3.12	-0.22	2.85	3.10	7	2	11.78 %	-0.4599
2.96	+0.53	2.85	3.10	41	1	11.04 %	0.4955	▾	169	▾	0.00	0.00	3.20	3.50	0	0	11.33 %	-0.5096
2.31	-0.26	2.35	2.50	17	438	10.68 %	0.4427	▾	170	▾	4.00	-0.85	3.60	3.90	2	36	10.77 %	-0.5641
1.58	0.00	1.80	2.00	0	1	10.22 %	0.3864	▾	171	▾	0.00	0.00	4.10	4.40	0	0	10.37 %	-0.6213
1.15	0.00	1.40	1.60	0	5	9.99 %	0.332	▾	172	▾	5.20	0.00	4.70	5.00	100	0	10.12 %	-0.6778
0.00	0.00	1.00	1.20	0	0	9.53 %	0.2737	▾	173	▾	0.00	0.00	4.50	5.70	0	0	7.96 %	-0.7902

After the share appreciation to $170, that March $170 strike call is probably going to be worth around $3.95 (this is a rough estimate— just roll[1] with it).

---

[1] Pun intentional.

Looking at your account, you have a $3.00 Feb $170 call showing a $1.75 loss, but you also see the March $170 call is going for $3.95. Why not roll out? You'll simultaneously buy back the $3.00 Feb $170 strike call and sell the March $170 call, netting you $95 into your account and giving VTI another month to do nothing, or potentially pull back below the strike price. Here's how that would look:

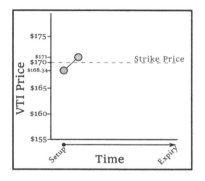

VTI Price: $171 ($2.66 per share gain)

Call Value: $3.95 per share (New $170 strike 64-day expiry call sold after BTC original $170 strike call for $3.00 per share)

Cash Balance: $220 (+125 original premium - $300 BTC cost + 395 new premium)

Account Value: +$91 ($0.91 per share gain = + $2.66 appreciation - $3.95 short call + $2.20/sh cash from roll out)

Setup:
-VTI Price: $168.34
-Call Value: $1.25/Share ($170 Strike, 36-day expiry)

Time Point 2 After Roll Out:
-Stock Price: $171
-Call Value: $3.95 (for new, $170 strike 64-day expiry call, sold after BTC original $170 strike call for $3.00)

In a world where everything works out for us, VTI would decrease to $169.99 on expiration day. In fact, *the best reason to roll out would be when you want to increase upside breakeven, are anticipating a decline back below the strike, and are patient enough to wait until expiration day while call value erodes away.*

If VTI stayed at $169.99 (below $170 strike), we'd get to keep the whole $3.95 plus the appreciation from $168.34 to $169.99 as below:

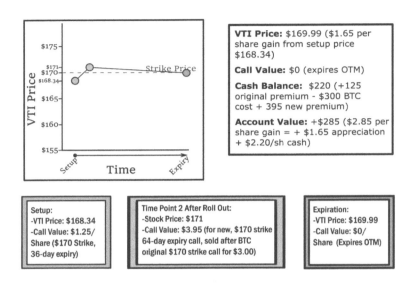

VTI Price: $169.99 ($1.65 per share gain from setup price $168.34)

Call Value: $0 (expires OTM)

Cash Balance: $220 (+125 original premium - $300 BTC cost + 395 new premium)

Account Value: +$285 ($2.85 per share gain = + $1.65 appreciation + $2.20/sh cash)

Setup:
-VTI Price: $168.34
-Call Value: $1.25/ Share ($170 Strike, 36-day expiry)

Time Point 2 After Roll Out:
-Stock Price: $171
-Call Value: $3.95 (for new, $170 strike 64-day expiry call, sold after BTC original $170 strike call for $3.00)

Expiration:
-VTI Price: $169.99
-Call Value: $0/ Share (Expires OTM)

Seems pretty snazzy, right? We didn't lower our cash balance[2] when we rolled up, and we actually got paid by selling more time value, and we increased our upside breakeven to $173.95...right? And our max profit to $5.61 (appreciation from $168.34 to $170, plus $3.95 premium)... right?

---

[2]Never forget that we always want to avoid "paying into" a position when portfolio overwriting.

Unfortunately no. Once we rolled, everything changed. Here's the setup, price rise, and BTC laid out. I'm separating the roll into the two separate transactions of BTC and selling a new call to highlight the fact that we decreased our cash value and accrued a loss the moment we BTC the ITM call:

SETUP	
SHARE PRICE	$168.34
CALL VALUE ($170 STRIKE, 30 DTE CALL)	$1.25
CASH	+$1.25
ACCOUNT VALUE	NO CHANGE

SP TO $171	
SHARE PRICE (+$2.66 APPRECIATION)	$171
CALL VALUE	$3.00
CASH	+$1.25
ACCOUNT VALUE ($2.66 + $1.25 - $3 = +$0.91)	+$0.91

BTC	
SHARE PRICE	$171
CALL VALUE	N/A
CASH ($1.25 - $3.00 = -$1.75)	-($1.75)
ACCOUNT VALUE ($2.66 - $1.75 = +$0.91)	+$0.91

The moment you BTC, you are actually negative $1.75 per share. You've booked a cash loss to "buy into" the appreciation and uncap your gains. The instant you sell to open the new call[3] this negative cash balance is remedied, but the loss is carried forward.

Although the new 60-DTE call you sold was worth $3.95 per share, the $1.75 negative cash value offsets it, leaving you with $2.20 cash.

BTC		STO 60 DTE	
SHARE PRICE	**$171**	**SHARE PRICE**	**$171**
CALL VALUE	**N/A**	**CALL VALUE** ($170 STRIKE, 60 DTE CALL)	**$3.95**
CASH ($1.25 - $3.00 = $1.75)	**-($1.75)**	**CASH** (- $1.75 + $3.95 = $2.20)	**+$2.20**
ACCOUNT VALUE ($2.66 - $1.75 = +$0.91)	**+$0.91**	**ACCOUNT VALUE** ($2.66 + $2.20 - $3.95 = +$0.91)	**+$0.91**

---

[3] This will be simultaneous if you are putting in the buy to close and the sell to open as one order with you brokerage

So your new upside breakeven[4] is only $2.20 over the strike, or $172.20. Additionally, your max profit is now only $3.86, as illustrated below.[5]

STO 60 DTE	$171 @EXPIRY	$173.95 @EXP
SHARE PRICE $171	SHARE PRICE $171	SHARE PRICE $173.95
CALL VALUE $3.95 ($170 STRIKE, 60 DTE CALL)	CALL VALUE $1.00 ($170 STRIKE CALL)	CALL VALUE $3.95 ($170 STRIKE CALL)
CASH +$2.20 (– $1.75 + $3.95 = $2.20)	CASH +$2.20	CASH +$2.20
ACCOUNT VALUE +$0.91 ($2.66 + $2.20 - $3.95 = +$0.91)	ACCOUNT VALUE +$3.86 ($2.66 - $1 + $2.20 = +$3.86)	ACCOUNT VALUE +$3.86 ($5.61 - $3.95 +$2.20= +$3.86)

If you are ok with the returns from the roll, this jives more with the passive style of overwriting that I would recommend for beginners that are paper trading (and maybe beyond if it fits your demeanor).

---

[4] Remember, this is the price the stock can be where our surplus cash received from call premiums can close a short call.

[5] The third picture here is serendipitously chosen with the share price at $173.95 at expiry. This is meant to illustrate that it results in the same max profit as a share price at $171 at expiry, but it is above your upside breakeven, as your $220 excess cash balance is insufficient to BTC a $3.95 call. Point is, the new $3.95 premium cannot be used alone for upside breakeven or maximum profit calculations if it is part of a position that has been adjusted (rolled). Part of the $3.95 premium was "spent" when you BTC the first call.

36.4   A Price that Continues to Rise After a Roll Out

What if the price rises even after you roll out? It means you're not psychic, but don't worry, that's normal. You can roll out again. You could also let shares get assigned, and I personally lean towards this option— I often won't roll out more than one or two months into the future when overwriting.[6] Keep in mind that when you rolled out, your return per month decreased (you went from $3.00 premium for one month to only $3.95 for two months, drastically decreasing your per-month returns), and the same thing will happen if you roll out again. You can check the math if you want— it's the time value inequality we've seen before.

And what if you roll and the price drops? Your sold call will be much cheaper, and you can buy it back cheaper, but you darn well better have been keeping track of how much you had been paid in premiums thus far, and compare that to the BTC cost. Read on to see why...

36.5   BEWARE THE ROLL!!!!!

As an intro to the chapter How to Lose Money with Calls let's do a little accounting. Say you did the roll out, got your $95[7] and are waiting until expiry. Maybe some time in the interim your sold call declined in value to $2.50, and you think the market is about to rally so you BTC (buy-to-close) that call. It looked like you had made $1.45 on the call when it's value decreased from $3.95 to $2.50. But guess what? You just lost $30!!!

---

[6]You can imagine how keeping track of P/L gets very messy very quickly.

[7]You paid $300 to BTC and got paid a new $395 premium, so the transaction shows +$95 overall when you actually perform the roll

36.6   Wait/Wut/How?

This should be familiar from previous examples as a concept, but here's what happened explicitly:

You initially got $1.25 (when you got paid your first call premium), but you then paid in $3.00 (to close that contract), then got another $3.95 (to sell a contract in March), then paid in $2.50 to close. So: $+1.25 - 3 + 3.95 - 2.50 = -0.30$

If you didn't follow the math, go back and reread it over and over again until you do, or it will cost you later.

You can also note that in the previous time-series tracking the roll, your cash balance is only +$220 after rolling out. As such, spending $250 BTC is a $30 loss.

Now that I've warned you, it's time to go over our last (and possibly my favorite) choice for position adjustment— rolling up and out. It's a combination of the two prior rolls, and a good way to get paid to roll up while still increasing your strike price— something that usually costs you money as an option seller. Also, this is going to be the last numbers-heavy, how-to chapter, so you can rejoice that the hard stuff is almost over!

CHAPTER 37

Rolling Up and Out

Eady for some real alchemy? Some real multi-dimensional call acrobatics? Time to combine the Roll Up and Roll Out into the chimera that is rolling up and out.

Deja-vu disclosure— this is the same setup as the last few articles.

Guess what? It's VTI chain time yet again! Looks like with a share price of $168.34, the 1-month $170 strike calls are going for $1.25 per share. If you sell one of those and then the share price goes to $171, what is your account going to look like?

Rolling Up and Out

The Chain:

		VANGUARD TOTAL STOCK MARKET ETF			AS OF 4 10 00PM ET 01/16/2020											
VTI	Q	$168.34 ⬆ 1.43 (0.86%)			More Quote Information											

Last	Change	Bid	Ask	Volume	Open Int	Imp Vol	Delta	Action	Strike ▲	Action	Last	Change	Bid	Ask	Volume	Open Int	Imp Vol	Delta
				CALLS					Feb 21 '20 (36 days)						PUTS			
4.86	0.00	5.40	5.80	0	75	13 31 %	0.7479	▼	164	▼	1.00	-0.30	0.95	1.10	1	19	13.00 %	-0.2478
4.38	+0.95	4.50	4.80	2	1,754	11.98 %	0.718	▼	165	▼	1.50	0.00	1.10	1.25	0	28	12.25 %	-0.2868
2.98	0.00	3.70	4.00	0	28	11.34 %	0.8698	▼	166	▼	2.01	0.00	1.30	1.45	0	8	11 60 %	-0.3347
2.90	+0.45	3.00	3.30	22	58	10 73 %	0.6124	▼	167	▼	1.64	-0.51	1.55	1.65	1	4	10.84 %	-0 3905
2.25	+0.58	2.30	2.50	11	37	10 08 %	0.5457	▼	168	▼	0.00	0.00	1.85	2.05	0	0	10 43 %	-0.4582
1.70	+0.28	1.75	1.90	15	18	9 70 %	0.4701	▼	169	▼	0.00	0 00	2.20	2.45	0	0	9.80 %	-0.5337
1.25	+0.35	1.20	1.35	72	79	9 06 %	0.3865	▼	170	▼	3.10	0.00	2.70	2.95	1	0	9.38 %	-0.6151
0 59	0.00	0.80	0.95	0	25	8 71 %	0.3038	▼	171	▼	0.00	0 00	3.10	3.60	0	0	8.62 %	-0.7072
0.55	-0.35	0.50	0.65	47	3	8.45 %	0.2271	▼	172	▼	0.00	0.00	3.60	4.30	0	0	7.58 %	-0.8141
0 30	+0.10	0.30	0.40	10	12	8 16 %	0.1584	▼	173	▼	0.00	0.00	4.70	5.10	0	0	8.43 %	-0.8484

The account after a price rise (we skipped the setup pic and went straight to this)

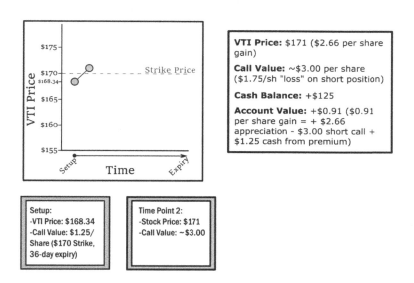

VTI Price: $171 ($2.66 per share gain)

Call Value: ~$3.00 per share ($1.75/sh "loss" on short position)

Cash Balance: +$125

Account Value: +$0.91 ($0.91 per share gain = + $2.66 appreciation - $3.00 short call + $1.25 cash from premium)

Setup:
-VTI Price: $168.34
-Call Value: $1.25/ Share ($170 Strike, 36-day expiry)

Time Point 2:
-Stock Price: $171
-Call Value: ~$3.00

Firstly, your sold call is now ITM. This is going to be a bit of a guess, but based on the extrinsic value in the first ITM call on the chain now, I'm going to ballpark the $170 strike call you sold for $1.25 will now be worth about $3.00 per share. Looking at the account, your VTI has a gain of $2.66 per share, but your call will show a loss of $1.75 per share.

You want to roll up, but you don't want to pay into your position. You want to roll out, but you'd rather have a higher strike price in case of more appreciation. What is an options wizard to do? Combine the arcane techniques by rolling up and out!

First, you look to the future's horizon and see that the farthest out you can sell calls for VTI in this example is June— there aren't any option chains past that month. On setup, the June $175 strike call was worth $2.20 per share, but that was when VTI was $168.34. Now that VTI is $171, the June $175 strike call is most likely going to be worth about $4.70.

		CALLS						Jun 19 '20 (155 days)			PUTS							
10.42	0.00	11.50	12.00	0	108	14.86%	0.7339	▾	160	▾	3.50	0.00	3.00	3.30	0	699	15.32%	-0.288
9.50	0.00	10.80	11.20	0	69	14.68%	0.7142	▾	161	▾	3.35	-1.05	3.20	3.50	1	90	14.98%	-0.3063
8.12	0.00	10.00	10.40	0	24	14.31%	0.6951	▾	162	▾	4.80	0.00	3.40	3.70	0	3	14.58%	-0.3259
7.80	0.00	9.30	9.80	0	40	14.06%	0.6738	▾	163	▾	6.10	0.00	3.50	3.90	0	84	14.03%	-0.3452
7.27	0.00	8.50	8.90	0	80	13.74%	0.6517	▾	164	▾	6.00	0.00	3.80	4.20	0	1	13.84%	-0.3682
6.88	0.00	7.80	8.10	0	32	13.36%	0.6285	▾	165	▾	4.40	-1.10	4.20	4.50	1	101	13.69%	-0.393
6.99	+1.09	7.10	7.40	10	79	13.08%	0.6033	▾	166	▾	4.70	-0.30	4.30	4.70	2	10	13.04%	-0.4162
5.50	0.00	6.40	6.70	0	127	12.73%	0.5768	▾	167	▾	4.99	-1.15	4.80	5.10	101	102	12.99%	-0.4445
4.53	+0.37	4.50	4.90	33	348	11.89%	0.4882	▾	170	▾	6.19	-3.01	5.80	6.20	100	12	11.84%	-0.5338
2.20	+0.35	2.15	2.40	65	135	10.57%	0.3203	▾	175	▾	10.50	0.00	8.40	8.80	0	14	10.37%	-0.7049

So take your $3.00 ITM call showing a $1.75 loss and trade it in for a further-dated $175-strike call going for $4.70 per share by rolling up and out! You'll get another $1.70 in your account, your new strike price will be $175, and your new upside breakeven will be $177.95.[1]

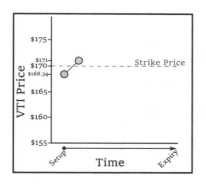

VTI Price: $171 ($2.66 per share gain)

Call Value: $4.70 per share (New $175 strike 155 day expiry call, sold after BTC original $170 strike call for $3.00 per share)

Cash Balance: $295 (+125 original premium - $300 BTC cost + 470 new premium)

Account Value: +$91 ($0.91 per share gain = + $2.66 appreciation - $3.95 short call + $2.20/sh cash from roll out)

Setup:
-VTI Price: $168.34
-Call Value: $1.25/ Share ($170 Strike, 36-day expiry)

Time Point 2 After Roll Up and Out:
-Stock Price: $171
-Call Value: $4.70 (for new, $175 strike 155-day expiry call, sold after BTC original $170 strike call for $3.00)

---

[1]Why not $179.70? It's a $175 strike plus a $4.70 premium, isn't it?

It is, but because you rolled you have to subtract the BTC cost from your received premiums. You were paid $1.25 for the first call you sold, BTC for $3.00, then sold a new call for $4.70, so $1.25– $3.00 + $4.70 = +$2.95 premium received, in total. $175 strike plus $2.95 premium = $177.95.

Another way to figure this out would be to add the $175 strike and the new $4.70 premium, and then subtract the $1.75 loss from BTC. $175 + $4.70 − $1.75 = $177.95

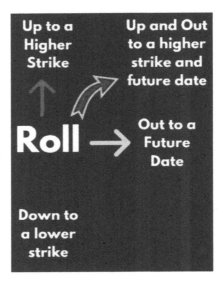

37.1   I'm a Fan

Overall, I really like rolling up and out. *Aside from not having to pay
from your starting cash balance to raise your strike price, the other
great benefit is that if there is a pullback in share price, your new,
farther OTM strike may lose extrinsic value and experience theta decay
at a much faster rate, often allowing for a profitable BTC.*[2]

Also make sure that you are tracking the cost basis of shares, because when you rolled up you effectively "paid into" them. The last
thing you want to do is BTC at more than they are worth just because
the short call looks like it shows a gain. That would make you feel
really dumb (it made me feel extraordinarily dim when I realized I had
been doing it).

---

[2]For this reason I would advocate holding on to your premiums instead of
spending them right away— in case you want to BTC.

37.2   Not for Everyone

But rolling up and out requires A LOT of patience, because it locks you into a position for longer. For a trader selling covered calls on actively traded stocks, this can be an issue, but as a FIRE-style index investor Boglehead, this should be one of your superpowers... so utilize it!

Remember that if shares of VTI close at $174.99 you get to keep the premium and your shares, and up to the upside breakeven of $177.95 you could BTC without using capital from your account. If shares drop, you get to keep the premium, and as an index investor you wouldn't care anyway— you know the drop is fake news (temporary in the long run).

Furthermore, if shares kept going up past your breakeven you would've made appreciation of $6.66[3] ($168.34 to the strike of $175) plus the premium of $2.95 ($1.25 from the initial call sale, plus $1.70 on the roll up and out), totaling $9.61/share. $961 is 5.7% of $16,834 (the original cost of 100 shares of VTI you needed to own in order to sell the covered call).

Where I come from, compounding a 5.7% return every 7 months is nothing to sneeze at. That's not even considering if you rolled again when June came around, or were able to BTC and then sell again, hitting a 2-for-1. Just to reiterate ad nauseum, remember to be careful when you BTC rolled calls, as the accounting can fool you into thinking you've made a profit if you aren't tracking your moves closely just like we saw in the last chapter.

---

[3]This is an unintentionally metal profit.

37.3   You Can't Keep Doing This

Word of warning: you should not expect to be in the habit of rolling up and out forever.

Firstly, not all indexes have LEAPS (options that go two years into the future) so you may only be able to do this a couple times before being stuck waiting or closing your whole position.

Secondly (and yes, this is the third time I'm saying it in this chapter), although rolling up and out may not look like it is costing you anything, you are using the premium from the new, farther up and further out call to pay for (buy into) the appreciation that made your first call end up in the money. To properly account for this, you need to add the amount you "paid into the roll" to the shares' cost when you BTC the short call.[4]

Thus concludes the last technical and trade-heavy article of the book. Time to move on to some housekeeping before we wrap up, starting with words of warning about how to lose money.

---

[4]Or just avoid it all and stick to No-Action overwriting.

CHAPTER 38

How to Lose Money Overwriting

---

ortfolio overwriting is not a silver bullet, and you can easily lose money if you don't know what you are doing.

Full Stop.

Repeat: you can lose money. I don't think that the options education out there sufficiently emphasizes and explains how. Aside from upside risk and downside risk, there are other, less straightforward ways to lose money. Oddly enough, most of them manifest when you are trying to actively manage your positions... so much so that I often wonder if No-Action Overwriting is truly the way to go?

I may never reach a conclusion on that philosophical dilemma. But in the meantime, we will explicitly cover the ways to make your account shrink with bad covered call trading.

Before I go into the specifics I want to point out that rolling (unless it generates enough premium to cover the cost-to-close) will always cause an initial loss because you "buy into" positions. Theta and appreciation may offset and eventually overtake that loss over time, but any time you pay into a position, it is in a way a "loss" if, after accounting for premiums received, it decreases your cash balance below where it was when you sold the initial call.

38.1   Rolling Risks

Firstly, let's criticize rolling down again. Rolling down can easily lock you into a loss. So easily, in fact, that I never roll down my index covered calls to a strike below cost basis. Whatever premium you received should have been enough when you set the trade up.

Further, even if the price of the underlying asset falls and you have to wait months for your shares to come back to their cost basis, you should be able to flex those passive FIRE investor muscles in the interim. Unless you are actively monitoring, adjusting, and rolling up and/or out constantly before price appreciation overtakes your strike; then you will find yourself in the money, and at a loss (that was a very intentional double entendre).

Rolling up has a different risk: you are paying into your position and raising your cost basis. Compare this to the idea of lowering your cost basis over time with call premiums – it's the exact opposite! Like I said, in general, we don't want to pay into our trades in the portfolio overwriting world. For other strategies, there are fitting times to adjust positions and pay into options, but for the purposes of FIRE overwriting I don't think it's a good habit to get into. You are gambling more money, hoping that you retain whatever appreciation made you roll up in the first place, and a simple drop in the security price can make whatever you paid into the position quickly evaporate.

Rolling out, or up and out, tends to keep you from paying cash from your account into your positions (but always realize you are still "paying" with the time value and original premium when you BTC and roll). This is generally better than rolling up alone. But you can only roll up and out so many times before you run out of months to roll to, and you eventually end up ITM. As a general rule, for the explicit goal of monthly income generation via portfolio overwriting, rolling out past a 90 DTE (expiration) usually isn't worth your time (literally).

Another problem is that the risk of loss for these adjustments shifts into the "lost profits" category. Why? Because of time value inequity. *The further into the future you roll, the less call premium per day you get.*

38.2   Time Value Inequality

This idea behind time value inequality is readily apparent if you take the premium for a call and divide it by the number of days until expiry, and then compare it to a longer-dated call. That premium per day will decrease substantially for longer-dated calls. Ergo, when we roll out or up and out, the total premium we receive will be less per day than the call we initially sold. And remember, it is the initial premium received plus the premium received when you rolled, **less the cost to BTC the first call.** It is not the total value of the new sold call. You will have technically "paid into" the new position with the initial premium received and potentially some of the new premium when you roll. You will need to recalculate expected ROI and decide if you are OK with the lower number before you make the trade.

38.3   Clerical Errors

Bad accounting can also be a risk when you are deciding whether to
BTC positions early. There are multiple examples in prior chapters,
but we will rehash it again here in case you aren't reading sequentially
or you need a refresher. After a roll, your new sold call's value in
your account is not equal to the amount of premiums you received
in your account, *if you are considering it to be a continuation of the
same position you had when you sold the first call.* You "paid into it"
when you rolled, and therefore closing it early may actually cause you
to spend more closing something than you made from theta decay.

From the earlier chapter: If you sell a call for $1.25, but it becomes
in the money and appreciates to $3.00 (a $1.75 loss to you), then roll
to a $3.95 contract at a later date, you would have only received $1.25
plus $0.95.[1] So, receiving $2.20 in premiums is good, but if you close
out that $3.95 position at any point before theta decay pares it down
to $2.20, you are losing money.

38.4   Losing Money By Biding Time

Finally, we need to dip into path-dependence, which is a consideration
of how the order of events (price moves) affects investment returns.
Consider the following time series. You buy VTI at $150 in January
and sell a call. It drops to $130 and stays there all year. Meanwhile,
you wait patiently for the share price to come back to your cost basis
of $150. Then, in December, it starts to rise. When it hits $150 you
get excited and sell a call again, capping your profits. It keeps going
up and ends at $180 for the year.

---

[1] In fact, the roll itself would only show a +95 transaction when you placed
the combination trade as a single order to BTC one call and sell to open another,
because you pay $300 to close and receive $395, netting you $95.

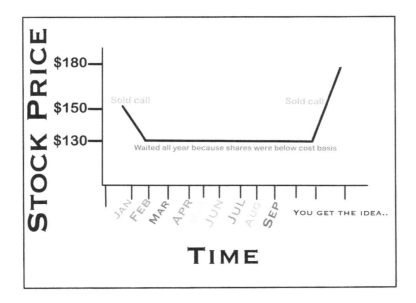

So, VTI did well for the year— it made 20%. You, as the call seller, didn't hit that mark, and only made two call premiums. This illustrates a lot of things to consider about how stocks make money, especially when considering when exactly to buy and sell. The first takeaway is that the first month when the index dropped, portfolio overwriting was a win. Secondly, if your cost basis was low enough that a $130 call was still OTM,[2] you could still have been selling calls and making premiums all year.

Third, buy and hold wins just from the one major move at the end of the year.[3] We saw an idealized example of this followed by an

---

[2]One nice thing I've noticed about portfolio overwriting for FIRE is that due to continuous dollar-cost averaging, most of the time your cost basis will be below market value.

[3]This is because the long shares are long volatility and delta positive, whereas a short call is the exact opposite. Selling the short call pays us to give up that one big, potential win in exchange for the smaller, certain return.

immediate dose of reality in the chapter on overwriting and returns. Because you don't know how the market will move, but as a Boglehead you do expect it to trend up, portfolio overwriting all your shares of something you have a long-term bullish outlook on would be counter-intuitive.

By extension, we also know that indexes pull back often, either as part of normal variance or due to the occasional financial crisis. Allocating a portion of your portfolio to covered calls will basically diversify your investments into an asset that outperforms ordinary shares on those pullbacks. So there is some serious logical financial justification[4] to be found beyond just income generation when it comes to portfolio overwriting (if you are looking for it).

Although this drastic move isn't the most common behavior for the total market, the concept is the key. But as you will see in the next chapter, we can try to minimize loss from these situations. I also introduce one more way you can get stuck trading covered calls.

---

[4] And just as many counter-arguments.

CHAPTER **39**

Martingales and Ladders

F you've been reading through, you might notice that I advocate not stressing over "lost profits" for portfolio overwriting shares. If I ran an investment fund with maximum profits in mind, this wouldn't fly. But since I am a retail investor like most of you, we don't need to maximize profits. We only need to hit 25x, and some extra monthly premiums on the way to FIRE are a completely different and completely attainable goal.

But missing out on upside can become a serious risk over time! Constantly buying lots of VTI at a higher price could potentially leave you stuck if you don't have enough cash to chase the rising price.

Imagine, if you will:

39.1   Running Out of Options

An investor with some fresh options wizard skills finally gets their first lot (100 shares) of VTI and rushes out to sell a call. Let's say VTI is $145 today (they have $14,500 in shares) and they sell an ATM $145–strike call for $200 ($2 per share). Everything is hunky dory, and VTI shoots up to $160 the next morning.

This options wizard doesn't mind much, and lets the shares get called, happy with the extra $200 in premiums and happy having sold shares for $145, which was above their cost basis in this imaginary example.

But the next Monday after shares were called, the options wizard is kind of screwed— their account has $14,500 from proceeds of the shares' sale, and $200 in premiums for a grand total of $14,700... but VTI costs $160 a share! Without $16,000 the options wizard can't buy another lot and sell another call!

This inability to buy more shares and sell more calls is similar to the Martingale betting strategy. You've probably heard of the Martingale betting system but not by that name— it is basically just doubling down, "knowing" that eventually you "should" win. Eventually, the gambler runs out of money and is unable to double down, and loses. In our case, the call seller without enough funds to buy another 100 shares and sell another all is similarly stuck, because he/she could not increase cost basis ad infinitum.

Worse, let's say that this happens consistently, month after month, and the options wizard is continually missing out on these $10 per share appreciation moves. After a year they missed out on $120 per share gains, $12,000 if they had just held their shares! Is this a disaster? What went wrong? This portfolio overwriting was supposed to be a good thing?!?!

Before you give up hope, a few things to realize, and some ways to avoid this. Firstly, a consistent rate of \$10/month gains in VTI from a starting price of \$145 is pretty unlikely.[1] VTI goes up, but unless it just crashed the move typically isn't that drastic, and we are holding it forever. So when consistently overwriting, the pullbacks and down months will become your friend. The US market seems to always go up over time... but it does like to go down a lot, too.[2]

39.2 Don't Sell Calls Against All Your Shares

Secondly, I would never recommend overwriting all your shares. In fact, I would say never overwrite more than half your shares if possible. Keeping it to less than 20% is probably optimal,[3] but that's just an empirical claim I'm making from experience. The more shares you own, the more calls you can sell, and the higher strike price you can sell them at to make a "meaningful" premium. Remember, that's the Mustachian secret weapon! We don't need to make % returns every month, we're just trying to make enough that it is meaningful to what should already be an otherwise frugal lifestyle,[4] or enough to buy more shares and speed up achieving FIRE.

Whatever the reason, trying to generate income when you don't need it can change the game drastically. To that point, overwriting

---

[1] Anything can happen.

[2] There is actually some evidence for skewed kurtosis in stock market returns. A bit complicated math–wise, but basically there may be more frequent down days, but as I understand it the magnitude of the less frequent up days more than compensates for it. That said, I've read conflicting information about this, which is surprising considering one would think it would be a pretty objective statistic.

[3] The less the better. This is a side hustle that you shouldn't let get in the way of FIRE. Everyone has a unique situation, so there's not a magic number.

[4] The beauty of compounding and FIRE is getting to watch compounded growth returns slowly overtake fixed costs of living if we can just manage to stay off the Hedonic Hamster Wheel.

doesn't even need to be something you consistently do. If you have a fear of losing out on any appreciation at any given time, then maybe for you overwriting is an infrequent thing. Maybe you only sell one or two calls a month, more for fun than anything else.

Selling calls could also only happen for you en masse when you think the market got excited and ran up too much. Or selling calls could be a life vest for when you have a serious need for some immediate income, and would rather chance a pullback or flat month than sell some of the nest egg shares outright. That's all up to you as an individual investor.

39.3   Ladder Those Calls!

Thirdly, there are different philosophies on when to sell your calls. The academic answer is that you should always sell calls at the beginning of the contract cycle. In theory, this maximizes the time value you receive in your premium.[5]

I disagree.

If you have 4 lots of shares you are planning to sell calls against, what's the problem with selling one the first week of the month, one the second week, a couple the third week... maybe even for next month's expiration in order to get the premium you want?

Answer: absolutely nothing.

This is a common practice known as "laddering". Laddering is great— it smooths out some uncertainty and gives you more access to call selling opportunities. More importantly, it is emotionally easier to handle (for me at least). Maybe the first call you sold wasn't optimal,

---

[5]It literally says this as a sky-is-blue capital-T Truth in one of the most well known standard academic textbooks on options. This is weird to me— it seems too simple; it lacks nuance.

Also, that textbook, like most on options, has precisely zero wizard cartoons.

but the next one could take advantage of the new circumstances. I find that I simply don't feel like I "missed out" as much when I ladder my calls across different dates and strike prices.

Since there are 4 weeks in each contract period, I often sell 25% of my calls the first week, 25% the next week, etc. I may sell further dated calls[6] to get the premium I want. If calls I sold have ended up in the money in the interim, I may roll them up and out, and as a result refrain from selling more calls next month in order to keep a healthy % of shares uncovered.

If I had a set in stone system, I'd tell you! Unfortunately this is something that, as far as I can tell, requires too much flexibility to be that rigorous. There is no secret formula to always maximize profits. You have to experiment and learn what works for you!

39.4   It's Not That Hard

Fortunately, I've found that it's not hard to make extra returns selling calls once you understand them and are familiar with how they work. *Managing positions, laddering and adjusting how far OTM you sell your calls are all levers you can pull to adjust your income/returns.* It's entirely possible to increase your returns over time pretty regularly without compromising the total market appreciation you are relying on for FIRE (Financial Independence/Retire Early).

Now that you know everything I know and have all the advice that I have... it's time to start putting it all together.

---

[6] 40–60 day calls usually provide a nice premium without losing too much to time value inequity.

CHAPTER 40

Putting It All Together

To buy 100 shares of VTI or some other index fund. [1]

Look at the options chain, and pick a strike price. Your decision will be based on the return you expect to make, what you think the underlying shares will do, and how much you want to manage your position.

Sell your covered call. Notice the money immediately deposited into your account. Maybe think of the guy that wrote this book on how to do this.

Watch the underlying and your sold call until expiration as much or as little as you want. If it goes down, wait and let your call expire,

---

[1] Or a stock you love if you aren't a Mustachian/Boglehead and still managed to get ahold of this book.

or buy it back. If it stays the same, watch time value eat away at your sold call as it slowly becomes profitable and let it expire worthless, or buy it back when you've made a satisfying profit from the call premium. If the underlying goes up, then let shares get called, or close out at a loss to retain appreciation, or roll up, out, or up and out. Figure out what works for you.

Repeat.

Use the extra money for whatever you like. Have a slightly cushier path to FIRE, or buy more of your index funds and speed up the process. Use your new skills, enjoy the rewards (monetary and otherwise), and try to make the world a better place.

Finally, some closing thoughts.

CHAPTER 41

In Closing

Figure 41.1: *It's a celebration! In case you didn't know, the options wizard has 2 cats.*

ou made it!

You know what an option is.

You know how to read an options chain.

You know how to sell covered calls.

You understand position management (rolling, closing or letting shares get called).

41.1   What Next?

If you only listen to one thing I say– let it be this: practice first.

Practice is the only way to honestly assess your skills. Unfortunately, you also need to know that practice is not the same as actually trading with your money, and never can be. Things get tricky when you are risking your cash; your emotions get involved.

That said, practice.

Do it with a spreadsheet, or better yet, get a free paper trading account.[1] Better still, sell covered calls on a lower priced stock before doing it with VTI. Even if you aren't a stock picker, trading on paper doesn't compare to trading with real money. No matter what you think, comparing the two is a fallacy. It would be akin to believing that reading about swimming can prepare you to jump into the ocean.

Hear me three times: practice.[2]

One of the interesting things about investing is that it has an objective measure, akin to weightlifting or dieting. There's a number, it doesn't lie to you. Unfortunately, objective measures can be hard to process for some people, but honestly self–assessing will always make you better in the end. Don't make any excuses– the numbers will be right in your face, exactly how much you've made or lost, so don't

---

[1] At the time of writing this, TD Ameritrade has a great app with a paper trading feature. This is my uncompensated, unbiased opinion.

[2] This is a reference to my favorite novel, Name of the Wind by Patrick Rothfuss. A great read, would recommend.

argue with them.[3]

After that, you'll be as ready as you can be to do some real portfolio overwriting.

41.2 Enjoy It

The first time you get a premium deposited in your account, it's a unique feeling. Having worked my whole life (since the age of 15), it was a thrill getting paid by making some clicks! It really motivated me to learn more and get good at it.

You're probably going to learn really quickly what you don't know. Then you're going to realize that I couldn't cover everything. You're also going to realize that there's no silver bullet, that there's an element of luck, and that it is possible to make some extra returns off of your index investing. If you want to pre–empt a lot of mistakes, find comfort in the fact that I made them myself when I was more into active investing and wrote about them in this book in the final supplemental chapters. You don't have to read them now (or at all), but you might be able to learn from my mistakes.

I hope some subset[4] of the FIRE community finds and appreciates this— I've always wanted to contribute to the movement. Frugality and the goal of financial independence have dramatically improved my life.[5] I came to Mustachianism relatively recently, long after I had been trading calls, and alchemically binding the two has always

---

[3]This should hint to you why I became a mostly Mustachian index investor after years of options trading. Also why I still sell covered calls against indexes, and not much else.

[4]I know this will likely not be everyone's cup of tea. The world can be a churlish place, so please be recognize this book is a genuine attempt to share what I know and find useful, and as such I implore you to be anodyne with any feedback.

[5]One of the biggest benefits was all the extra time you have for the important things in life when you aren't constantly trying to beat the market. Life is short— spend it with friends and family and doing things you love, not seeking alpha.

seemed natural to me. Hopefully someone agrees with this (mostly) reformed active investor.

Until then, have fun with selling calls.

And Good Luck!

Figure 41.2: *My "good luck" maneki neko collection. Feel free to soak up some good fortune vibes from it.*

CHAPTER 42

Supplement – Emotionally Intelligent Investing Part 1

Figure 42.1: *"Most of my problems in life come from confusing what I want and what I need"*—- *David Foster Wallace. If you haven't heard his 2005 Kenyon College commencement speech "This is Water" I'd highly recommend it. I revisit it often.*

42.1   When Investing, You Need
a Destination.

ver try to achieve something unfamiliar? Pop psychology and motivational literature will tell you the importance of concrete goals, and they're right. "Stop eating fast food and prep all your lunches" is superior to the nebulous "eat healthier". "Do thirty minutes of cardio three times a week" is better than "exercise more".

Not only does a discrete destination allow you to better map out your approach, but actionable goals also make you more likely to move in the right direction because it's easier to measure your progress objectively. Investing is no different – you need a plan. That plan needs to suit you and your goals.

FIRE adherents use the 25x rule and the 60%/12 year savings rate[1] as concrete goals. They recognize that they are much more likely to meet those quantitative goals than if their plan was just "save more" and "spend less". I'd like to apply this thinking to covered call selling.

So what is our goal? Not maximizing returns.[2]

Yep, I said it.

Chasing alpha (alpha is investing lingo for a return in excess of the returns of the overall market) as high as you can take it is a fool's errand in portfolio overwriting. In a world of retail investors vs quants, it's like using a javelin to hunt deer when the competition has heat–seeking missiles... and oddly enough, most of the time, simply

---

[1] Per networthify.com's free early retirement calculator— a great tool to play with.
[2] We covered this already a few times. Funds set aside for portfolio overwriting are transmuted into a primarily "income generating" investment with the *potential* for capital appreciation to the strike, fundamentally different than growth-focused, long-term, buy-and-hold index investments.

owning the market wins over time.[3]

42.2 The Less You Want, The Freer You Are

Besides the buy-and-hold superpower, there is another major advantage the FIRE crowd has over the typical investor. We are shooting for a fixed number, i.e., 25–30x spending. This is a much more achievable and mentally less burdensome goal than "maximum profits" or "infinite returns". Don't jump on that hedonic treadmill— it doesn't go anywhere!!! Money should allow you to do what you want and be a means to an end, rather than an end itself.

The early retirement methodology is not about acquiring as much wealth as possible, only what is needed to separate yourself from a traditional income stream. Likewise, portfolio overwriting is not an options trading strategy that is leveraged for huge returns, but rather a means to generate modest income from held shares.

42.3 So What Should We Aim For?

Enough.[4]

So how much is enough? Before you figure out a number, you actually need to do some introspection. Setting goals requires you to

---

[3]I strongly encourage you to read about Buffet's big bet, detailed in the 2016 Berkshire Hathaway shareholder letter. It is available free online, with the big bet story starting on page 20 of the pdf under the heading "The Bet (or how your money finds its way to Wall Street)." Of note, one can deduce that Renaissance technologies did *not* participate in this challenge because they usually do beat the market. They are an outlier.

[4]See Kurt Vonnegut and Joseph Heller's conversation on the topic

balance income you wish to generate with a trading strategy you can stick to.

The "sticking to" part is hard, but it's the best way to keep from making bad decisions, and it lets you assess your results if you transparently track your returns. Without an internalized method, there's a big chance you'll do bad things. You might average up your positions, or roll calls down, or close calls you rolled up for an overall loss. But eventually, if you avoid past mistakes and repeat what works, I think you'll do well.

Consider the tradeoff.[5] How much time and emotion do you want to put into learning and trading and what do you expect to get out of it?

To me, the effort spent learning options was not effort, and I had the time. Trading can be fun, and portfolio overwriting does not require a lot of position adjustment if you lean towards selling further OTM calls like I do.[6] For you, that may not be the case, and that's ok as long as you know your predilections.

42.4   To Thine Self, Be True

This all involves a good amount of self-surveying. You need to consider how good you are at a few of the hardest pieces of investing. You'll see that most of them boil down to patience, confidence, and not chasing profits.

How good are you at waiting? Can you hold off on buying and selling calls until your index is at or above your cost basis, or will you grow impatient and sell calls below cost average and risk assignment at a loss?

---

[5]Instead of ROE (Return On Equity, more appropriate for companies) I think in terms of the much more human ROH— Return on Hassle/Headache.

[6]Honestly it takes me less than an hour a month.

How good are you at doing nothing? If the underlying moves past your call strike, can you let the shares get assigned at a call that meets your percent return goals with appreciation, or will you want to roll because you are "missing out" on profits? Can you wait and see if the underlying falls back below the strike before expiration without stressing about it?

If you do roll up and out, how long are you willing to hold a covered position? Can you wait until the underlying drops again and you can BTC? Alternatively, will you handle it well if the underlying moves past your strike yet again, leaving you with no more months to roll up and out to?

If you are patient, most of these issues won't be a problem. If you aren't chasing maximum profit, most of these issues won't be a problem. If you are confident in your trading plan, your ability to stick to it, and are satisfied with the returns you are targeting, then most of these issues won't be a problem.[7]

42.5 So How Much Money is Enough?

Do you need to sell calls at the first strike above the current price for maximum premium (and do you need the stress of movements every day until expiration)? Or do you need the peace of mind of selling 2-month calls at a higher, farther OTM strike, garnering less returns? Is there an immediate financial need in your life, or are the returns from portfolio overwriting merely a "bonus" to your net worth?

---

[7]If you are a mustachian at heart, the problems outlined in this section shouldn't affect you. It's more of a warning to people portfolio overwriting individual stocks, or FIRE adherents with a gambling inclination that might be tempted by the dark arts of active investing and excessive position management.

42.6   How Does Your Personality Play Into the Returns You Want?

Do you need to be an investing genius that seeks alpha at every opportunity, or do you need to come to terms with the fact that you are not Jim Simons, not Spencer Greenberg, not Benoit Mandelbrot, not Ed Thorpe, not Nassim Taleb, but instead a learned, responsible investor with a safe plan that he/she has the discipline to stick to? [8]

42.7   Considering All That, Let's Look at Some Numbers:

Typically the farther OTM you sell calls, the less active trading you have to engage in (because the shares are less likely to reach the strike and require adjustment). So you can either make more selling closer ATM calls that require more time, or you can make less and spend less time position adjusting. Returns and effort are factors you can balance to suit your individual needs.

Alternatively, if you are comfortable having your shares assigned, you can devote less time to adjusting positions (a strong argument for trading within an IRA). You can just sell calls and not look at your account until it is time to sell calls again.

---

[8]I know that I personally want to be perceived as clever, and I have to actively keep that desire in check.

Figure 42.2: *This is a picture I took of some ghost pipes in the Cuyahoga National Forest. The are a mycotrophic wildflower. They can't photosynthesize, but have almost all the same structural features as a regular flower. Mushroom hunting is a wonderful hobby that is free and gets you outdoors, and sometimes lets you take pictures that do a good job filling an awkward blank space in the pages of a book you are writing. Dysart woods is definitely the best place to mushroom hunt in Ohio. It is one of the oldest growth forests in the state, and has off-the-charts biodiversity. I would recommend going in early fall the day after it's had some rain, and taking only pictures.*

With those things in mind, let's look at the different choices of what call to sell on the chain below:

For illustration's sake, let's say Investors A, B, and C all have acquired 10 lots (100 shares per lot, 1,000 shares total) of VTI, and can therefore sell 10 calls each month.

42.7.1 Investor A

Investor A wants the maximum returns and loves to trade, so Investor A always sells the ATM strike. She also loves to get the most out of extrinsic values, and thinks it is best to just capture all the time premium now, so she sells calls against all her shares today, about 5 weeks out. So investor A gets $2,500 in her account right now.

Investor A Advantages

- Maximum immediate returns from the premium, that do not require shares to appreciate

- Typically the most downside protection and extrinsic value

- Better opportunity to collect two premiums in the contract cycle if the share value decreases quickly and then increases in value again.

Investor A Disadvantages

- Loses money to upside risk (lost profits) as soon as VTI shares appreciate

- Misses more lucrative opportunities to sell calls if the price of the underlying rises during the contract period

- Will require either a lot more management, or the ability to let shares get called. But we said she loves to trade, so no big deal!

42.7.2 Investor B

Investor B doesn't like to trade as much. He finds it stressful. He already has a well-paying job and a low cost of living, and good habits with regards to spending.

As such, the reduced stress and the ability to have just a few more dollars each month is the goal. If he sells ten of the $176 calls for $0.70 per share, that extra $700 would take his lifestyle from a frugal lunch–packing, dinner–cooking, bike–riding Mustachian lean to a couple fun nights out a week or (god forbid) a few good lattes from the local coffee shop, or maybe even a couple baller vacations each year! For Investor B, an extra $700 a month is enough.

Investor B Advantages

- Less stress managing positions (that is, if you consider position management a stressor like we said investor B does, or you simply don't have the time)

- Potential of high returns from price appreciation. If the shares do go all the way from $171.60 to the $176 strike, that's a 2.5% monthly return ($4,400 on $171,600 to be exact).

- Farther OTM calls undergo theta decay faster. He could close out sooner and leave shares uncovered, or possibly go two–for–one if the underlying rises after BTC.

Investor B Disadvantages

- Less than one-third the monthly premium of Investor A (this is not necessarily a disadvantage; we stated $700 a month was enough for him)

42.7.3   Investor C

Investor C kind of likes to trade, but from a position of comfort. Investor C also knows that a lot can happen in a month. Investor C suspects that the investor A textbook mindset of "capturing the maximum premium because there is the most time value" might not be true. Although the future is a mystery, a $2 increase in VTI would offset all of investor A's premiums.

Investor C also knows that BXY, the 2% OTM index actually beats the S&P depending on the time horizon and transaction cost assumptions. Investor C doesn't know how to program backtesting, but did a lot of paper trading and found that no strategy based on specific numbers and percentages worked every time, so they spread out their call selling, known as "laddering". Always OTM and above cost basis, Investor C sells a couple calls for $173 strike at $1.90 a share and a couple at $175 strike for $1.00 a share. Next week, they'll maybe sell a couple more at a higher strike if the stock moves up. Or maybe sell the call for the next month out to get more time premium if VTI has declined.

Investor C Advantages

- Calls are "spread out", with more opportunity to pick a favorable strike

- Emotionally easier for some, because all the eggs aren't in one basket with one strike price

- More flexibility within the strategy

- Lots of trading opportunities (investor C enjoys adjusting positions)

Investor C Disadvantages

- Harder bookkeeping

- Less concrete trading strategy

Whether you are an A, B, or C, or some other combination or permutation, just remember that you need to balance your returns – what you consider to be enough – with what you want, and what you can handle as an investor. If you do some trading, you'll find out quickly what does and doesn't work for you.

Figure 42.3: *Pholiota squarrosa, aka shaggy scalycap. Also found in the Cuyahoga national forest.*

CHAPTER 43

Supplement – Emotionally Intelligent Investing Part 2

Few more random musings on emotional investing, and some embarrassing stories about yours truly. These are mostly tales about my active investing foibles, something I barely partake in anymore aside from managing my "legacy" positions[1] from my past life as an active trader.

---

[1]These are positions that are comprised of "free" shares bought with proceeds from other strategies, or positions so large that liquidating them would cause to experience seriously dangerous levels of regret and emotional instability if the "went to the moon" after I sold out.

43.1   When You Look at the Market, How Does It Make You Feel?

Until I learned options trading, the prevailing emotion surrounding trading was somewhat helpless.[2] All I could do was buy something, wait, and hope it went up. Unfortunately, some of the best investments don't go up for a long time, or they have major pullbacks on irrelevant news, or no news at all. You can weather the storm with extreme confidence, but if you run out of cash or your account value drops, no amount of confidence will fix it. When actively trading, I always remind myself of what John Maynard Keynes purportedly said, "Markets can stay irrational longer than you can stay solvent."

Figure 43.1: *The notorious JMK. Did you know he wrote a book on the philosophy of probability?*

And even if I held a security and it did go up, then it was time for me to fret about when to sell.

---

[2]The funny thing is now that I'm mostly an index investor, I've come full-circle and am Zen about the whole thing. "Zen" is probably the nice way to say "not worried about not being in control" if you're a Stoic.

This was the recurring theme for me (and I'm guessing it is for the majority of investors) until I found out about options trading. Covered calls were like manna from heaven for me because they allowed me to "cash in" on some of the gains without exiting my position, and it was *very* appealing to me. Selling calls also offered some downside protection in the event of a share price decline, so even better!

The sense of control and the alleviation of trying to predict a good exit point[3] or trying to concoct some strategy of stop-loss orders made the whole experience so much more pleasurable that I started to learn everything I could about options. After I understood covered calls, I learned about puts, the inverse instrument. Puts allow you to enter positions more cheaply, or protect you from share price decline, or place a limited–risk bet on a stock's value decreasing. Fast forward past about a decade of trying to beat the market with options and here I am, typing to you about indexing and selling the occasional call for income.

Additionally, selling calls can alleviate macro fears about the market. Afraid that the US market will stagnate and have minimal or no growth in the next decade? Great news buddy! Covered calls win out over buy and hold in those scenarios! It's nice having an alternative plan for the periods when being a Boglehead flounders.

Even more to the point, the premiums you receive are usable immediately[4] (only recommended if you don't mind assignment) opening even more doors for you. If your underlying rose enough you can simultaneously buy a put and call to create a collar, which will lock in profits and make you money on the downside, or buy another call in

---

[3]Selling an ITM call after appreciation from your cost basis is, in a way, a surrogate for profit-taking that features the possibility of retaining your shares, if you think about it.

[4]If your account has very little extra cash, I wouldn't recommend spending premiums until the contract expires, as you may not have the funds to buy-to-close if the opportunity presents itself.

anticipation of a further move up. The possibilities are near limitless with options.[5]

43.2   Be OK With Your Plan. The Good News Is That This Plan Suits the FIRE Crowd

To the point of redundancy: don't do anything you emotionally can't do. The first application of this if you are overwriting is not selling calls on anything you wouldn't own anyway. This is one of the main reasons I am approaching portfolio overwriting in a way that jives with the FIRE/index investor community. Over time, the market wins, and there is a large movement of people who are completely happy buying and holding VTI forever, convinced that they don't care what happens in the short term... which is exactly the indifference needed to be good at portfolio overwriting.

That said, there are other schools of thought and types of covered call selling strategies out there. Some traders buy different stocks and sell different covered calls each month, but this monthly churning requires a different type of discipline, namely no attachment to the underlying (this is actually how I started trading options, way before I found MMM). Honestly, I'm not convinced that it's the best way to sell covered calls – it may be, I just haven't decided and I didn't log wild success over the long run when I was done experimenting with it.[6]

---

[5]But surprisingly the simplest and first one I ever learned, covered calls, is the only one that worked consistently and made sense to take with me on the path to FIRE.

[6]I had some dangerously good streaks. Dangerous because it motivated me to stay in the game long after the streak ended. I am intentionally using the term "streak" to parallel the idea of a winning streak in gambling.

Imagine you buy 100 shares of something, sell a call, and then shares plummet. Then you are either closing out at a loss (difficult) or holding onto something you don't want to be holding onto in the first place, waiting for the price to appreciate back to breakeven (also difficult). Further, the 1–4% a month you make on 4 covered call trades might get entirely wiped out and then some by share price depreciation of the fifth. In summary, the risk/reward seemed off to me, so I don't trade that way anymore.

43.3   Minimize Regret

> *If you want to know what someone really thinks, observe their actions, not their words. Unless someone has lived through a specific scenario, their opinion about it is meaningless.*
>
> *Scars signal skin in the game.*
>
> —Nassim Nicholas Taleb

The above quotes from Taleb are there to illuminate why I want to regale you with tales describing how I'm not a perfect investor.

I've read my fair share pop psychology books that synthesize studies on human emotions. One theme that rings true to me from my own life experience is that people tend to emphasize bad experiences more than good ones. I apply this axiom to my trading in ways that reduce my chances of having a long–term regret. Here's what I've learned:

Firstly, I have learned to always leave room to run. I initially learned this when selling covered calls, and the lesson was reinforced when selling diagonal calendar spreads (selling a call against a call you own instead of against shares you own— explained more in the next paragraph).

When you sell a covered call, you need to be ok with the underlying getting called at that price. After trading on some riskier securities, I learned I am much happier if I leave some shares uncovered. Reason being, I want to be able to participate in any run-ups in price above the strike of the call I sold, and/or sell another call after a major run–up. These steep rises in price selling covered calls that I missed out on were typically only 10–20% gains. But as you will see, you miss out on much larger gains trading diagonals because of the leveraged nature of long calls. The following personal experience really pounded the lesson into my thick head.

Diagonal calendar spreads are one of the most interesting forms of options trading. Probably one of the most complex, too. When you trade a diagonal it's a lot like a covered call, but you don't own any stock. Instead of owning stock and selling calls against it, you own a call and sell calls against the call you own.

With that background on diagonals, it's story time about capping gains! My big epiphany about leaving things uncovered came in the form of missing out on big gains twice, in rapid succession. I know that book learning can teach you the theory, and paper trading can teach you the mechanics and allow some testing. All well and good, but nothing makes you learn better than doing. As such, I decided to commit a large portion of my tradeable retirement to a limited margin IRA to try different options strategies. Cheaper than the cost of formal education, and honestly less money than I could save if I were a real ramen noodle–eating bike riding Mustachian badass, I deemed it worth the cost even if I lost it all. My investment was $25,000.

43.4   Great Picks, Poor Choices

I had purchased a few LEAP calls for DXCM around the time it was in the $110–$130 range, and some AMD LEAPs when it was floating in the $25 range. Silly me sold short term calls against all of these LEAPs at or shortly after the time of purchase, effectively capping profits. I was learning diagonals, and didn't know better.

Unfortunately, I was about to learn the hard way. When DXCM hit $150, selling a call against my LEAP and locking in the $1,500–$2,000 profits per call seemed great, and when AMD hit $35, the same $1,000 return per call sounded nice (especially considering the lower cost LEAP I purchased to enter the trade). The problem was that when AMD hit $59, I had to look at the long call value up more than $2,500 each (10% return on my original entire account value per call) and just accept the fact there wasn't much I could do. If that doesn't sound frustrating enough, DXCM went up... and up... and up some more to a high of $400. That represents roughly $25,000 return on each long call (you know, just a measly 100% return on my account per call, of which I had 3!) and I knew I couldn't participate in any of that.

43.5   The Takeaway

So I learned if I am trading with an inherent long bias, I don't cap all my profits.

As such, trading with an inherently bullish bias on VTI, never sell calls against all your shares or you might miss out and regret it.[7]

---

[7]Yes, I realize the total US market doesn't typically double or triple in value over the course of a few months, but the lesson is still applicable. Over time you could miss out on long-term compounded gains.

43.6   Minimize Regret with Negative Visualization

Familiar with stoic philosophy? I sure am! Ever since MMM recommended A Guide to The Good Life by William B. Irvine, I have run through a few books on the topic and picked up some solid insights. The most pragmatic and actionable one is probably negative visualization.[8]

This is the great Stoic thought experiment you can try at home! Are you afraid of a bad thing happening? Imagine the bad thing happening. In theory, this is supposed to make you familiar, comfortable with, prepared for, and indifferent to said tragedy.

For me, it was less effective as the "exposure therapy" it was intended to be, and actually more of a useful way to "test" how I would feel under different outcomes. This is different than the "exposure therapy" negative visualization was originally intended to be. I use negative visualization to aid in decision making – namely to minimize regret. I first imagine myself dealing with the outcomes of decision A and the outcomes of decision B.

But I don't do what most people do by trying to pinpoint what would bring me the most joy or "happy feels". Instead, I think about which situation would lead to the most regret, and typically avoid that one like the plague.

I'm not sure if this works for everyone, but it works pretty well for me. As an example of how it applies to trading, I sometimes would keep positions open that I had lost on but still hold the potential for profits. I used to have a small penny stock account that I would trade in roughly $50–$200 increments almost purely for fun/small returns. If I bought $100 worth of stock and the position decreases 75% to

---

[8]Malorum Praemeditatio

$25, I usually considered the opportunity of reinvesting the $25 better allocated to the potential of a rebound, and avoiding the bad feelings that come with missing out and locking in a loss. To be clear, I do not recommend you hold on to shares like this– it's just something that I did.

It was in fact horrible, irrational investing. Reasonable if you are trying to protect yourself emotionally...but if you're doing things like that, you probably shouldn't be actively investing!

43.7   Story Time Part Deux!

I learned this lesson with EMIS,[9] probably my best trade to date in terms of % return. I immediately bought 500 shares at a price of 50 cents per share when I dispensed Eligen at work one day. (I'm a pharmacist in real life.) This company I had never heard of potentially circumvented the need for B12 injections in anemic patients lacking intrinsic factor! I found out when I got home that they didn't market it as an FDA approved drug. As such, sales lagged due to a lack of traditional reimbursement, and I forgot about the shares I bought for years. Until one day I noticed my penny stock account went up by a few thousand dollars.

Turns out EMIS partnered with a big pharma to develop an oral semaglutide (a drug to regulate blood sugar in diabetics) using their carrier molecule technology.

Additionally, Eligen had become a bestselling Amazon product. At the time of writing, it was going for $60 a bottle ($2 a pill). I sold enough to make back my initial $500, plus $500 at $2 per share price. Although they are traded on the OTC market and don't regularly

---

[9] I am comfortable mentioning an individual ticker here because Emisphere pharmaceuticals has since been acquired, and is no longer a tradeable ticker.

report financials, making it difficult to assess enterprise value, I decided
to keep some shares for fun. It eventually went to $10, and I was able
to use that to pay for part of my pre-wedding honeymoon.

So I felt smart (in reality lucky), and validated (in reality lucky). I
was also 100% sure that if I had missed out on that run it would have
made me kick myself until my foot (or ass) fell off. In fact, I'm still
sad I didn't buy more back in 2012, but c'est la vie.

43.8   Leave Some Wiggle Room

Depending on your interests and affinities, once you are able to trade
and consistently make money from calls (only losing on upside potential), I would not advocate close position tracking and trading strategy
analysis unless you personally want to do it and find it fun/rewarding.

To put it another way, breaking down your trading strategy to
the point that you construct a system of explicit fixed rules is usually
a Sisyphean task. The movements of the stock market are random
enough to render most schemes invalid over time, and maximizing
returns is best left to the quants.

Much better would be laddering strikes. Much easier to manage
would be setting attainable goals (consistently making some extra disposable cash whilst not selling shares at a loss), and simply seeing how
your account value has changed over time. You can always sequester
your portfolio overwriting shares to a different account and compare
it's performance to the underlying index if you desire.

43.9   How Much Are You Making, Mr. Options Wizard Writer Guy?

Have I sat down and figured out my returns vs buy and hold? Yep—roughly. They're usually on par, more often a bit more, sometimes a bit less than VTI, depending on the time frame.[10] But it's only part of my investments; most of my index funds are in a retirement account

---

[10]I want to address why this isn't plastered on the front of my book, but rather near the end in a footnote.

People who are looking for a "how much have you made over time" are in search of a consistently profitable long-term trading strategy. I'm not claiming or selling that— it doesn't exist, and as you probably know the closest thing we have is index investing.

What I am describing is the way to sell a call and get paid cash in your account for doing it. If your cost basis is above the ATM strike, you might not be able to make much, if anything. Some months, your index might go past your strike and your shares may get called, causing your overall position to lag buy-and-hold.

This book details every aspect of that, but I am reticent to suggest "make $X per month consistently forever" because there's not a works-every-time way to do so. The unfortunate thing is that some people want that, and if they are desperate enough to believe anyone who gives them what what they want, there will be no shortage of people that will have absolutely zero qualms selling it to them. I'm lucky to be in a position where sales of this book are not my source of survival, so I can engage in this type of poor marketing, which comes with the benefit of genuine (albeit unprofessional) communication that the type of person I am appealing to will likely appreciate, and maintains my ability to sleep at night.

Selling calls generates income. If you sell strikes above cost basis, your account may lag your underlying index, but you won't *lose* money you have. Overall, this seems like a pretty good deal to me.

With that out of the way— it's usually + or – 5% vs buy–and–hold over years I've been able to compare. When the market is flat, I do a bit better than buy-and-hold. When the market rises too fast and surpasses the strikes of the calls I sold, I do worse. It's how calls work— it's not rocket science. This does not include use or reinvestment of premiums. Over longer time periods, it trends toward +0.25% to 0.75% per month, which jives with our 0.5% per month goal,

It's horrendously complicated to figure out. I've been selling calls for about a decade, recently shifted most of it from individual securities to index funds, and have unfortunately spent a fair amount for daily expenses, mortgage, etc. I also used to try lots of other options strategies in my accounts. And I have 3 tradeable investment accounts. And I don't always reinvest my premiums (In the past I usually spent them or used them to fund other strategies, which sometimes have stellar returns or complete losses).

I can't trade.

More importantly, I haven't factored in the utility of the premium. Using it to buy more shares of the underlying index and the compounding returns. Or using premium to buy long calls, and returns if those pay off. Or the interest costs I've saved by using premiums to make extra principal payments on car loans, mortgage payments, student loans.[11]

And even if I rigorously did that math, it wouldn't take into account the non–monetary returns. The satisfaction I derive from knowing that I can trade options. Or the emotional security of knowing that I can generate income independent of an employer. Or the fun I simply have trading and adjusting positions in the casino that I access from my phone.[12]

Simply put, I am comfortable with some level of ignorance because I'm happy with the current results. The aggregate benefits outweigh the negatives for me so much that I don't obsessively track returns in the way lots of active traders do. I'm doing well and making extra premiums— what else could I want out of life?[13]

Most importantly, selling covered calls is not meant to beat buy and hold index investing over the long run.[14] I never claimed it did, and almost nothing does over the long run. Most of my retirement and

---

[11]We need to change the student loan system. Not only is it the one type of loan you can't declare bankruptcy on, but my interest rate after consolidating is greater than 6.5%. I know student loan forgiveness is political and controversial, but I feel like we could all agree that interest rates shouldn't be onerous. A interest rate greater than 6% on student loans when I can get a mortgage at less than 3% is usury.

[12]I despise casinos. At least with trading there's some chance the odds are sometimes in your favor, maybe.

[13]More importantly I have my health (money can't buy this) and a wonderful partner (I think it's easier to become a millionaire than it is to find that special someone that is just lovely, and willing to put up with you and all the time that you spend writing silly books about covered calls).

[14]I think this is the umpteenth time I've said this

investments are just index funds. Portfolio overwriting is simply a way to generate income with a different risk profile than other alternative investments and (hopefully) less drag on one's portfolio than simply cashing out funds.

> **Don't get too deep into it and whittle the precious, limited hours of your life away trying to maximize gains. Just make some extra premiums and be happy.**

43.10 Lottery Tickets are a Magical Thing to Have in Your Back Pocket

Ever buy a lottery ticket?

I rarely do anymore, but hyper-introspection[15] made me realize that I often liked having a lottery ticket tucked above the sun visor in my car more than I actually liked scratching it off (and usually losing). Kind of like how Charlie waited to open his Wonka chocolate bar.

Without getting too abstract, possibility equates to a partial reality in our perception of the world. We often account positively for things that have the potential to happen, even if they never do. Hope is powerful.

This has interesting consequences– consider the dead–end job, that may be high paying or have good benefits, but can still be emotionally difficult. For someone able to forecast monotony until retirement it can be a mind–killer, unless they think retirement holds the potential for something great.

The FIRE path was like this for me. Doing the math and seeing the drudgery laid out before me made me engineer the potential for a quicker exit into my plan. This wild card of portfolio overwriting

---

[15]Introspection is one of my superpowers.

returns makes the journey emotionally easier for me. It also made me commit to accumulating shares and grow my indexes more seriously, and that was probably the biggest benefit at the end of the day.

CHAPTER 44

Supplement – "Lost" Profits

44.1   Oh Noes! I Could Have Made...

N a particularly good day, when I was feeling supremely affluent, a younger me would buy a scratcher ticket at the gas station. I know the odds are against me, but it was a cheap habit I picked up in high school, and as far as vices go, it was fairly innocuous. When I strolled out with that ticket, I would jump in the car and immediately throw it above my sun visor and let it sit for a while. Only when I felt the need for a dopamine rush would I scratch it.

Inevitably, if the winning numbers are 5, 10, and 15, I would reveal a 6, 11, and 16, and irrationally think to myself "if only it was one number higher, then I could've won..." Although the stock market is no less random than the lotto ticket, I see the same thought pattern among investors.

So did I just miss out on winning the lottery? Did you just miss out on making that big win in the market?

I would say "no". In one sense, the real answer is yes, but "no" is in quotation marks for a reason. It's a special kind of "no" that will make disciplined portfolio overwriting much easier . By very disciplined, I mean:

- only selling OTM calls above your cost basis with a percentage goal that meets your needs

- not buying back at a loss

- never rolling down

In order to confidently stick with the premiums you've made, rather than chase profits, you need to take into account the infinite possible outcomes that could have happened. Specifically, consider all the ones where you lost, and weigh those against your choice to stick with a smaller return rather than adjust your position. This accounting of probabilities is the only real way to assess choices in the face of randomness.

Unfortunately, humans aren't designed to think that way, and it's difficult to rewire your thinking.

44.2   A Related Thought Experiment:

Thought experiment time!

Imagine you never, ever saw the price of the underlying after you sold a call. How would that change your trading? I would posit that it might make you better. Better from an emotional perspective, and perhaps from a technical perspective as well. I have a hunch that most retail traders would be better suited to this "mystery" investing because most people are wired to place more emotional emphasis on loss than gain.

The funny thing is, even if a stock went to zero after you sold it, your satisfaction at jumping ship at the right time would be vastly outweighed by your regret if the stock skyrocketed without you.[1] Seeing how prices behave may give you some insight over time if you can identify repeating patterns (to the extent that such patterns actually exist). But the absolute discipline of seeing only the money risked and the resultant reward gained, and the path between a mystery, would give you an entirely different – and potentially more useful – perspective.

44.3 A Second Related Thought Experiment:

More to the point, imagine that your covered call trades were always "locked in". Once you sold a call, it either expired as worthless or got called away, but involved absolutely no position adjustment. This is counter to the typical mode of thinking where you can buy and sell your option in a contract cycle, rolling or closing as the underlying stock price moves. This could be great if it kept you from doing dangerous things like rolling down, or buying back at a loss to roll up.

As the popular investing aphorism goes "pigs get fat, hogs get slaughtered" – meaning greed will catch up with you.[2] Being unable to adjust your sold call might change your thinking from a fluid, dynamic

---

[1]See my footnote in the previous chapter about my legacy positions. I'm unfortunately stuck with holding them to avoid crippling regret.

[2]No one wins forever.

trading attitude to more of a "horse race" attitude. Imagine trading where you place your bets and then the betting window closes while you watch em' run. With explicit risk and reward you would probably consider a lot more carefully before locking yourself into a position.

44.4   Application:

Having considered those two scenarios, now consider what you want to make per month. Then write it down on a tiny piece of paper, and hide it in your wallet. With portfolio overwriting, 1% would be great[3], especially if you compounded it twelve times per year, but I'll let you choose the return.

Then, every time you make a trade, think of it as casting a vote for (or against) your goals and the type of trader you want to be. You can even keep a tally on the piece of paper if you want. Try and see how many times you adjust positions, risking more in the hopes of a bigger return. It's very tempting, but if you don't consider the lost profits as something within your reach, they won't lead you astray.

Now, this is all a wee bit flighty and theoretical, and there are trading strategies where upside risk matters. But for portfolio overwriting, and especially for FIRE, keeping these mindsets explicit should benefit you. If anything, looking at things through a different lens will push the boundaries of your typical thought processes, which I always advocate.

Even if you don't act on these ideas, it's always useful to see things from as many angles as you possibly can.

---

[3]0.5% would be more realistic, 0.2% even more so.

CHAPTER 45

Supplement – Technical Analysis

He following quote resonated powerfully with me after about a year and a half of trying to learn technical analysis. It galvanized my frustration and led me to give up the whole endeavor.[1]

---

[1] There's another important lesson here. Even one of the sharpest logical minds to have ever lived can sometimes miss the nuance that other types of thinking are attuned to. Besides recognizing the inadequacy of his perception (humility), the fact that Mr. Thorp holds his spouse in high regard, and values her for her qualities (qualities far removed from the world of a quantitative mathematician) is downright heartwarming.

Thinking about momentum led me to wonder whether
past prices could somehow be used to predict future
prices. To test this, I looked at charting, the art of using
patterns in the graphs of stock (or commodity) prices to
forecast their future changes. I was introduced to this by
Norman, a Canadian resident living in Las Cruces,
while I was teaching at New Mexico State University.
After months of examining his data and predictions, I
was unable to find anything of value. As [wife] Vivian
said at the start, "This is going to be a waste of time.
Norman's been doing this for years and you can tell he's
barely getting by. Just look at his worn–out shoes and
shabby clothes. And you can tell from the quality of his
wife's old and outdated outfits that they were once better
off."

—Ed Thorp, *A Man for All Markets*

2

---

[2]The best autobiography I've ever read, and another one of my favorite books.
It's even better as an audiobook because Thorp narrates it himself, and there's
some raw emotion in there. Pairs well with "Fortune's Formula", a book detailing
the derivation of the Kelly Criterion and the other characters and influences in
Thorp's life. And if you want to read Thorp directly to round out the trifecta,
"Beat the Dealer", the book that described his card counting method for blackjack,
is very accessible to the average human.

Of note, Nassim Nicholas Taleb wrote the forward.

Figure 45.1: *Artist's representation of Ed Thorp, the man with the plan.*

Some people swear by technical analysis, and some of them are successful traders. Some of them are *very* successful traders.[3] But they are rare. I do not think believing in or using technical analysis means you will not be successful; they are not mutually exclusive. There is some credence to the notion that if everyone is using the same momentum indicators, then they could constitute a self-fulfilling prophecy. However, in my experience technical analysis works... until it doesn't.

---

[3]See "Unknown Market Wizards" by Jack D. Schwager

45.1   What Works, When?

I realize technical indicators have value for some people. If they at
minimum add confidence when entering positions, or at most actually
do predict future prices, that's great. But I would submit to you
the following evidence against their use as a retail investor.[4] Firstly,
they don't always work, so then the question is raised "does technical
indicator X work more often than not? If so, in what situations, with
what % of success?"

Show me a technical analyst who publishes all his predictions and
results in a completely transparent manner and I'll show you someone
I'd climb Mount Everest to learn from. Furthermore, if there are
some high–probability technical indicators, I'd assume an algorithm
has figured them out. Couldn't what they are and when they should
be applied, in theory, be automated in a way that we can't begin to
compete with as retail investors?

45.2   It's All About Perspective

Secondly, most technical analysis is HIGHLY subjective. Anyone can
draw lines on a chart to identify trends (stockcharts.com is a great free
tool for this, and very fun to play with), but the level of individual
interpretation at play is too much to make it anything but an art in my
estimation. Simply changing the time frame gives you totally different
patterns on a chart, so I just never understood how one knows they've
picked the relevant trend, or pattern, or cup and handle etc, etc.

But there is also a very dark side to technical analysis that this
individual interpretation lends itself to: advertising to retail investors.

---

[4]This is all personal experience, N = 1. Plus I'm not a genius so maybe I just
didn't learn it well enough? *shrug*

Whenever you see any ads for something akin to Surefire Trading
Patterns or Killer Chart Strategies, I would advise you to run.

45.3   A Great Review

If you need a more entertaining reason to run, head on over to In-
vestimonials.com,[5] one of the most amazing websites ever created in
regards to paid investment advice services. Here you can see a lot
of great reviews of questionable validity . Interspersed within these
rave reviews there's inevitably a furious investor who was grifted for a
significant sum of money trying to learn aforementioned Killer Chart
Strategies. I remember reading about technical analysis-based trade
alert services (at the time, I was considering paying for one in order to learn and be competent myself – I'm glad I never did). In
searching, I came across a long, exasperated review nestled in a group
of overwhelmingly positive ones for a popular service that was being
targeted-advertised to me nonstop on a popular internet video site.

45.4   This Poor Guy

The reviewer said he bought the initial program, then paid for a sub-
scription service. Then paid for all the extra "advanced
strategy" DVDs. In the hole for close to $1,000 (I looked through the
reviews at the time of writing but this one had ominously
disappeared, so forgive me for going off memory), he then paid even
more to go to an in–person seminar so he could learn from the face of
the company live, and have a chance to bring his own examples and
ask why the strategies didn't work. Said guru proceeded to tell him

---

[5]It's not what it used to be- I checked when writing this book and most of the
candid reviews are absent.

he incorrectly identified patterns, mainly because he chose the wrong time horizon (among other reasons).

This is a great "out", as changing the length of data completely changes the trend, and no one will ever give you a real answer of when to choose what horizon. Guru then ridiculed the person in front of other attendees for his inability to learn the simple trading secrets. Finally, when confronted about his trade alerts, which often were emailed to subscribers seconds before (or after!) a price changed, the guru claimed that with multiple positions open, no one could have a 100% win rate. The investor should have diversified his risk better (position sizings were not included in the alerts) and been more nimble entering and exiting positions. Additionally, they were told that they should rely on the skills that they learned. The alerts were also of an educational nature, not a trading strategy.

45.5 Allow Me To Rant

I find this infuriating. If you are truly going to claim that you have the secret to making money in the markets you would probably have to do the following[6]

- Understand risk diversification, which involves learning higher level mathematics, including The Kelly Criterion

- Do historical testing on the probability of your trading patterns being successful

- Apply that to your strategy

- Develop a self-correction mechanism for your strategy. Backtesting is similar to regression analysis— it tells you what worked the past, not what is going to work in the future

- Tell the subscribers of your fantastic service exactly what the portfolio allocation should be. All buys, sells, entries, exits, percentage weighting of positions. The whole shebang... and

- Get a third party to verify it.

> *"Don't tell me what you think, tell me what you have in your portfolio."*
> —Nassim Nicholas Taleb, *Skin in the Game*

More importantly, tell them exactly what your portfolio allocations are. Not the trading one you are hocking, but your actual, real life

---

[6]Anyone that can actually do all this likely wouldn't waste their time selling "trading secrets" to the masses.

retirement portfolio.[7]

Further, tell them exactly what percentage of that portfolio's returns are based on the service you are selling.

Worried about our weird morals surrounding money? I'm sure someone could make a program that would blind the actual dollar value and convert it all to percentages for educational purposes. In fact, it's a stellar business idea, and you could sell it to all the trading gurus on social media so they can share ALL their trades and retain privacy.

When that exists, then I'll be chomping at the bit to sign up for some trading services.

Unfortunately, most guys selling a trading service don't do this (let me know if there is one). What you see more often than not is a combination of moving averages, MACD, and doji candlestick patterns.

45.6   Keep Your Cash

Don't fall for it.

I can teach you how to trade covered calls. I don't know what will maximize profit every time.[8]

---

[7]About 85% of my entire portfolio is Boglehead stuff. The other 15% is tradeable. Every year the index funds get larger and the tradeable portion gets smaller as buy-and-hold slowly wins. That tradeable 15% (down from 25%, partly due to halting contributions, partly due to the 2021–2022 biotech bear market) is comprised mostly of biotechs (options wizard is a BCOP in real life, and thinks he has some sort of an edge— he doesn't), and index funds (yep, more Boglehead) that I sell calls against just like I described in this book.

What's in my portfolio? In the spirit of transparency and "tell me what's in your portfolio" if you send me a nice email I will likely tell you what my current positions are with the caveats that 1. It's not investing advice and 2. know that with the exception of the occasional outsized return, I've always done better long-term with mostly index investing and a lil' portfolio overwriting.

[8]No one does.

Now, I can't make blanket claims, and there may in fact be awesome subscription-based services out there. But if you are going to pay for one, be careful. If you find some technical indicators that work, or services that are worth the price, awesome. Please drop me an email about them. In the meantime, be careful, and don't buy any "secrets". I personally don't sell any services like this or boast about investing returns because I can't tell the future, I can only describe *how* to sell call options.

45.7 Caveats, Galore

That being said, there are guys on twitter who trade stocks mostly on a combination of TA (technical analysis) and due diligence, post their trades, and are successful... sometimes. That gives me a creeping feeling of dread that I'm missing something. I just don't know, and that's hard for me to say because I sincerely tried to understand and couldn't. I respect these guys because they are transparent, free, have some good picks, and have made me some money.[9]

But I've also lost just as much on their bad calls. So, if you are a huge proponent if T.A. don't construe this chapter as me thinking technical analysis is BS. Like most things it's complicated, and it just may be the case that I don't understand it.

45.8 Takeaway

In closing, like Ed Thorp, I was unable to find anything of value.[10]

---

[9]When I used to follow along and trade their plays for fun— I don't anymore.

[10]I'm dumb, but I know for damn sure that Ed Thorp is one of the smartest humans alive and one of the best investors to ever live. Also of note, Thorpe did develop a trading system dubbed MIDAS which may have included some technical analysis. He describes it as follows "....indicators we systematically analyzed, several correlated strongly with past performance. Among them were earnings

45.9   Spoiler Alert: The Last Lesson

When asked to sum up the investing lesson one could take from Ed
Thorp's autobiography a friend who read it the same time as me (hi-
lariously) replied: "Be as smart as Ed Thorp".

Although this isn't possible for most people, you *can* take Ed
Thorp's advice, contained in the last chapters of the book.[11] Spoiler
alert— it's the same as Mr. Money Mustache's take on the topic.

Invest in index funds.

---

yield (annual earnings divided by price), dividend yield, book value divided by
price, momentum, short interest (the number of shares of a company currently
sold short), earnings surprise (an earnings announcement that is significantly and
unexpectedly different from the analysts' consensus), purchases and sales by company officers, directors, and large shareholders, and the ratio of total company
sales to the market price of the company. We studied each of these separately,
then worked out how to combine them. When the historical patterns persisted as
prices unfolded into the future, we created a trading system called MIDAS (multiple indicator diversified asset system) and used it to run a separate long/ short
hedge fund." So maybe he did crack the code... Like I said, it's complicated.

[11]Everyone should really read it, and although I prefer actual, physical books,
in this case the audiobook is even better because Thorp narrates it himself.

Acknowledgments

I really enjoyed writing this text, and I don't imagine myself an island. The following people (those I know and those I don't) deserve my thanks for all of the various ways that they made this project possible.

This will likely be the only book I ever write, so I hope you'll forgive a long "Acknowledgements." It may be my only chance to get these all in, and I couldn't pass up the opportunity to share the people who have influenced my thinking. My hope is that readers may find one of the recommendations that I make here changes the way they see the world.

First and foremost, thanks my editors, Bruce Smith[12] and Amanda Kay Metskas.

I'm not an innately skilled writer, nor have I spent much time honing the skill outside this book. Knowing what the first draft was like[13], they are miracle workers.

To my family, who have always been there for me: Thank you.

To my chosen family (friends): I realize the impact and impression

---

[12]Available for contract editing at https://www.linkedin.com/in/brucesmith9/
[13]Imagine a dumpster. Now imagine it on fire.

you've had on me.

> *"If I'm the sum of all my friends, then all my friends*
> *are some of me"*
>
> —The Matches, You (Don't) Know Me,
> from the album Decomposer

To anyone I have been lucky enough to count among my friends throughout life: I have nothing but gratitude for you. Special thanks to the longtime emotional support pillars and life-decision consultants: August Brunsman, Joe Camerlengo, Michael Donohoe, Katie Gritti, Sarah Hammond, Adam Kucharski, Amanda Kay Metskas, and Brian Rutledge.

Special thanks to Trisha Kennedy, Shelley Lang, and Heather McConnell for getting me through pharmacy school. Class would have been unbearably boring without you guys. Back Row Ki [14] was wildly successful in retrospect.

And in the spirit of naive optimism and relentless positivity, thanks to all the people I'm not huge fans of for providing me valuable life lessons and examples of what not to be, *via negativa.*

To all my intellectual idols and inspirations[15] Thank you for making me smarter by allowing me to see through your many different lenses. Life is complicated, and it helps to have more blind men grasping at the elephant.[16]

First, many thanks to Pete Adeney (aka Mr. Money Mustache). My only wish was that I had found you sooner. I hope to pay a visit to the co-working space in Longmont as an early retiree someday.

---

[14] A coed service fraternity we formed in response to the onerous demands of the actual academic pharmacy fraternity, Rho Ki.

[15] People who are smarter than me, and think differently than me, that I have the privilege of learning from.

[16] If you aren't familiar with the story of the blind men and the elephant here's a place to start:https://en.wikipedia.org/wiki/Blind_men_and_an_elephant

I owe a debt of gratitude to Rudy from Alpha Investments. He runs a Youtube channel[17] detailing mainly his long-term investments in Magic the Gathering cards and other collectibles. But it's secretly a channel about financial education, investing, and how to truly grow wealth. I personally have never owned MTG cards[18], though I plan on getting some sealed product once I have more disposable passive income. I haven't played an in-person MTG game either, but always love and recommend his videos to anyone interested in investing.

He may look like a hairy guy that lives in a basement and can't afford a haircut, but he has professional finance experience and an accurate view of the way the world works. More importantly, he's a genuine guy who is willing to share what he knows.

My personal admiration for Rudy stems from one specific video, "Timmy's are Losers." One of the first Alpha Investments videos I ever watched, it detailed the difficulty of going long options. I already knew everything he covered at an intellectual level, but I saw it at precisely the right time in my life, namely when the tide had turned on my overall P&L for all my active investing and options trading adventures (all the losses were due to buying long calls). It really made me realize how hard the game was, and the mindset I was functioning in. Immediately after that, I watched "Story Time: I almost BANKRUPTED Alpha Investments"[19] and it was just what I needed to hear.

I naively thought I took a very measured bet after explicit, extended deliberation. I was hoping I could speed up the clock on FIRE, since I had come to the idea later in life. My decision was influenced by my acute awareness of just how short life is (thanks to my day job), and an unhealthy amount of hubris. But realizing I was in the "Timmy" mindset (making bets, thinking only of upside, "needing" a big win to happen) and that everyone makes mistakes that they can (hopefully) move on from really helped shake me out of the delusion that I was not only going to be able to make back my losses, but also

---

[17]https://www.youtube.com/@AlphaInvestments69
[18]I do own one of the limited edition Rudy playmats, though.
[19]https://www.youtube.com/watch?v=6o148ck50dQ

going to be clever enough to beat the market, and make endless long-term profits buying options and trading spreads.

Selling covered calls is easy. Buying long calls is pure risk. Alpha Investments gave me the nudge I needed to get me serious and committed to wealth accumulation and FIRE. For that, I owe The Rudy a taco or three.[20]

> **Admitting you were wrong and changing is simultaneously the hardest thing and the most important thing to do in life.**

At the time I'm writing this, over to 2 years into the process, Rudy just released a video "Wealth and Poor People", which describes, among other things like margin equity loans[21], how very wealthy people will sometimes sell covered calls against their index holdings to collect roughly a 0.5% premium as income (using the % gain as a surrogate indicator for minimizing chances of assignment)! So, as an autodidact who had been portfolio overwriting for FIRE and decided to write a book on it, that was... vindicating.

To Nassim Nicholas Taleb: Your writing changed the way I think about the world, not only via the introduction of new ideas, but it also galvanized many of the intuitions I already held. The sometimes gruff delivery and strong moral compass was neither foreign nor off-putting to me, as my father was a biker in the '70s. I'm currently working at a state institution and writing a book, so really taking your advice on

---

[20]Other amazing videos of his include "CEOs of Brokerage firms do not own mutual funds," "Timmy Learns about Credit Card Manipulation," and "Royal Caribbean Cruise Lines: Let's Talk about Bonds." Basically any time you see a whiteboard and Rudy wearing a pink 80's visor you're about to get a free education worth more than most MBA programs. Also, for anyone wondering, Rudy consistently refers to his love of tacos in his videos, in a self-deprecating way.

[21]Anyone interested in FIRE should know about margin equity loans. Mr. Money Mustache recently discovered these and wrote about using one to buy a home for cash in the January 29th, 2021 post titled "The Margin Loan: How to Make a $400,00 Impulse Purchase"

barbelling. If I make it to FIRE, the first thing I'm doing is getting a degree in math. Hopefully I'll see you at the Real World Risk Institute someday.[22]

To Ed Thorp, who had the audacity to see a card game people had been trying to beat for centuries and take an honest shot at it... and succeed. The application of the Kelly Criterion[23] to finance remains simultaneously one of your greatest and (somehow) least well-known contributions to the field of risk.[24]

As I am finishing the final edit of this book, my focus is shifting to learning the math necessary to understand the Kelly Criterion more thoroughly.

Although one may not be as natively intelligent as Mr. Thorp, the spirit of inquiry and experimentation is the real takeaway. One should always try. Even if you end up like Icarus, I'm sure you'll get a once-in-a-lifetime view before you get too close to the sun.

> "How will I know limits from lies, if I never try?"
> —Thrice, The Melting Point of Wax,
> from the album The Artist in the Ambulance

Thank you to Matt Hollerbach and the Breaking the Market University[25]. Most of his writings deal with rebalancing premium, Shannon's Demon, CAGR, and the Kelly Criterion (which I suspect is one of the most important ways to look at investing). My long-term

---

[22]Likely NNT will never see this, and with him being an applied expert in higher-level derivatives trading, I would probably be embarrassed if he did. What I'm doing is basically drawing with crayons while he is painting the Sistine Chapel.

[23]The Kelly Criterion is a formula that can gauge the optimal size for a bet that will produce long term growth of a bankroll after repeated rounds of play.

[24]I really think expected value is pervasively used simply because it's just much, much easier to calculate. But you are not the probability-weighted sum of all possible outcomes- you are only one person, with one bankroll at the casino, one portfolio to retire on, and one life to live. Measure risk accordingly, or you will go bust.

[25]https://breakingthemarket.com/breaking-the-market-university/

"mathematical goal" is to intuitively understand the primary paper[26] his work builds on.

Ole Peters[27]— I am looking forward to your book, and hope to see more episodes of Ergodicity TV[28] soon! The video "Random Multiplicative Dynamics" caused one of the biggest lightbulb moments I've ever had with regards to probability, growth, and statistics. Specifically, it helped me understand how an economy can grow overall as the majority of actors lose. The world needs more simple visualizations of what are extremely important, but often ignored, concepts.

To Grant Sanderson (aka 3blue1brown[29]) who has a love for teaching, and the ability to make maths beautiful and unintimidating: You are a national treasure, and were kind enough to email me back when this book was in its early stages.

To the Math Sorcerer, who makes great reviews of mathematics books (and some other random stuff) on Youtube:[30] I can appreciate the wizard vibe. Your videos helped me compile a small library of things to work on, including an absolutely awesome book on proofs, which has become my favorite mathematics textbook–*Proofs: A Long-Form Mathematics Textbook* by Jay Cummings.

To Ross Enamait, who made the best books on fitness that ever existed as a labor of love and a service to people looking to become athletic anywhere, with any amount of equipment (including none): I remember reading your books as a teenager and thinking that it would be cool if someday I would be passionate enough about something to write a book like yours.[31] I hope that you would find this book to be

---

[26]Dubikovsky, Vladislav and Susinno, Gabriele, Demystifying Rebalancing Premium and Extending Portfolio Theory in the Process (May 20, 2015). Available at SSRN: `https://ssrn.com/abstract=2927791` or `http://dx.doi.org/10.2139/ssrn.2927791`

[27]Another mathematician I found through Taleb whose work is directly in my area of interest

[28]`https://www.youtube.com/@ErgodicityTV`

[29]`https://www.youtube.com/@3blue1brown`

[30]`https://www.youtube.com/@TheMathSorcerer`

[31]Interestingly, he also hit on a lot of the tenets of Crossfit before Crossfit existed.

as standalone and gimmick-free as your own. That was certainly my aspiration.

Thank you to Jacob Lund Fisker, whose fantastic book Early Retirement Extreme (also formatted in LATEX) also served as inspiration for me to write something unique and put it out into the FIRE-verse.

To Jacob Lund Fisker, whose fantastic book Early Retirement Extreme (also formatted in L^AT_EX) served as inspiration for me.

Also thank you to FIRE bloggers like Early Retirement Now[32] and Financial Velociraptor, who are willing to think outside the index fund box a little bit.

Early Retirement Now covers FIRE and alternative investments strategies with a quantitative and experimental bent, usually so thoroughly and simply explained that even I can understand it. His website also includes tracking his put-selling portfolio, which is functionally equivalent to covered call selling, from a risk profile. He also sent me some nice email replies in the past.

Financial Velociraptor retired with less than 25x, but maintained his income via options trading.[33] He posted his positions and monthly finances in a way that was so simple and transparent that no other finance blogger has ever even come close.[34]

To Lane, the author of Reminiscences of a Stockblogger: Your web-

---

I remember doing Tabata intervals, box jumps and GPP in high school, only to be re-introduced to them as a "novel" concept 7 years later when I joined one of the first "Box" gyms that opened in my hometown.

[32] https://earlyretirementnow.com/

[33] Including a simple and ingenious UVXY put-buying strategy, that unfortunately no longer worked as well once the leverage of UVXY was reduced. The (formerly) 3x leverage of the fund resulted in easily foreseeable long-term price erosion, so buying long-dated puts printed money for him for a while. A beautifully simple strategy hidden in plain sight.

[34] His site is now sadly defunct due to technical issues with web hosting, but he still posts financial transparencies on Facebook.

site was another motivation for me to make something myself. He's a good (internet) friend and very insightful guy, applying high-level, classical valuation to his area of expertise. I will never be as good at his style of valuation-based investing as he is, but I hope he writes a book someday. It's a passion project for him, but lots of investors out there would likely benefit from learning what he knows. [35]

I'm also grateful to all the other thinkers that are iconoclastic and well-intentioned, especially and specifically Hamilton Morris. For the first 5 years of my career I dealt with terminally ill patients, face-to-face. This can have profound effects on a person. Realizing life is short, and that you would not like to spend the majority of it working is one of them. A true sense of the despair and hopelessness thanatophobia brings to the people unable to process and accept their prognosis is another.

Without discovering Hamilton's work, I would not have a well-educated or in-depth viewpoint on the history, potential, medicinal chemistry, and pharmacology of what are generically referred to as psychedelics. Understanding these pharmaceutical compounds has made me hopeful for their potential in treating the distress of confronting imminent mortality, as well as the myriad of other mental disorders our society is currently facing. Psilocybin for anxiety and depression in terminally ill patients, MDMA for PSTD, and ketamine for treatment resistant depression and alcohol abuse are the forefront of the field, with a stream of novel compounds as the next wave of potential treatments. I'm hopeful not only for patients, but the people I personally know who have benefited from these compounds, or could have before their lives were cut short.[36]

Hamilton's work helped me develop a reasonable and objective view of the topic. Mr. Morris possesses the otherworldly skill of presenting a logical and non-judgemental analysis of what is an emotionally, politically, and morally charged subject. This is truly the sign of a good

[35]His site is private to keep comments engaged and quality, but you can request access directly via https://reminiscencesofastockblogger.com/

[36]I hope to live to see the day these compounds are available to "healthy normals."

journalist and anthropologist.[37]

His mini-documentary series Hamilton's Pharmacopeia is beautifully produced.. I really hope someone reading this checks them out.[38] How can you not love understated humor provided in a sonorous baritone contralto narration when learning the actual chemical synthesis of pharmacologically active substances? [39]

One example of a mind that was lost too soon to depression and alcoholism, who may still have been with us today were it not for the unavailability of a viable treatment,is David Foster Wallace. I include him here because his Kenyon University commencement speech "This is Water" is something I listen to at least monthly to remind me that as Dylan says, "you gotta serve somebody."[40] His way of thinking about our human experience, and subsequent ability to crystallize and convey those ideas, was singular.

I initially thought Infinite Jest[41] was "just ok," but once I started to watch interviews of him to understand the book better, I had the realization that he had the insight and predictive capacity to perceive cultural issues ongoing and incoming long before they materialized. DFW's 2003 unedited interview for the German TV station ZDF[42] made me realize that I could potentially learn the most from hearing people who were far smarter than me in some dimension opine on things adjacent to (or altogether different) from their primary exper-

---

[37] The value of a de facto ethnography was something I underestimated when I was younger, foolishly favoring the "hard" sciences and being too dismissive of the power our culture plays in our life.

[38] I especially recommend viewing Season 2 Episode 1 and Season 3 Episode 1 in succession.

[39] He has psychoactive toad (bufo alvaris) t-shirts for sale as well at https://shop.creamforever.com/collections/protect-the-sonoran-desert-toad. All the proceeds go to Parkinson's research and Sonoran Desert Toad habitat preservation— they make great gifts!

[40] I prefer the Pop Staples version. Hoodoo Soul Band arguably does the best live performance on the planet.

[41] This book removed my sense of shame surrounding the excessive use of footnotes, for better or for worse.

[42] https://www.youtube.com/watch?v=iGLzWdT7vGc&t=4190s

tise.[43]

Jonathan Laroquette and Seth Romatelli of Uhh Yeah Dude and The McElroy Brothers Griffin, Justin and Travis[44]— thanks for bringing me lots of joy, and keeping me from being too serious. Laughter is carbonated holiness.

Kate Ma[45] for colorization and cartoonization of my fiancée's great wizard cartoons, and of illustrations and various thinkers.

Amy Pielow and r/latex for on-demand help with LaTeX

Finally, thanks to Curo and Shade for being good kitties.

Email me at `calltofirewizard@gmail.com`

[43]It's more about *how* one thinks about things than *what* one thinks about things.

[44]The Adventure Zone's First Season, The Balance Arc, started out as a joke with a lot of low-brow humor and morphed into one of the most beautiful stories ever told. Worth your time.

[45]Contact `signskate8@gmail.com` for commissions.